Hanging by a Thread

Ohio University Research in International Studies

This series of publications on Africa, Latin America, Southeast Asia, and Global and Comparative Studies is designed to present significant research, translation, and opinion to area specialists and to a wide community of persons interested in world affairs. The editor seeks manuscripts of quality on any subject and can usually make a decision regarding publication within three months of receipt of the original work. Production methods generally permit a work to appear within one year of acceptance. The editor works closely with authors to produce a high-quality book. The series appears in a paperback format and is distributed worldwide. For more information, contact the executive editor at Ohio University Press, 19 Circle Drive, The Ridges, Athens, Ohio 45701.

Executive editor: Gillian Berchowitz
AREA CONSULTANTS
Africa: Diane M. Ciekawy
Latin America: Brad Jokisch, Patrick Barr-Melej, and Rafael Obregon
Southeast Asia: William H. Frederick .

The Ohio University Research in International Studies series is published for the Center for International Studies by Ohio University Press. The views expressed in individual volumes are those of the authors and should not be considered to represent the policies or beliefs of the Center for International Studies, Ohio University Press, or Ohio University.

Hanging by a Thread

COTTON, GLOBALIZATION,
AND POVERTY IN AFRICA

Edited by

William G. Moseley and Leslie C. Gray

Ohio University Research in International Studies
Global and Comparative Studies Series No. 9
Ohio University Press
Athens

The Nordic Africa Institute
Uppsala

© 2008 by the
Center for International Studies
Ohio University
www.ohioswallow.com

Published in Europe by:
The Nordic Africa Institute
P O Box 1703
S-751 47 Uppsala
Sweden
www.nai.uu.se
ISBN: 978-91-7106-614-5

18 17 16 15 14 13 12 11 10 09 08   5 4 3 2 1

The books in the Ohio University Research in International Studies Series
are printed on acid-free paper ⊚ ™

Library of Congress Cataloging-in-Publication Data

Hanging by a thread : cotton, globalization, and poverty in Africa / edited by William G.
Moseley and Leslie C. Gray.
    p. cm. — (Ohio University research in international studies. Global and comparative
studies series ; no. 9)
  Includes bibliographical references and index.
  ISBN-13: 978-0-89680-260-5 (pb : alk. paper)
  ISBN-10: 0-89680-260-4 (pb : alk. paper)
    1. Cotton trade—Africa. 2. Cotton—Economic aspects—Africa. 3. Poverty—Africa. I.
Moseley, William G. II. Gray, Leslie. III. Title: Cotton, globalization, and poverty in Africa.
IV. Series: Research in international studies. Global and comparative studies series ; no. 9.
  HD9087.A2H35 2008
  338.1'7351096—dc22

                                                                            2007048114

Contents

Part III
Alternate Futures:
Genetically Engineered and Organic Cotton

Preface and Acknowledgments

Both of us have long been interested in the role of cotton in African rural livelihoods. Bill was first introduced to cotton when, as a U.S. Peace Corps "gardening" volunteer in the 1980s, he was assigned to a state agricultural extension agency in southern Mali that was largely preoccupied with the sale and production of this crop. He would again encounter cotton as a dominating force in rural livelihoods as an aid agency worker in central Zimbabwe. Leslie initially became familiar with African cotton cultivation as a relief worker in the mid-1980s in Sudan, where she traveled around the Gezira scheme (an irrigation project begun by the British in 1925). She would later work in the cotton-growing region in Burkina Faso. While neither of us set out to make cotton production a focal point of our master's and doctoral research in the 1990s, we kept bumping into it along the way: as Bill studied indigenous knowledge systems and poverty-environment questions in southern Mali and as Leslie examined land degradation and population growth in southwestern Burkina Faso.

In the early 2000s we collaborated on a journal's special issue exploring and questioning the theorized relationship between poverty and environmental management. Here again, cotton seemed to be an important issue in a number of African countries. At about the same time, the humdrum crop we had long recognized as a significant variable in a number of African livelihood systems seemed to burst onto the international scene as a major subject of contention between actors in the global North and the global South. West African cotton farmer unions were working with international allies to put pressure on their governments to improve producer prices. African leaders editorialized in a major U.S. newspaper about unjust American cotton subsidies. Cotton farming supports became a significant issue during the Doha round of world trade negotiations. Finally, the UK-based nonprofit Oxfam launched an international campaign highlighting the hypocritical nature of European and North American agricultural subsidies (particularly U.S. support for its cotton farmers). To say the least, it was becoming clear that the cotton production and supply chain represented an interesting thread connecting African rural livelihoods, national-scale politics, and international markets. Hence, the idea was born to assemble a series of case studies from across sub-Saharan Africa that used cotton as a way to understand the evolving dynamic between African livelihoods and the global economy.

Most of the contributions to this volume stem from papers given in two organized sessions on Cotton, Natural Resources, and Society in Sub-Saharan Africa at the November 2004 annual meeting of the African Studies Association in New Orleans. We are grateful to the two panel discussants at this conference, Torbjörn Engdahl and Allen Isaacman, who provided insightful comments on these papers. We further express our thanks to two anonymous reviewers who provided constructive feedback on all chapter drafts. We also acknowledge Gillian Berchowitz, senior editor, and Nancy Basmajian, managing editor (both at Ohio University Press), who recognized the value of this project and helped it see the light of day. We further thank Birgit Mühlenhaus, cartographer at Macalester College, who produced many of the figures in this book. Bill is especially indebted to the innumerable small farmers in the Djitoumou and Siwaa areas of southern Mali, who, during his various visits and longer stays between 1987 and 2003, patiently showed him the ins and outs of their farming systems. Leslie acknowledges the farmers of the Province of Tuy in southwestern Burkina Faso for their patience and willingness to talk openly and honestly about their concerns surrounding cotton production. Finally, we recognize the direct and indirect contributions of our family members to this book project—Bill to Julia, Ben, and Sophie; Leslie to Michael, Elliot, and Sukie.

Contributors

Thomas J. Bassett, Professor, Department of Geography, University of Illinois, Urbana, Illinois.

Jim Bingen, Professor, Department of Community, Agriculture, Recreation, and Resource Studies, Michigan State University, East Lansing, Michigan.

Duncan Boughton, Associate Professor, Department of Agricultural Economics, Michigan State University, East Lansing, Michigan.

Brian M. Dowd, PhD Candidate, Department of Environmental Studies, University of California, Santa Cruz, California.

Marnus Gouse, Research Fellow, Department of Agricultural Economics, Extension and Rural Development, University of Pretoria, Pretoria, South Africa.

Leslie C. Gray, Associate Professor, Environmental Studies Institute, Santa Clara University, Santa Clara, California.

Dolores Koenig, Associate Professor, Department of Anthropology, American University, Washington, DC.

Scott M. Lacy, Assistant Professor, Department of Anthropology, Emory University, Atlanta, Georgia.

William G. Moseley, Associate Professor, Department of Geography, Macalester College, Saint Paul, Minnesota.

Colin Poulton, Research Fellow, Centre for Environmental Policy, Imperial College, London, UK.

Bhavani Shankar, Lecturer, Department of Agricultural and Food Economics, University of Reading, Reading, UK.

Corinne Siaens, Consultant, Poverty Group of the Latin American and Caribbean Region, World Bank, Washington, DC.

Colin Thirtle, Professor, Centre for Environmental Policy, Imperial College, London, UK

David Tschirley, Professor, Department of Agricultural Economics, Michigan State University, East Lansing, Michigan.

Quentin Wodon, Lead Specialist, Poverty Reduction and Economic Management Unit of the Africa Region, World Bank, Washington, DC.

Introduction

Cotton, Globalization, and Poverty in Africa

William G. Moseley and Leslie C. Gray

Cotton is the mother of poverty.

—*Allen Isaacman*

It is clear that the cotton sector has contributed to alleviating poverty. The expansion of the cotton sector is not harming the production of food crops, quite the contrary.

—*Government of Burkina Faso*

GM cotton is, in truth, at best irrelevant to poverty in the area, and at worst is lowering wages and job prospects for agricultural laborers, who are some of the most impoverished people in South Africa.

—*Aaron de Grassi*

Coton est le clé du développement. [Cotton is the key to development.]

—*Drissa Keita, general director, Malian Cotton Company*

Africa's greatest value to Europe at the beginning of the imperialist era was as a source of raw materials such as palm products, groundnuts, cotton, and rubber. . . . The need for those materials arose out of Europe's expanded economic capacity . . . [and] . . . one of the important factors in that process was the unequal trade with Africa.

—*Walter Rodney*

Cotton is our ticket into the world market. Its production is crucial
to economic development in West and Central Africa, as well as to
the livelihoods of millions of people there.... This vital economic
sector in our countries is seriously threatened by agricultural subsidies
granted by rich countries to their cotton producers.

—*Malian president Amadou Toumani Touré*
and Burkina president Blaise Compaoré

Cotton production here will have to shrink
eventually because the soil is being exhausted.

—*Orou Guere, secretary of a local farmer's cooperative in Benin*

COTTON IS CURRENTLY THE SUBJECT of a number of debates concerning sub-Saharan Africa (SSA),[1] where the crop is simultaneously
depicted as an agent of development, poverty, wealth, change, trade
disputes, and environmental destruction. These cotton discourses
reflect national, regional, and international discussions pertaining to
various subtexts in the globalization debate, namely privatization,
structural adjustment, food security, biotechnology, agricultural subsidies, poverty alleviation, and sustainable development.

The idea that cotton is controversial may come as a surprise to
some readers. In fact, cotton probably does not strike most people as
a topic that could keep one captivated for an entire book. Cotton does
not have the gastronomic allure of, say, coffee, chocolate, or tea, which
attract loving aficionados. But cotton, like any cash crop, is not just a
lowly plant in the ground. In Africa the history of why cotton is grown
in which locales, by whom, in what quantity, and with which techniques involves international politics, colonial power, environmental
factors, and, in many instances, coercion. Cotton is grown by people
and families who take risks to grow it (in terms of money borrowed,
impacts the crop may have on the land, and pesticide exposure in the
fields) and who depend on the income it generates. For many farmers
it is the route to wealth; for others it keeps them poor.

Cotton links farmers to the international economy. African farmers sell their cotton to private companies and parastatals whose stakeholders[2] depend on the sale of the crop and who may have instituted a number of policies and programs to guarantee the continued production of this crop and the flow of money into their coffers. Multilateral banks have an interest in the crop if it means that their loans to African governments are repaid on schedule. African cotton is sold on international markets at a price largely related to the actions of the global powers (e.g., whether China will be exporting or importing cotton in a given year and the level of American subsidies to its cotton farmers) and to the whims of international consumers (e.g., whether they prefer cotton or synthetics). So cotton is not just a crop, it is a commodity rooted in African soil, with consequences for local livelihoods, that is situated in an international web of economic transfers reflecting historical and contemporary power structures.

For better or for worse, Africa is connected to the global marketplace. These links are fairly transparent and long standing, as the continent is highly dependent on the export of two groups of commodities: energy and mineral resources on the one hand, and cash crops on the other. Africa's energy and mineral resources tend to be controlled by state companies or private corporations (Maponga and Maxwell 2001) and, as such, the income generated by the extraction and export of these assets is often captured by these entities. While these industries employ labor, workers in these sectors account for a very small proportion of the African labor force. In contrast, cash crop production (which also engages the state and private corporations) involves a much higher proportion of that workforce. Seventy-five percent of the female labor force, and 62 percent of the male labor force, in SSA is involved in agriculture (USAID 2004). Nearly all of Africa's approximately six million commercial farmworkers, and a very large proportion of its 140 million smallholders (USAID 2004) have some involvement with cash crop production. Commodity crops are a major strand linking Africa's farmworkers and small farmers with global markets. Furthermore, agriculture, in any context, is a major means by which humans transform the landscape. Therefore, a study of cash crop production in the African context provides one with significant insights into the processes of globalization, poverty dynamics, and land management.

Cotton can be seen as one important thread of the globalization process in Africa. Through a set of linked case studies, we can comprehend the nested dynamics of the crop in the soil, in local African communities, in national political economies, and in international circuits of power and commerce. Thus, the overarching conceptual framework of the volume is that of the commodity chain.

The commodity chain approach follows a product from one point to the next, examining the dynamics at each level and between levels. Commodity chain studies may also involve an analysis of price formation at different stages in the production and delivery process. Particular attention is given to the impact of political economy, history, and power relations on the geography, input-output structure, and governance of the commodity chain (Hartwick 1998; Gereffi and Korzeniewicz 1994; Bair 2005). There is also a related and growing literature on alternative consumption, for example, on fair trade and organic production (Bryant and Goodman 2004). Global commodity chain analysis bears some resemblance to the *filière* approach. The main difference is that the filière approach has generally been restricted to national scale and the emphasis has been on restructuring production systems, and supporting institutions, in the name of development (Raikes, Jensen, and Ponte 2000).

This volume employs a modified commodity chain approach, focusing on the social, economic, and environmental dimensions of cotton production in Africa, and the links between this production and the global market. Individual chapters may examine one or multiple levels in the commodity chain and employ different theoretical approaches, from ethnography, to agroecology, to political ecology, to classic economic analysis. We want to acknowledge, however, that while the commodity chain is an important part of cotton dynamics, it is not the only force at work in African cotton. There are new and interesting developments outside the commodity chain that work for change. Networks of African farmers are linking up with international activists and nongovernmental organizations (NGOs) to change how cotton is grown, working to reduce pesticide use, limit genetically modified organisms, and affect international pricing policies, particularly the subsidies that the developed world gives to their farmers. This is a new and dynamic form of globalization that has direct implications for the livelihoods and well-being of Africa's cotton farmers. We finally note that this book also seeks to update the story of cotton in Africa. While previous texts have provided a historical overview of the development of cotton production Africa—most notably Isaacman and Roberts's *Cotton, Colonialism, and Social History in Sub-Saharan Africa* (1995)—this volume offers an analysis of the situation in the postcolonial period.

African Cotton Production Systems in Global and Historical Context

Cotton was first cultivated in South Asia and South America. Cotton fragments found in the Indus Valley date to 3000 BC. The two species used in South Asia were *Gossypium herbaceum* and *G. arboreum*. *G. herbaceum* originated in Africa. Trade in cotton fabrics between Asia and Europe was established during the time of Alexander the Great. In the 1600s, Europeans discovered that cotton plants were also being grown in the Americas. These New World cotton cultivars were superior for mechanized cloth production because of their longer fibers. New World cotton varieties were introduced into Africa in the 1800s, eventually displacing local varieties.

The textile industry was one of the first manufacturing activities to become organized globally, with mechanized production in Europe using cotton from the various colonies. As others have described (e.g., Isaacman and Roberts 1995), textile manufacturing initially became industrialized in late-eighteenth-century England. A series of technical innovations and the development of factory-style production approaches (which quickly spread from England to continental Europe) created a mass market for cotton textiles by driving down their price. These changes fueled an ever-increasing demand for cotton lint. The British were the first to develop cotton production in their colonies, most notably the United States, India, and Egypt (with the United States quickly becoming the largest producer).

A significant shock occurred between 1861 and 1865, when the American Civil War and a Northern blockade of exports from the South, greatly reduced supplies of raw cotton to European textile manufacturers. As raw cotton prices climbed, many European mills were forced to close and lay off workers. This lack of employment led to what has been called the Cotton Famine. This difficult social situation, and the concerns of industrialists, put pressure on European governments to develop new sources of cotton. Increasingly, sub-Saharan Africa was seen as a supplier of cotton for European mills.

As Porter (1995) notes, "In the global drama of cotton production, African colonies were mainly bit players." In the late 1920s, African cotton production accounted for only 1 percent of global production. This proportion climbed slowly to 2.6 percent from 1934 to 1938 and 4.1 percent in 1959. As table 0.1 indicates, African cotton producers now account for nearly 16 percent of global cotton exports. In terms of export revenues, cotton is now the second-most-important cash crop in Africa after cacao. The growing prominence of African cotton is arguably related to a combination of state-led approaches (most evident in francophone West Africa) and export promotion policies pushed by the World Bank and the International Monetary Fund (IMF).

As the data in tables 0.2 and 0.3 suggest, export-oriented cotton production is most developed in francophone West Africa, where four of the top five producers are found (Mali, Côte d'Ivoire, Benin, and Burkina Faso). The growth of production in these areas may be attributed to the seriousness of the French colonial effort, the level of state control in the cotton sector, and, to some extent, a lack of other export alternatives for Mali, Benin, and Burkina Faso. In most of these countries, cotton production is managed by a partially government-owned parastatal that has monopoly control over the provision of credit, the sale of inputs, and the purchase of farmer output (Bingen 2004). In East and southern Africa, cotton production is organized differently as private companies are authorized by a government board or agency to manage their own cotton production, collection, processing and export (Bingen 2004).

Table 0.1 Export value of SSA agricultural commodities, 1999–2003

Commodity	1999	2000	2001	2002	2003	5-yr. avg.	% of world exports
Cacao	$2,186,792	$1,569,003	$1,761,311	$2,721,587	$3,130,812	$2,273,901	70.8
Cotton	$1,113,017	$968,226	$999,956	$959,169	$1,182,449	$1,044,563	15.6
Tobacco	$967,701	$1,100,229	$1,148,009	$873,613	$1,001,909	$1,018,292	4.8
Coffee	$1,374,735	$1,107,091	$596,297	$515,011	$600,716	$838,770	12.2
Tea	$600,444	$648,081	$623,331	$284,669	$595,930	$550,491	20.1
Sugarcane	$103	$42	$485	$293	$273	$239	6.1

Source: FAO 2005.

Table 0.2 Production of cotton lint in SSA, 1998–2005
(thousands of tonnes)

Country	1998/99	1999/2000	2000/1	2001/2	2002/3	2003/4	2004/5	7-yr. avg.
Mali	217	197	102	240	200	217	228	200.1
Côte d'Ivoire	157	173	125	173	162	165	168	160.4
Benin	123	152	141	172	137	149	159	147.6
Burkina Faso	119	109	116	158	144	146	149	134.4
Zimbabwe	115	138	135	75	132	132	132	122.7
Cameroon	79	79	95	102	83	95	97	90.0
Chad	64	74	58	68	60	70	72	66.6
Togo	78	56	49	70	64	71	74	66.0
Nigeria	65	50	55	60	55	63	63	58.7
Tanzania	35	42	45	63	67	67	67	55.1
Zambia	36	30	24	35	43	47	50	37.9
South Africa	53	30	36	18	21	24	27	29.9
Mozambique	36	12	24	25	21	22	23	23.3
Uganda	15	22	19	20	22	22	22	20.3
Ethiopia	16	16	18	20	20	20	20	18.6
Guinea	16	11	11	14	11	12	—	12.5
Senegal	5	6	9	15	13	19	19	12.3
Cent. Afr. Rep.	17	9	10	14	10	10	10	11.4
Ghana	15	14	14	6	7	10	10	10.9
Madagascar	16	14	11	11	5	8	9	10.6
Kenya	4	4	4	5	5	5	5	4.6
Congo, DR	3	3	3	3	3	3	3	3.0
Niger	2	1	1	1	1	1	1	1.1
Angola	0	0	0	0	1	1	1	0.4
Total	1,286	1,242	1,105	1,368	1,287	1,379	1,409	1,298.4

Source: International Cotton Council.

Table 0.3 Area in cotton production in SSA, 1998–2005
(thousands of hectares)

Country	1998/99	1999/2000	2000/1	2001/2	2002/3	2003/4	2004/5	7-yr. avg.
Mali	504	482	228	532	468	500	525	462.7
Zimbabwe	330	369	389	363	400	400	400	378.7
Benin	394	372	337	384	323	350	375	362.1
Tanzania	250	182	430	392	400	400	400	350.6
Nigeria	300	280	350	375	338	338	338	331.3
Burkina Faso	355	245	275	356	338	345	352	323.7
Chad	298	300	240	312	281	286	292	287.0
Côte d'Ivoire	271	291	248	283	280	286	291	278.6
Mozambique	333	148	235	222	200	210	221	224.1
Uganda	250	202	202	200	200	200	200	207.7
Cameroon	173	172	199	210	200	204	208	195.1
Togo	159	154	135	165	160	163	166	157.4
Zambia	150	150	125	114	150	158	165	144.6
Ethiopia	80	80	100	113	113	113	113	101.7
South Africa	137	85	73	44	51	58	67	73.6
Kenya	30	50	50	50	50	50	50	47.1
Cent. Afr. Rep.	55	47	39	48	35	35	36	42.1
Senegal	48	18	22	32	36	45	46	35.3
Ghana	45	40	35	22	30	30	30	33.1
Guinea	33	27	21	30	27	28	-	27.7
Madagascar	34	35	29	28	14	20	22	26.0
Congo, DR	10	10	10	10	11	11	11	10.4
Niger	5	3	2	3	3	3	3	3.1
Angola	1	1	1	1	2	2	3	1.6
Total	4,245	3,743	3,775	4,289	4,110	4,235	4,314	

Source: International Cotton Council.

Today, cotton is cultivated in more than one hundred countries worldwide on approximately 2.5 percent of all arable land. This makes it one of the world's most significant crops in terms of surface area, after food grains and soybeans. The total area globally devoted to cotton has fluctuated, yet has shown no tendency to permanently rise since the 1950s (as climbing global production has been more closely related to improving yields). While cotton is grown in thirty-seven different African countries, five of those countries (Mali, Côte d'Ivoire, Benin, Burkina Faso, and Zimbabwe) account for nearly 60 percent of sub-Saharan Africa's production. Three other countries are notable: South Africa, because it has the most experience with genetically engineered cotton; Uganda and Tanzania, because they account for 92.8 percent of Africa's organic cotton production. In contrast to the rest of the world, the area devoted to cotton production in Africa has been rising. See figure 0.1 for the current spatial distribution of cotton production in Africa.

A group of former French colonies in West and Central Africa (WCA)[3] have increased production almost fivefold from the early 1980s to 2002, from two hundred thousand metric tons to almost one million tonnes. Together this group constitutes the seventh-largest producer of cotton in the world after China, the United States, India, Pakistan, Uzbekistan, and the European Union. With about 15 percent of global exports, the WCA countries are the second-largest exporter after the United States (USAID 2004).

Africa's major commodity crop exports are cotton, cocoa, coffee, and tea (USAID 2004). While Africa's share of world agricultural trade fell by 50 percent from 1980 to 2000, its share of cotton trade rose by 30 percent (FAO 2002). Over this period, production grew three times more rapidly in SSA than the world average (Goreux and Macrae 2002). In contrast to other parts of the world, cotton is a predominantly smallholder crop in SSA, with over two million rural households (or roughly fifteen million people) (Brottem 2005) depending on it as their main source of cash income (Tschirley, Poulton, and Boughton, this volume). To put this in context, SSA has 140 million smallholders who occupy 90 percent of the agricultural land.

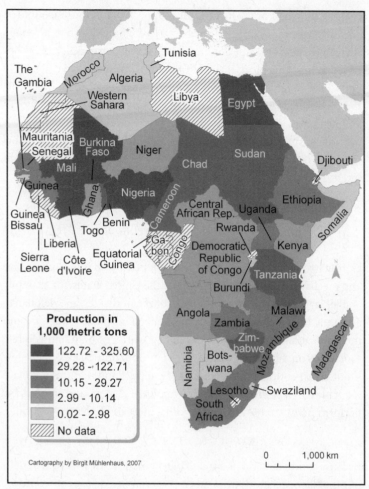

FIG. 0.1. Average cotton lint production in sub-Saharan Africa, 2000–2005. (Based on data from FAOSTAT 2006, the FAO's online database, at http://faostat.fao.org. Data is a five-year average.)

While Africa accounts for only about 15 percent of global cotton exports, its contribution to global markets has been climbing over the years, and the crop is of critical importance to many African countries (UNCTAD 2005). Most African cotton is exported in its raw form; only 5 to 10 percent is locally made into end products. Cotton is one of the most important cash crops in West Africa, where it contributes to more than half of the income for roughly two million smallholders who cultivate an average of one hectare of land (Martin et al. 2005). African cotton is of superior quality because it is hand picked (as opposed to machine picked) (UNCTAD 2005). West African cotton is of particularly high quality, having a longer fiber length than other cotton types that are characterized in the same category (Bassett 2005).

In sum, Africa, the least developed of the world's major regions, is now increasingly engaged in the production of cotton for the global market. The debates about the pros and cons of this trend continue to intensify.

Cotton, Poverty, and Rural Livelihoods in Africa

Cotton production in much of the developed world is input intensive and mechanized. Cotton cultivation in the United States, for example, applies large amounts of irrigation, fertilizer, pesticides, and defoliants, and uses highly mechanized means such as airplanes, tractors, and mechanical harvesters. In the developed world, human hands rarely touch cotton fiber. In Africa, cotton production is extremely low input. Most cotton is rain fed, uses few inputs and requires high levels of human labor to guide ox-drawn plows, seeders, and weeders (or perform many of these activities with a hoe) and to harvest cotton.

COTTON LIVELIHOODS

Because cotton tends to be a smallholder crop in Africa, it is different in terms of labor relations from other cash crops in Africa that are grown on larger farms or plantations. Given the quicker return on investment, annual crops such as cotton and tobacco tend to be more appropriate for small farms than tree crops such as rubber and oil palm, which are more likely to be grown on plantations. Tea, cacao, and coffee are well suited to both. The average wealth of African cotton farmers is less than that of those who focus on other cash crops (USAID 2004).

While women historically grew cotton in small gardens in many areas of West Africa, the crop is now largely grown by male-headed households and by young men (Moseley 1993; Bassett 2001). This transition, from a crop that is grown by men and women to one that is almost exclusively grown by men, relates to the change during the colonial era from cotton being grown for local cloth production to its cultivation as a cash crop (Isaacman and Roberts 1995). Colonial authorities, and postcolonial African governments, targeted men over women for extension services. Agricultural credit, needed to purchase inputs for export-oriented cotton production, was also largely inaccessible to women. Even though cotton is now a "male" crop, male heads of households use both family and hired labor to harvest cotton by hand. Women and girls work harvesting cotton on the household farm.

Besides cotton's shift from a "female" crop to a "male" crop, there is another significant change in the gendered division of labor of cotton production. Throughout West Africa, during the cotton harvest period, gangs of women hire themselves out as labor during the harvest period. Women are often preferred for harvesting cotton (as are children) because their smaller fingers can harvest cotton bolls faster and with less damage. This new labor system has several significant implications for the household. First, women are removing themselves from family work to work as laborers and in some cases even charging their own husbands for work on household fields. Second, women have access to significant income, which has implications for the household as a whole.

Some have argued that, because cotton is essentially a smallholder crop in Africa, increased production will have a significant impact on poverty (USAID 2004). West African governments also suggest that cotton production is really the only strategy they have for moving up the economic ladder (e.g., Touré and Compaoré 2003). Minot and Daniels (2005), though, demonstrate that whether cotton alleviates poverty is highly dependent on world prices. When world cotton prices declined by 40 percent during 2001/2, rural poverty in cotton-growing regions of Benin increased by 8 percent. This illustrates how linked issues of poverty and cotton in Africa are to international pricing policies. However, Siaens and Wodon (in this volume) contend that farmers were buffered from world price decreases because of currency devaluation, cotton reforms that resulted in higher producer prices, and overall production increases.

Others have documented an increasing debt problem for many smallhold cotton producers. Gray (in this volume) discusses how over 50 percent of farmers in her sample were indebted. Lacy (in this volume) notes that there is an increasing divide in many villages in southern Mali between poor indebted farmers and wealthier farmers. This has led to the breakup of village-level cooperative structures in many instances. Given normal rainfall variation in most cotton-growing areas, and the relatively high levels of inputs (and associated credit) required to grow cotton, it may be that cotton generates wealth only for those able to operate at a certain scale.

A key question is, why, if farmers have such difficulty with cotton production, do they continue to grow it? Koenig (in this volume) gives some insight to this in her chapter, where she describes how cotton systems provide a whole set of infrastructures that complement farmers' other activities. Through cotton, farmers have gained access to agricultural credit, equipment, fertilizer, as well as broader infrastructural improvements such as roads, telephones, schools, and health centers. Thus cotton, while not always lucrative by itself, needs to be viewed as part of a larger political economic system.

As cotton's ability to generate wealth for its custodians is ultimately tied up in the productivity of the land, any discussion of cotton, poverty, and wealth generation must also touch on the impact of this crop on the environment.

COTTON AND THE ENVIRONMENT

Cotton is grown primarily in tropical and subtropical climates. It is a crop that is threatened by excessive cold or heat (although resistance to these extremes varies from species to species). Excessive moisture or dryness at certain junctures in the growing season may also affect cotton quality and yields. The cotton plant has remarkable nutrient and moisture uptake; it can quickly exhaust the soil in the absence of sound management practices (including fertilizers, organic inputs, and crop rotation). The root systems of cotton plants are particularly well developed and penetrate deeply into the soil (often double the above-ground height of the plant). Seeds need warm temperatures and moisture during the germination phase (one to four weeks). Flowering starts one and a half to two months after planting. After flowering, the inner part of the bloom develops into a fruit, or boll. The bolls burst open at maturity, revealing cotton fibers (UNCTAD 2005).

Improved varieties of cotton are vulnerable to a number of insect pests, particularly foliage feeders and bollworms, and are frequently grown with regular pesticide applications. For example, Oerke and Dehne (2004) estimate that African cotton producers are at risk of losing 85 percent of their cotton crop to pests and diseases, but sacrifice only about 50 percent because of pesticide use. Cotton accounts for more pesticide use than any other crop, about 10 percent of global pesticide consumption when measured by weight of active ingredients (International Cotton Council, pers. comm., 2004).

Globalization critics often talk about a "race to the bottom," in which companies leave the global North in search of places that have lower environmental and labor standards. As such, one might assume that environmentally problematic crops such as cotton would quickly be outsourced to the developing world. One of the ironies of cotton in West Africa is that it generally does not follow that model; while cotton production in Africa uses pesticides and other inputs, the overall amount of inputs used pales in comparison to what is used in the global North. Indeed, Kutting (2003) argues that compared to other regions, farmers in Africa are "too poor to pollute."

Being too poor to pollute does not mean that cotton holds no environmental hazards. Cotton is at the center of debates about land degradation, pesticide use, and biotechnology in Africa. In terms of land issues, cotton cultivation is intersecting with population growth and land scarcity to create increasingly anthropogenic landscapes (Gray 1999). At the heart of the debate is whether cotton production is increasing or decreasing soil quality. In this volume, Moseley argues that cotton production in Mali has increased use of animal traction and chemical inputs by wealthier farmers. This has combined with the high nutrient demands of cotton and the abandonment of beneficial practices such as intercropping and minimum tillage to reduce soil fertility.

Another serious hazard of cotton production is the use of pesticides. Throughout the developing world, where farmers use pesticides on cotton, deaths and illnesses have been reported (Mancini et al. 2005; Ton, Tovignan, and Vodouhê 2000). Although pesticides are applied at fairly low rates, the way they are applied and their toxicity endanger human health. Furthermore, there is little education about the negative effects of pesticides. Pesticides used on cotton in Africa include chemicals from the organochlorine and organophosphate classes, both of which are extremely toxic. Endosulfan organochlorine pesticides were introduced in 1999 in francophone West Africa after cotton bollworms were found to be resistant to pyrethroids. Endosulfans are highly toxic neurotoxins and are banned in many countries. A government agency in Benin estimated that thirty-seven deaths occurred due to pesticide poisoning in one province during the 1999 season (Ton, Tovignan, and Vodouhê 2000).

Illnesses from pesticides occur in several ways. Before applying pesticides, farmers must generally mix chemicals with water, leading to direct skin contact. Then farmers apply these pesticides using backpack sprayers that frequently leak. Most farmers do not have access to protective gear during application; few farmers wear the recommended respirators, goggles, gloves, boots, or long sleeves in the hot tropical sun. This puts farmers at risk of either inhaling or coming into skin or eye contact with pesticides. Another risk of pesticide poisoning exists after application. When used in the developed world, there are strict rules about entering fields after pesticide application. In Africa, no signs are put out to warn those who might enter a field that it has just been treated.

Pesticides are frequently used for crops for which they have not been approved. Studies in Senegal, Ghana, and Benin have demonstrated that significant numbers of farmers used cotton pesticides on other crops, around the household for pest control, to preserve postharvest grain crops, and that they reuse pesticide containers for other purposes (Ton, Tovignan, and Vodouhê 2000; Williamson 2003). Part of the shifting of pesticides to other uses results from the large black market in cotton pesticides; many farmers obtain pesticides on credit and sell them either because they are cash constrained or because they have used their entire stock of pesticides. This means that anyone with enough cash can go to the marketplace and buy whatever pesticide they would like, even if they do not use it on cotton. In Ghana, for example, many farmers use cotton pesticides on food crops such as cowpea (Williamson 2003). The inappropriate use of pesticides is quite serious in the case of endosulfans, which are persistent and do not easily wash off with water. Because of concerns about pesticide use, there are efforts to introduce organic cotton into sub-Saharan Africa. Dowd, in this volume, addresses this issue, illustrating how one of the main motivations for the introduction of organic cotton is the reduction in pesticide-related illnesses.

One of the newer cotton technologies that will be introduced in many African countries in the coming years is genetically modified (GM) cotton (also referred to as genetically engineered or biotech cotton in common parlance). Already in use in South Africa, several countries in West Africa are undertaking field trials of GM cotton. The main type of GM cotton used in Africa is Bt cotton. The genetic modification in this variety comes from *Bacillus thuringiensis,* a soil bacterium that is toxic to insects of the bollworm family (Qaim and Zilberman 2003). Because the Bt gene produces toxins in the cotton plant that affect such insects, insecticide spraying is potentially reduced.

This new technology holds both promises and perils and has been quite controversial in some arenas. The promise lies in the potential ability of GM cotton to reduce insecticide use, thus reducing costs to farmers in the form of pesticides and labor, increasing yields and also reducing exposure to toxic pesticides. In South Africa, the only African country where GM cotton is widely in use at this point, both insect infestation and pesticide poisoning have been reduced and early studies indicated increased profits for farmers (Bennett et al. 2003; Thirtle et al. 2003).

The big environmental question concerns resistance. It is extremely likely that bollworm insects will eventually develop a decreased susceptibility to the toxin in Bt cotton (Tabashnik et al. 2003). The most common way of preventing resistance is to implement refuge strategies, where farmers dedicate a portion of their farmland to growing non-Bt cotton. Refuges work on the theory that in any given population, there are individuals that are not resistant to a given toxin. By having a refuge, nonresistant insects can survive to reproduce, eventually diluting the resistance of the population. One large question is whether African farmers have the institutional support to adopt the sorts of practices that will delay resistance.

Another big question about GM cotton is whether it can reduce poverty levels in sub-Saharan Africa. Gouse, Shankar, and Thirtle's chapter (in this volume) seems to indicate that the early promise of GM cotton due to reduced pesticide use and cost savings has been diminished somewhat by problems in institutional structures in South Africa and by the effects of different climatic conditions. A long-term perspective on the effects of GM cotton is therefore important.

Bingen (this volume) is likewise skeptical of GM cotton use in sub-Saharan Africa. He points to concerns of West African farmers about proprietary control, where after the introduction of GM cotton, farmers will be required to purchase seed at a higher price. In particular, farmers in West Africa seem concerned that they must agree not to save seed for replanting or give seed to anyone else. Bingen points to questions about the undemocratic nature of technology transfer, where farmers have little say in their future livelihoods. He asserts that decisions about what technology will be adopted and ultimately used are externally driven, particularly by large corporations and the U.S. government. He notes that it is interesting that farmers have become greatly involved in global politics, yet seem unable to have a voice in domestic political decisions. These decisions are essentially undemocratic and leave the small farmer completely out of the decision-making process about something that will affect them for years to come.

Globalization Debates and African Cotton Production

There is a considerable literature devoted to understanding the phenomenon of globalization and Africa's relationship with that process (e.g., Carmody 2002; Logan 2002: Cheru 2002; Reed 2003; Mbaku and Saxena 2004). In its most general sense, globalization refers to the increasingly international nature of the world economy (or the interconnectedness of national economies), as well as the growing global flow of ideas and culture. There are at least three debates in the globalization literature that relate to (or are informed by) studies of African cotton production in a global context. First, to what degree is Africa involved in the globalization process? Second, what is the nature of global trading regimes and Africa's relationship with them? Third, to what extent do African governments and farmers passively accept unequal treatment or use the tools of globalization—international media and networks of NGOs, for example—to try to mobilize against the negative forces of globalization.

GLOBALIZATION AND AFRICA

To what degree is Africa involved in the globalization process? Many view Africa as operating at the margins of globalization (Grant and Agnew 1996; Cook and Kirkpatrick 1997). In other words, Africa is an increasingly minor player in terms of its share of global trade and investment. In the case of agricultural products for example (which traditionally have been considered the continent's strong suit), Africa's share of global trade fell by 50 percent between 1980 and 2000 (FAO 2002). Africa's declining share of world trade (as a marker of globalization) may be interpreted in a number of ways.

The orthodox economic interpretation of this situation is that African producers have a comparative advantage in the area of commodity crop production. While African farmers should be leading the globe as producers for some crops, interventionist policies and government inefficiency has led to the decline of African economies, a point made in the oft-cited Berg report (World Bank 1981). African states have historically used agriculture as a way to extract revenue for government operations and to subsidize urban dwellers. World Bank and IMF structural adjustment programs (which advocate a smaller role for government, export orientation, and currency devaluation) have been major policy instruments aimed at rebolstering Africa's position as a commodity crop producer. One of the pillars of structural adjustment has been to increase commodity prices for agricultural producers, which, in theory, should increase commodity production and bring in the financial resources necessary for poverty alleviation and the strategic investments needed to advance African economies. In sum, proponents of this perspective argue that Africa is operating at the margins of the global economy because of internal inefficiencies. They further assert that African economies will benefit from international trade if they can reduce such inefficiencies and more vigorously engage international markets as commodity producers. In addition to internal inefficiencies, supporters of this perspective also often acknowledge that subsidized production in countries of the global North has led to an unfair situation in the global training arena.

An alternate interpretation is that Africa is neither excluded from, nor a minor player in, the globalization process. Rather, Africa is playing the *integral* role of the peripheral commodity producer. Peripheral in this instance does not imply an area outside the globalization process but rather a zone from which resources are being extracted (Frank 1979; Wallerstein 1979). In other words, Africa is not a minor or marginal player in the globalization process, it has just been dealt the role of commodity producer. The globalization of markets for agricultural commodities thus constructs a new terrain of uneven development at the global scale (FitzSimmons 1997). The reality is that Africa's level of commodity production has not declined in most cases. However, its share of global production has decreased in some instances as other areas in the global South have increased production (e.g., this is the case for coffee, where Vietnam has recently become a large producer) (USAID 2004). More significant than production changes have been noticeable and consistent declines in terms of trade for commodity crops (Africa is receiving less for the products it exports and paying more for its imports).

It has been estimated that declining terms of trade cost non-oil-exporting African countries 119 percent of their combined GDPs between 1970 and 1997 (FAO 2002). More specific to the case of African cotton, Oxfam (2002) determined that for the six African countries that depend on cotton for more than 20 percent of their total revenues (Benin, Burkina Faso, Central African Republic, Chad, Mali, and Togo), they increased export volumes by 40 percent during the 1990s, yet saw their export revenues decline by 4 percent during the same period. As such, Africa's declining export revenues are most closely related to declining prices for its products, even though (in many instances) it is producing more of such commodities. Therefore, it seems reasonable to conclude that Africa is not outside the globalization process (because material flows of goods are increasing) but is simply at the wrong end (because less and less money is flowing in for the increasing flow of agricultural commodities going out). Indeed some critics of globalization contend that it "searches out differences—in living standards, in the defensive strength of political institutions, in the resilient and resistant practices of people in place—to achieve the old mercantile goal of buying cheap and selling dear" (FitzSimmons 1997, 160). One of the discussions heard in African cotton-producing countries is that unless African economies can find some way to add value to cotton production, through industrialization, they will remain in the role of peripheral primary commodity producer.

TRADE AND AFRICA

What is the nature of global trading regimes and Africa's relationship with these? The 1990s were a particularly notable period for globalization (Gallagher 2001). In the early to mid- 1990s, a new round of negotiations under the General Agreements on Tariffs and Trade (GATT) created the World Trade Organization (WTO). The main mission of the WTO was to create the conditions for free trade and mediate trade disputes among different countries. At the regional level, new trade agreements were initiated in different parts of the world, including Africa.

Critics noted that these agreements tended to focus on areas where the industrialized world had a comparative advantage, leaving agriculture, the main economic export activity of Africa, alone. At the same time, African governments came under pressure from international financial institutions (IFIs) to initiate structural adjustment programs (SAPs). These SAPs played a key role in opening up African economies to global markets (Roy 1997; Bracking 1999), particularly as they pressured producing countries to liberalize their domestic marketing and price policies. What came to be known as the Washington Consensus aimed to increase agricultural production through increased prices for agricultural producers and reduced state intervention in agricultural markets (Daviron and Gibbon 2002). The irony of course is that while developing countries have liberalized their agricultural production to meet the demands of donor governments, and become more efficient producers because of these domestic policy changes, agricultural production in developed countries was and still is heavily subsidized. As such, agriculture, in addition to intellectual property rights, remains one of the last frontiers for free-trade negotiations. Reducing agricultural subsidies for North American and European farmers has been particularly challenging. For more than a century in Europe, and for a shorter time span in the United States, the persistence of agricultural subsidies has been explained in terms of the relative power of farmers in these countries. Some have seen that as a paradox (or agrarian question), as the influence of farmers was growing just as their economic power was waning (Kautsky 1988; Koning 1994).

Since the mid-1990s, global cotton prices have declined by 50 percent. Part of this can be blamed on international trends away from cotton toward synthetic materials, and by increased cotton production in China. However, much of the blame can also be put squarely at the feet of subsidies given by the wealthy countries of the world (particularly the United States) to their agricultural producers (Baffes 2004). This latter view has been effectively communicated in the international arena by a series of influential reports, editorials, and the vocal role that West African leaders have taken against subsidies.

One of the most influential and effective campaigns against cotton subsidies has come from Oxfam as part of its Make Trade Fair campaign. Oxfam has highlighted the injustice of cotton subsidies given to American farmers in several provocative reports (2002, 2004). They blame the plummet in world prices directly on the increase of cotton production in the United States (Oxfam 2004). Blaming declining world prices solely on the U.S. subsidies is somewhat simplistic as both China and the European Union also subsidize their cotton producers, yet it is clear the magnitude of U.S. subsidies has led to increased cotton exports. Goreux (2005) reports that in 2003/4 the United States. exported 75 percent of its cotton production, compared with only 37 percent four years earlier.

Increased exports have largely resulted from changes made in the 1990s and reaffirmed in the 2002 U.S. farm bill, making cotton more profitable than other competing crops such as soybeans or corn (Badiane et al. 2002). Current U.S. farm policy guarantees farmers a minimum price above market prices. Above that farmers in the United States are then given a payment that brings them to a target price. As a result, American cotton farmers have received up to 73 percent above world market price (Oxfam 2002). This is in stark contrast to African farmers, who receive no subsidies and receive well below the world market price. These subsidies result in the United States spending between US$3 and $4 billion each year supporting cotton farmers. Without subsidies, cotton production would not be profitable in the United States. The World Bank estimates that removing subsidies would generate an extra $250 million per year in added revenues for cotton farmers in West Africa (Minot and Daniels 2005). However, removing subsidies may not be the magic bullet in increasing incomes of cotton farmers that many are proposing. Bassett (in this volume) sees a short-term benefit to increased cotton prices but points out that these additional revenues may be captured by others in the commodity chain. West African farmers have historically received a low proportion of world cotton prices; there is no reason to believe that this will change if world prices increase. Bassett argues that in order for farmers to benefit from increased world prices, they must increase their share of the world market price at the national scale. Furthermore, others make the point (e.g., Moseley in this volume) that these added revenues would be temporary as others farmers will increase production as global prices rise.

As such, the global trading regime has often been portrayed as unfair to African producers in at least two ways. The first and more radical critique is that Africa will always be at a disadvantage if it continues to focus on undifferentiated commodity production. The second perspective suggests that trade in commodities makes sense but that it is not working well for African producers because all countries do not play by the same rules.

One response to the more radical critique is the suggestion that Africa would be best served by disengaging from the globalization process. Advocates of the disengagement position (e.g., Bond 2002) argue that involvement with the global economy has only hurt Africa and that the global trade flows are not free but structured in a way that benefits the North. They assert that the continent is better served by a move toward self-sufficiency and regional trade. Such an approach might also entail a return to import substitution, an idea that some are beginning to look at again anew (e.g., Bruton 1998). While this argument may be appealing, whether or not disengagement is actually happening, and whether or not this is a real option, is another story. As mentioned above, while African revenues from agricultural trade (in dollar terms) are declining, the quantity of goods it is producing for international markets is increasing. Moreover, there is ample evidence to suggest that most rural economies in Africa are becoming increasingly monetized, a trend that points toward the increasing integration (not disengagement) of African producers in the global market.

GLOBALIZATION, AGRICULTURAL TRADE, AND AFRICAN AGENCY

Globalization is often portrayed as a hegemonic process, one where African farmers and governments are negatively affected by globalized processes. What is becoming clear with cotton, however, is that African farmers and governments do not passively accept unequal treatment and are quite adept in using the tools of globalization to try to mobilize against the negative forces of this process.

West African political leaders have been outspoken about the injustice of cotton-pricing policies in the United States and the negative effects that they have on poor West African farmers. In a *New York Times* editorial, the presidents of Mali and Burkina Faso put the production practices of small farmers in West Africa and large farmers in the United States in stark contrast (Touré and Compaoré 2003). Smallhold family farmers in West Africa can produce high-quality cotton for a 50 percent lower cost than can large corporate farmers in the United States, where farms generate little employment and have large environmental impacts. The two presidents further highlighted the injustice of the policy by claiming that most of the subsidies go to the wealthiest farmers. Indeed, the top 10 percent of farmers receive 79 percent of cotton subsidies, while the top 1 percent of farmers in the United States receive 25 percent of the subsidies (Oxfam 2004).

The presidents of Mali and Burkina Faso illustrated how cotton policies of the wealthy countries reveal the basic inequities in the world-trade system, where free-trade rules are generally applied to products of interest to the wealthy countries but not to products where the poorest countries have a comparative advantage.

Four West African countries—Benin, Mali, Burkina Faso, and Chad—demanded recourse from the WTO, presenting a proposal in 2003 that asked for an elimination of cotton subsidies and for compensation for exporters of cotton as part of the Doha round of trade negotiations (WTO 2003). The unwillingness of the developed world to make concessions on this issue led to the collapse of the trade negotiations in Cancun in 2004. Cotton subsidies were one of the issues cited by the world's developing countries as illustrating the basic inequities of agricultural policies of the developed and developing worlds. Indeed the public relations campaign mounted by the West African countries has been remarkably effective. The plight of West Africa peasant farmers has been highlighted in forums ranging from a series of editorials in the *New York Times* entitled "Harvesting Poverty" to public appearances by members of the farmers' unions in Cancun. These public pleas, however, left farm policy in the United States fundamentally unchanged.

What eventually changed farm policy in the United States was a decision by the World Trade Organization against U.S. cotton subsidies. Leading to that decision was a suit, brought by Brazil, that challenged the "peace clause," an agreement granted to the developed countries in the Uruguay round of negotiations. The peace clause basically allowed countries to give their farmers agricultural subsidies as long as they did not exceed 1992 levels. Brazil argued that the current cotton subsidies granted by the most recent U.S. farm bill exceeded the cap and constituted an illegal payment. The WTO ruled in favor of Brazil, and in March 2005 the WTO ruled against an appeal by the United States. If the United States did not reform its agricultural policies that give large subsidies to cotton farmers, it is likely that Brazil would retaliate with sanctions. At this time, it is unclear what type of agricultural reform will emerge as cotton farmers, particularly those from Southern states, such as Texas and Mississippi, wield a great deal of political power. Research by Ledermann (2005) suggests that, while the U.S. may comply with the letter of international trade law, the repackaging of subsidies may lead to little or no decline in government support for U.S. farmers.

One way to think of global cotton is as a vertically integrated set of farmers, national private-public partnerships, or marketing boards and international corporations that process and market cotton. While global forces are clearly an important part of the cotton story in West Africa, they are only part of the story. As the activism of West African cotton farmers suggests, we need to have a more nuanced view of globalization to counter the idea of globalization as a hegemonic force that is unaffected by local actors; instead we must show that globalization is uneven and contested (Whatmore and Thorne 1997). In African cotton struggles, networks of farmers and international NGOs are an equally important part of this story. Bassett (2001) largely represents the peasant cotton revolution in Côte d'Ivoire as a success due to the agency of local producers who made demands on state actors to raise cotton prices. When prices were too low, farmers responded by protest and withdrawal from the cotton market, using their market power to create new alliances with state actors.

Somewhat ironically, farmers' unions may have more power when the state is overly dependent on a commodity they produce. This is arguably the case in Mali and Burkina Faso. Alternatively, the over-dependence of the treasury on commodity crop revenues could conceivably also lead to state-sponsored violence or coercion to ensure continued production. This was the case in some colonies during the colonial era, although such a strategy was never that effective as it resulted in farmers' diverting their production to the black market as well as a generalized subsistence crisis (Isaacman 1996; Bassett 2001).

At this time, producer groups in countries such as Burkina Faso and Mali are asserting their power. Unions of cotton growers are using their influence to determine local price policy by bargaining with national governments and international policymakers. Thus, West African farmers are going global. Mirroring the fair trade movement in other commodities such as coffee, West African cotton producers are utilizing alternative networks to create new markets for cotton production. For example, while members of West African farmers' unions are attending WTO meetings to change policy, they are also attending international meetings of organic farmers, marketers, and textile makers seeking to move away from chemical-intensive cotton production toward organic production. These efforts work side-by-side with their more conventional efforts to change the pricing policies of developed countries. These alternative networks have emerged from groups of NGOs, such as Oxfam, which has pushed its Make Trade Fair campaign for cotton, among other commodities. Dowd, in his chapter, illustrates how European NGOs are organizing organic cotton cooperatives in East and West Africa. Very interestingly, organic cotton production has been easier to establish in areas where the state is less active in the promotion of conventional cotton production, making East Africa more favorable for this type of production than West Africa.

Notes

The epigraphs to this chapter are drawn from Isaacman 1996; Government of Burkina Faso, "Strategic Framework for the Development of the Cotton Sector in Burkina Faso" (Ouagadougou, 2004); Aaron de Grassi, "Genetically Modified Crops and Sustainable Poverty Alleviation in Sub-Saharan Africa: An Assessment of Current Evidence," Working Paper, Accra: Third World Network—Africa, 2003; Drissa Keita, "La filière cotonnière est le clé du développement du Mali," interview, *Jeune Afrique économie,* June 1–14, 1998; Walter S. Rodney, *How Europe Underdeveloped Africa* (Washington, DC: Howard University Press, 1982); Touré and Compaoré 2003.

1. Hereafter we will refer to sub-Saharan Africa simply as Africa.

2. African and non-African governments, civil servants, local business people, and multinational corporations.

3. These countries are often discussed as a group because they have a similar history and organization of cotton production. They also participate in the global cotton market as a group. The vast majority of production in this group hails from four West African countries: Benin, Burkina Faso, Côte d'Ivoire, and Mali.

References

Badiane, Ousmane, Dhaneshwar Ghura, Louis Goreux, and Paul Masson. 2002. "Cotton Sector Strategies in West and Central Africa." World Bank Policy Research Working Paper 2867, Washington, DC.

Baffes, John. 2004. "Cotton: Market Setting, Trade Policies and Issues." World Bank Policy Research Working Paper No. 3218, Washington, DC, February.

Bair, Jennifer. 2005. "Global Capitalism and Commodity Chains: Looking Back, Going Forward." *Competition and Change* 9 (2): 153–80.

Bassett, Thomas J. 2001. *The Peasant Cotton Revolution in West Africa: Côte d'Ivoire, 1880–1995.* London: Cambridge University Press.

———. 2005. "Price Formation and Power Relations in Cotton Value Chains of Mali, Burkina Faso and Côte d'Ivoire." Report prepared for Oxfam America, Boston.

Bennett, Richard, T. Joseph Buthelezi, Yousouf Ismael, and Stephen Morse. 2003. "Bt Cotton, Pesticides, Labour and Health: A Case Study of Smallholder Farmers in Makhathini Flats, Republic of South Africa." *Outlook on Agriculture* 32 (2): 123–28.

Bingen, James. 2004. "Pesticides, Politics, and Pest Management: Toward a Political Ecology of Cotton in Sub-Saharan Africa." In *African Environment and Development: Rhetoric, Programs, Realities,* ed. William G. Moseley and B. Ikubolajeh Logan, 111–26. Aldershot, UK: Ashgate.

Bond, Patrick. 2002. *Unsustainable South Africa: Environment, Development, and Social Protest.* Merlin Press and University of Natal Press.

Bracking, Sarah. 1999. "Structural Adjustment: Why It Wasn't Necessary and Why It Did Work." *Review of African Political Economy* 26 (80): 207–26.

Brottem, Leif. 2005. "The Limits of Cotton: White Gold Shows Its Dark Side in Benin." *Foreign Policy in Focus,* June 30.

Bruton, Henry J. 1998. "A Reconsideration of Import Substitution." *Journal of Economic Literature* 36:903–36.

Bryant, Raymond L., and Michael K. Goodman. 2004. "Consuming Narratives: The Political Ecology of 'Alternative' Consumption." *Transactions of the Institute of British Geographers* 29:344–66.

Carmody, Padraig. 2002. "Between Globalisation and (Post)apartheid: The Political Economy of Restructuring in South Africa." *Journal of Southern African Studies* 28 (2): 255–75.

Cheru, Fantu. 2002. *African Renaissance: Roadmaps to the Challenge of Globalization.* Zed Books.

Cook, Paul, and Colin Kirkpatrick. 1997. "Globalization, Regionalization and Third-World Development." *Regional Studies* 31 (1): 55–66.

Daviron, Benoit, and Peter Gibbon. 2002. "Global Commodity Chains and African Export Agriculture." *Journal of Agrarian Change* 2 (2): 137–61.

FAO (Food and Agriculture Organization of the United Nations). 2002. *FAOSTAT.* http://faostat.fao.org.

FitzSimmons, Margaret 1997. "Commentary on part 2: Region in Global Context? Restructuring, Industry and Regional Dynamics." In *Globalising Food: Agrarian Questions and Global Restructuring,* ed. Michael Watts and David Goodman, 158–68. London: Routledge.

Frank, Andre Gunder. 1979. *Dependent Accumulation and Underdevelopment.* New York: Monthly Review Press.

Gallagher, Kevin. 2001. "Globalization and Sustainability." In *A Survey of Sustainable Development: Social and Economic Dimensions,* ed. Jonathan Harris, Timothy Wise, Kevin Gallagher, and Neva Goodwin. Washington, DC: Island Press.

Gereffi, Gary, and Miguel Korzeniewicz, eds. 1994. *Commodity Chains and Global Capitalism.* Westport, CT: Praeger.

Goreux, Louis. 2005. "Cotton in Burkina Faso." Paper. Organisation for Economic Co-operation and Development.

Goreux, Louis, and John Macrae. 2002. "Liberalizing the Cotton Sector in SSA." Part 1: "Main Issues." Mimeo, World Bank, Washington, DC.

Grant, Richard, and John Agnew. 1996. "Representing Africa: The Geography of Africa in World Trade, 1960–1992." *Annals of the Association of American Geographers* 86 (4): 729–44.

Gray, Leslie C. 1999. "Is Land Being Degraded?: A Multi-scale Examination of Landscape Change in Southwestern Burkina Faso." *Land Degradation and Development* 10:329–43.

Hartwick, Elain. 1998. "Geographies of Consumption: A Commodity Chain Approach." *Environment and Planning D: Society and Space* 16:423–37.

Isaacman, Allen. 1996. *Cotton Is the Mother of Poverty: Peasants, Work, and Rural Struggle in Colonial Mozambique, 1938–1961.* Portsmouth, NH: Heinemann.

Isaacman, Allen, and Richard Roberts, eds. 1995. *Cotton, Colonialism, and Social History in Sub-Saharan Africa.* London: James Currey.

Kautsky, Karl. 1988. *The Agrarian Question.* Trans. from the German by Peter Burgess. 2 vols. London: Zwan. (Orig. pub. 1899.)

Koning, Niek. 1994. *The Failure of Agrarian Capitalism: Agrarian Politics in the United Kingdom, Germany, the Netherlands and the USA, 1846–1919.* London: Routledge.

Kutting, Gabriella. 2003. "Globalization, Poverty and the Environment in West Africa: Too Poor to Pollute?" *Global Environmental Politics* 3 (4): 42–60.

Ledermann, Samuel T. 2005. "Agricultural Subsidies and the Doha Round: A Historic Breakthrough?" Honors thesis, Department of Geography, Macalester College, Saint Paul, MN.

Logan, B. Ikubolajeh, ed. 2002. *Globalization, the Third World State, and Poverty-Alleviation in the Twenty-First Century.* Aldershot, UK: Ashgate.

Mancini, Francesca, Ariena Van Bruggen, Janice Jiggins, Arun Ambatipudi, and Helen Murphy. 2005. "Acute Pesticide Poisoning among Male and Female Cotton Growers in India." *International Journal of Occupational Health* 11 (3): 221–32.

Maponga, Oliver, and Philip Maxwell. 2001. "The Fall and Rise of African Mining." *Minerals and Energy* 16 (3): 9–26.

Martin, Thibaud, Germain O. Ochou, Angelo Djihinto, Doulaye Traore, Mamoutou Togola, Jean Michael Vassal, Maurice Vaissayre, and Didier Fournier. 2005. "Controlling an Insecticide-Resistant Bollworm in West Africa." *Agriculture, Ecosystems and Environment* 107 (4): 409–11.

Mbaku, John Mukum, and Suresh Chandra Saxena. 2004. *Africa at the Crossroads: Between Regionalism and Globalization.* Westport, CT: Praeger.

Minot, Nicholas, and Lisa Daniels. 2005. "Impact of Global Cotton Markets on Rural Poverty in Benin." *Agricultural Economics* 33 (3): 453–66.

Moseley, William G. 1993. "Indigenous Agroecological Knowledge among the Bambara of Djitoumou Mali: Foundation for a Sustainable Community." Master's thesis, University of Michigan, Ann Arbor.

Oerke, Erich-Christian, and Heinz-Wilhelm Dehne. 2004. "Safeguarding Production—Losses in Major Crops and the Role of Crop Protection." *Crop Protection* 23(4): 275–85.

Oxfam. 2002. "Cultivating Poverty: The Impact of U.S. Cotton Subsidies on Africa." Oxfam Briefing Paper 30.

———. 2004. "Finding the Moral Fiber: Why Reform Is Urgently Needed for a Fair Cotton Trade." Oxfam Briefing Paper 69.

Porter, Philip. 1995. "Note on Cotton and Climate: A Colonial Conundrum." In *Cotton, Colonialism, and Social History in Sub-Saharan Africa,* ed. Allen Isaacman and Richard Roberts. London: James Currey.

Qaim, Martin, and David Zilberman. 2003. "Yield Effects of Genetically Modified Crops in Developing Countries." *Science* 299:900–922.

Raikes, Philip, Michael Friis Jensen, and Stefano Ponte. 2000. "Global Commodity Chain Analysis and the French Filière Approach: Comparison and Critique." *Economy and Society* 29 (3): 390–417.

Reed, Richard. 2003. *Economic Change, Governance and Natural Resource Wealth: The Political Economy of Change in Southern Africa.* London: Earthscan.

Roy, Sumit. 1997. "Globalization, Structural Change and Poverty: Some Conceptual and Policy Issues." *Economic and Political Weekly.* 32 (33–34): 2117–35.

Tabashnik, Bruce E., Timothy J. Dennehy, Yves Carriere, Yong Biao Liu, Susan K. Meyer, Amanda L. Patin, Maria A. Sims, and Christa Ellers-Kirk. 2003. "Resistance Management: Slowing Pest Adaptation to Transgenic Crops." *Acta Agric. Scand., Sect. B, Soil and Plant Sci. Supplementum 1,* 51–56.

Thirtle, Colin, Lindie Beyers, Yousouf Ismael, and Jennifer Piesse. 2003. "Can GM-Technologies Help the Poor? The Impact of Bt Cotton in Makhathini Flats, KwaZulu-Natal." *World Development* 31 (4): 717–32.

Ton, Peter, Dansinou Silvère Tovignan, and Simplice Davo Vodouhê. 2000. "Endosulfan Deaths and Poisonings in Benin." *Pesticides News,* no. 47: 12–14.

Touré, Amadou Toumani, and Blaise Compaoré. 2003. "Your Farm Subsidies Are Strangling Us." *New York Times,* July 11.

UNCTAD (United Nations Conference on Trade and Development). 2005. *Cotton: Info Comm—Market Information in the Commodities Area.* http://ro.unctad.org/infocomm/anglais/cotton/crop.htm.

USAID (U.S. Agency for International Development). 2004. "Poverty Reduction and Agricultural Trade in Sub-Saharan Africa: Recommendations for USAID Interventions." Discussion paper, USAID, Washington, DC, May.

Wallerstein, Immanuel M. 1979. *The Capitalist World Economy: Essays.* New York: Cambridge University Press.

Whatmore, Sarah, and Lorraine Thorne. 1997. "Nourishing Networks: Alternative Geographies of Food." In *Globalizing Food: Agrarian Questions and Global Restructuring,* ed. Michael Watts and David Goodman. London: Routledge.

Williamson, Stephanie. 2003. "Pesticide Provision in Liberalized Africa: Out of Control." ODI Agricultural Research and Extension Network, Network Paper 126, 1–20.

World Bank. 1981. *Accelerated Growth in Sub-Saharan Africa: An Agenda for Action.* Washington, DC: World Bank.

WTO (World Trade Organization). 2003. *Brief from West African Countries.*

Part I

Global Cotton, Local Crises

1

Producing Poverty

Power Relations and Price Formation in the Cotton Commodity Chains of West Africa

Thomas J. Bassett

"If I export a kilogram of raw cotton I am paid US $1.20. If you make yarn, you get three times that. If you weave, the value goes up six times and if you make the garment the value goes up ten times," Museveni said, complaining that unfair tariff barriers make Africa a continent of "donor" nations that give jobs and income to the industrial west.

—*Ugandan president Yoweri Museveni*

Ann and I will carry out this equivocal [*sic*] message to the world, markets must be open. The United States will not tolerate favoritism and unfair subsidies. We want to compete, and we want our farmers to compete on level ground.

—*U.S. president George W. Bush*

THE 2003 WORLD TRADE ORGANIZATION (WTO) meetings held in Cancun, Mexico, collapsed because cotton growers of the global South insisted on a level playing field in agricultural trade. Led by the trade ministers of Brazil, Benin, Burkina Faso, Mali, and Chad, a group of twenty countries declined to take up the North's agenda until progress was made in implementing the Doha Declaration.

Penned at the end of the 2001 WTO ministerial conference held in Doha, Qatar, the declaration committed the North "to correct and prevent restrictions and distortions in world agricultural markets . . . with a view to phasing out, all forms of export subsidies; and substantial reductions in trade distorting support" (WTO 2001). Yet the United States and European Union continue to give billions of dollars in subsidies to their cotton growers, ginners, and exporters, leading to overproduction, dumping, and depressed world market prices. The cotton subsidy issue was again center stage at the 2005 WTO Hong Kong meetings (Bradsher 2005; Ricard 2005). But despite the exhortations of African cotton growers, little progress was made in settling this dispute.[1] Some observers of farm subsidies have argued that if all cotton subsidies were eliminated, world prices would increase by 11 cents (Oxfam 2003; FAO 2004). Even if that came to pass,[2] major questions remain about the distribution of this eleven-cent cotton bonus. Would it trickle down to African cotton growers or end up in the pockets of other actors in the cotton commodity chain?

Cotton Broils

Cotton cultivation is central to the farming systems and rural economies of West Africa. With few cash-earning alternatives, cotton is often the only source of agricultural credit and is pivotal to reducing poverty and improving livelihoods for hundreds of thousands of rural and urban households (Pfeifer 2005). Income from cotton sales pays for health and education expenses and determines whether a metal or thatch roof covers the home. When cotton incomes are low, sick children are not taken to health clinics because their parents cannot afford to buy medicines. Low incomes also force parents to take children out of school because they cannot afford to pay for school fees and supplies. Cotton is also a major source of foreign-exchange earnings for West African governments, ranging from a fifth of Mali's exports to more than a third of Burkina Faso's. This dependence of cotton growers and governments on world markets makes them vulnerable to declining prices and unfavorable exchange rates since, cotton is traded in dollars.

Cotton growers in the United States depend more on government subsidies than on world market prices. In most years, U.S. farmers are unable to produce cotton at a cost that is below the world market price. Between 1997 and 2004 world market prices for cotton averaged 54 cents per pound.[3] The average cost of production (ex-gin) in the United States fluctuates around 70 cents per pound (Estur 2005). In the absence of subsidies, U.S. cotton is not profitable. U.S. cotton growers would have lost $827 per acre every year since 1997 without government subsidies that amounted to between $2 and $3 billion annually (UNDP 2005). The 2002 Farm Act assures that U.S. cotton growers are compensated for their high production costs no matter what the market price. The number and variety of income support programs (direct payments, countercyclical payments, marketing loans) encourages farmers to sustain production levels despite falling world market prices (Wescott, Young, and Price 2002). Cotton-ginning companies and exporters reap their own subsidies through the Step 2 and export credit programs. In fact, all the major actors in the U.S. cotton industry, from growers and ginners to warehouse operators, domestic mill owners, and international traders, receive some government payment in what one observer calls the "most 'vertically integrated' program of any commodity" (Thompson 2005, 11). The proponents of these programs, notably the industry's lobbying arm, the National Cotton Council, argue that these subsidies are "essential tools of the U.S. [cotton] industry" (National Cotton Council 2005, 9–10).[4] By dumping price-depressing surpluses onto the world market, U.S. cotton growers and exporters prevent West African cotton growers from reaping the widely touted rewards of free trade. To understand the relationship between world prices and producer prices in West Africa, we need to understand how prices are formed in the cotton commodity chain.

The Global Commodity Chain Approach

The global commodity chain (GCC) is an analytical tool for uncovering price formation at different stages of the production and marketing processes. By dividing the chain into its constituent activities, we can see where profits are made and how they are distributed among various actors. The regulation and coordination of a GCC, also known as chain governance, is strong when a particular firm or institution has significant influence on price formation. Chain governance is very strong in West Africa where parastatal cotton companies have historically regulated cotton production through input supply-credit schemes and monopsonistic control over seed cotton markets. One of the World Bank's objectives in restructuring West Africa's cotton sectors is to modify chain governance by giving market forces as well as cotton growers more power in price formation (see below).

The GCC approach derives from world systems theory and the political economy of development/underdevelopment studies of the 1970s and 1980s. It is distinguished from the global value chain approach by its focus on the political-economic dimensions, history, and power relations that shape the input/output structure, geography, and governance structures of GCCs (Bair 2005; Gereffi and Korzeniewicz 1994). GCC analysis is closely allied to the commodity-based filière approach, derived from French colonial agricultural development policy (Raikes, Jensen, and Ponte 2000). While GCC is tending toward developing a coherent theoretical framework (Bair 2005; Gereffi, Humphrey, and Sturgeon 2005), the filière approach is more of a mesolevel analytical tool used by policymakers for restructuring production systems and institutional frameworks in the name of development. Until recently the filière approach restricted itself to the national scale, since producer prices were set and trade controlled by state institutions such as government marketing boards. In the context of economic restructuring driven by the neoliberal polices of international financial institutions like the World Bank, the filière approach is increasingly concerned with issues of price formation and trade issues that transcend the national scale (Raikes, Jensen, and Ponte 2000, 404). A good example of the filière's expanded scope is the series of studies conducted by the Centre International de Recherche en Agriculture pour le Développement (CIRAD) from 2001 to 2003 of the cotton commodity chains of a half dozen West African countries (Fok and Taze 2003). Table 1.1 illustrates this multiscale scope of the filière approach.

Table 1.1. Cotton commodity chain, Côte d'Ivoire

Activity	Actors	Competition	Regulation	Price formation
Importation of inputs	HydroChem, STEPC, SIMCHEM	—	UNIPHYTO rules for quality control	5% tariff; low TVA (11.1%); none since 2002
Local acquisition of inputs	UNIPHYTO, HydroChem, STEPC, SIMCHEM, Novartis, Callivoire, Chemivoire, Aventis, Fortichem, cotton companies, farmer organizations	Some via bidding process; limited entry	INTERCOTON monitors and mediates bids and price formation; phytosanitary manufacturing laws	Prices negotiated by INTERCOTON; input-supply credit to growers (with 6–10% interest levy)
Seed production	CIRAD, CNRA, cotton companies, selected growers	None	No seed certification or contracts	Officially free but 5 FCFA/kg charge enters seed cotton price
Distribution of seeds and inputs to farmers	Cotton companies, transporters, co-ops, INTERCOTON	Some between transporters union and cotton companies	INTERCOTON mediates cotton chain actors; farmer unions organize distribution and credit recovery	6–8% charge on cost of inputs factored into grower price
Production of seed cotton	1,750 producer co-ops; 5 farmer federations	None	R&D links with CNRA & companies; extension agents monitor input supply; co-op contracts with input suppliers	R&D and extension costs entered into cotton company costs in negotiating seed cotton price
Marketing of cotton	Ivoire Coton, LCCI, Nouvelle CIDT, URECOS-CI	Some? Geographical monopolies challenged by URECOS-CI; DOPA	Cotton company regional monopsony linking input-credit system destabilized	Administered prices (BNETD/HORUS formula); co-ops receive 6–8 FCFA/kg for primary marketing; 2 cotton grades; supplementary payment

Forging the West African Cotton Commodity Chain

The historical development of the West African cotton commodity chain is key to our understanding of its current configuration, in which parastatal cotton companies play key governance roles (Bassett 2001). We can date the emergence of these firms to the waning years of French colonial rule in West Africa, when the French Company for the Development of Textile Fibers (CFDT) and the Institute for Research on Cotton and Textile Fibers (IRCT) developed a high-yielding cotton package consisting of seeds, fertilizers, and insecticides. The Allen cotton program, named after the *G. hirsutum* variety that was the centerpiece of this package in Côte d'Ivoire, involved important innovations in the production and marketing of cotton. For example, before the Allen program, seed cotton could be purchased by any trader. The Mandé-speaking Jula outcompeted French traders by offering higher prices for seed cotton. French traders gained the upper hand when the CFDT signed a cotton development contract with the independent Ivorian government in 1962. Arguing that it needed to control seed cotton varieties and agricultural inputs to prospective cotton growers, the CFDT succeeded in becoming the exclusive buyer of cotton in the country (Bassett 2001, 103–6). The CFDT's monopsony allowed the company to give credit to cotton growers for the purchase of fertilizers and pesticides at the beginning of the growing season and to recuperate these loans at the time of harvest, when producers sold their crop to the company. This input supply-credit scheme, which tied producers to cotton companies in an informal system of contract farming, became the hallmark of the cotton commodity chain in West Africa until the end of the twentieth century.

Parastatal control over cotton markets and input supply enabled cotton companies to erect a vertically integrated commodity chain. Their activities included cotton varietal research and development, input delivery, extension services, village-level marketing, transportation, ginning, and selling cotton fiber on world markets. The CFDT's marketing arm, the Compagnie Cotonnière (COPACO), served as the commission agent for three new national cotton companies: CIDT (Côte d'Ivoire), CMDT (Mali), and Sofitex (Burkina Faso).[5] In conjunction with government marketing boards or stabilization funds, these cotton companies exercised considerable power in setting agricultural input and seed cotton prices. The constituent parts of this buyer-driven commodity chain are diagrammed in figure 1.1.

The commodity chain segments shown in figure 1.1 trace the major activities involved in the production of seed cotton, its ginning, and its delivery to ports. The closure of the chain at ports reflects the export-oriented nature of cotton production in West Africa. Ninety-nine percent of Mali and Burkina Faso's cotton is exported onto the world market. For Côte d'Ivoire, 15 percent of the cotton crop enters domestic textile mills; 85 percent is exported.

This system of strong single-firm governance of all aspects of the commodity chain became the target of World Bank structural adjustment reforms during the mid-1990s and early 2000s throughout West Africa. The bank requires governments to break up parastatal cotton companies by selling off groups of gins to private investors. To make the sale attractive, the governments delimited cotton-growing zones in which investors would have the right to buy seed cotton from "their producers." The zonal model of partial privatization that characterizes the World Bank's liberalization scheme was first pioneered in Côte d'Ivoire (Bassett 2003, 246–50). In Burkina Faso the parastatal cotton company Sofitex saw its national monopoly partially reduced in 2004 when it sold three of its gins to two different companies: Faso

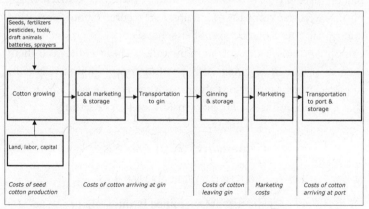

FIG. 1.1. The cotton commodity chain: farm inputs to FOB.

Coton and SOCOMA (Société Cotonnière de Gourma). The share-holders of Faso Coton are the Swiss cotton-trading firm Paul Rein-hart (29 percent), International Promotion Services (21 percent), the Burkinabè transportation company SOBA (20 percent), the fertilizer company Amerfert (formerly Agridis) (20 percent), and the Burkinabè cotton growers' union (UNPCB) (10 percent). The major shareholders of SOCOMA are Dagris (ex-CFDT) (55 percent) and UNPCB (20 percent). The remaining shares are held by private Burkinabè investors. Despite the reform, Sofitex continues to dominate the cotton economy. The area it controls accounted for 82 percent of national cotton production in 2004/5. SOCOMA and Faso Coton's zones produced 11 percent and 7 percent of Burkina's cotton that year.

Like Côte d'Ivoire, Burkina's privatization scheme retains the vertically integrated form of the former parastatal. Rather than a national monopoly, there are now three regional monopolies. Each cotton company has a clearly delimited zone of intervention and control (fig. 1.2). Cotton growers obtain inputs from the company that controls their area and to which they are obliged to sell their seed cotton. Pan-territorial pricing facilitates this process. The zoning model is primarily designed to manage the key input-supply credit and reimbursement relationship that links producers to specific cotton companies. If this link is broken (e.g., when producers sell their cotton to a company other than the one that provided them with credit), then cotton companies will be unable to recover their loans. Under the regional monopoly model, cotton company profits are more secure. Nationwide pricing and a guaranteed market also offer some security to producers who can obtain credit from cotton companies as long as they sell them their crop. The involvement of the cotton growers' union (UNPCB) in price-setting negotiations also introduces a degree of transparency that reduces producer-company tensions over price setting.

Commodity Chain Analysis

AGRICULTURAL INPUTS

Of the three segments that are examined in this section, agricultural inputs are perhaps the most important and least studied. Cotton is

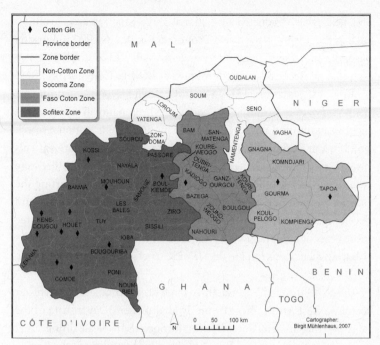

FIG. 1.2. The cotton zones in Burkina Faso, 2005.

an extremely demanding crop in terms of agrochemical inputs. It alone accounts for 60 percent of all fertilizers and 80 percent of all insecticides used in the West African agriculture. As a result, cotton growers spend large sums of money each year purchasing these inputs. Depending on the yields and purchase price, agricultural inputs consume 35 to 45 percent of cotton growers' gross revenues. The high costs of inputs, as well as low producer prices, have been the catalyst of repeated market boycotts in Côte d'Ivoire and Mali in the 1990s and early 2000s (Bassett 2001, 162–64; Bingen 1994).

Cottonseed. Cottonseed is distributed freely to producers in Côte d'Ivoire and Mali. However, cotton companies in both countries claim a research and development expense that is factored into their costs during producer price-setting negotiations. Cotton growers in Burkina Faso pay 30 West African francs (FCFA) per kilogram for linted seeds and FCFA 70 for delinted seeds.[6] The companies fund cottonseed research

The Cotton Commodity Chains of West Africa | 43

and field trials conducted by national agronomic research institutes such as the Institut Nationale d'Economie Rurale (INERA) in Burkina Faso, the Institute d'Economie Rurale in Mali (IER), and the Centre National de Recherche Agronomique (CNRA) in Côte d'Ivoire. Seed multiplication is contracted out to growers, who receive a premium for their seed cotton. Beginning in 2002 large multinational seed companies (Monsanto and Syngenta) began to fund transgenic cotton research programs in Burkina Faso at INERA's Fara Koba and Kouaré agricultural research stations. After three years of experimentations that were considered successful by INERA, Monsanto is currently inserting the Bt gene into two Burkina varietals (FK 37 and Stam) at its research and development facilities in the United States. INERA anticipates three more years of field trials with these local Bt cotton varieties before distributing them to cotton growers (INERA, pers. comm., June 18, 2005).

Fertilizers. Outside of Nigeria, three large firms dominate the fertilizer sector of West Africa: Yara (formerly HydroChem), an affiliate of the large Norwegian firm NorskHydro; the Société Tropicale d'Engrais et de Produits Chimiques (STEPC), a Côte d'Ivoire affiliate of the French Société Commerciale des Potasses d'Alsace, which is itself an affiliate of the Entreprise Minière et Chimique (EMC) group; and SENCHIM, a commercial affiliate of the Senegalese firm Industries Chimiques du Sénégal (IFDC 2002, 11). Each firm specializes in certain fertilizer components. Yara is the world's largest producer of nitrogen fertilizer. STEPC is a leading producer of potassium. SENCHIM specializes in phosphate.

Cotton companies in Mali and Burkina maintain a monopoly in the distribution of fertilizers. In Côte d'Ivoire, national producer organizations (*les faitières*) and cotton companies furnish fertilizers on credit to growers via their cooperatives. Through a process of international bidding, cotton companies select both local and international firms to furnish specific fertilizers to specific locations. The winning firm(s) supply the fertilizer on credit (sometimes backed by local and international banks) to cotton companies, which have 360 days to pay their creditors.[7] Fertilizer companies typically charge a 15 to 20 percent transaction fee. The high fee is explained in part by the long repayment period and in part by the fact that transactions take place in CFA francs that are eventually converted into euros or U.S. dollars.

Cotton companies, in turn, supply fertilizers to village-scale producer associations on credit that contain a 10 to 11 percent service fee (Résocot 2003a, 2003b). Local-level farmer organizations typically add a handling charge for their role in distributing fertilizers to producers. In sum, producers pay a 25 to 30 percent credit fee for the fertilizers they use in their cotton fields. Not surprisingly, one of the major complaints of producers is the high cost of inputs.

Although difficult to verify, insiders speak of collusion among input suppliers and between suppliers and cotton companies in price setting. For example, the international bidding process typically elicits bids from both the parent company and its local or regional affiliate. Thus, although there appear to be many firms competing against each other, in fact there are very few firms involved. The bidding process is further compromised by the participation of agrochemical companies that are also important shareholders of the cotton companies seeking bids. For example, one of Burkina Faso's major fertilizer suppliers, Amerfert, holds a 20 percent share in one of the country's new cotton companies, Faso Coton.

Pesticides. The supply of pesticides is dominated by multinational agrochemical firms such as Syngenta, STEPC, SENCHIM, and Callivoire that work through affiliates and distributors within the region. These local affiliates mix the active ingredients, which are generally imported from Europe and the United States (IFDC 2002, 12). Cotton companies obtain pesticides with a supplier credit that is guaranteed by local and international banks.

As in the supply of fertilizer, cotton companies in Mali and Burkina have a monopoly in the distribution of pesticides to producers. Pesticide suppliers are selected through a process of international bidding. However, questionable intrafirm practices exist in which cotton companies select suppliers in which they have an investment. The case of Sofitex and the pesticide company Saphyto is illustrative.

Saphyto (Société Africaine de Produits Phytosanitaires et d'Insecticides) is located in Bobo-Dioulasso and is jointly owned by the

French company Calliope (65 percent) and Sofitex (35 percent). It accounts for 50 to 70 percent of the pesticide sales in Burkina (IFDC 2002, 29). Sofitex goes through the process of international bidding and selects a company that offers the best products for the best prices. Sofitex may purchase 25 percent of its pesticides from the winning firm. It will then buy up to 75 percent of its remaining pesticide needs from Saphyto at the same price offered by the successful bidder.

Cotton companies typically supply pesticides (insecticides and herbicides) to cotton grower groups on credit and charge a 10 to 11 percent service fee (Résocot 2003a, 2003b). The producer cost per kilogram or liter is typically negotiated between producer organizations and cotton companies so that there is a unique, pan-territorial price for these inputs. As noted above, companies automatically deduct the input credits from the payments they give to producers for their seed cotton.

If farmers do not sell sufficient cotton to repay their credit, the cotton grower group at the village scale is obligated to pay for its defaulting members. That is, the earnings of successful farmers are deducted to pay back the loans of less productive, or free-riding, farmers, who may have diverted inputs to their food crop fields or sold them in parallel markets. The collective guarantee for input supply credits is a frequent source of conflict among farmers within a community. It often leads to the exclusion of chronically indebted cotton growers from producer groups and the constant reorganization of these groups (MacRae and Marmignon 2004, 10–12).

COTTON PRODUCTION

This segment of the commodity chain includes farming systems and expenses. Cotton is a rain-fed (nonirrigated) crop in all three countries. It is grown in the Sudano-Guinean climate zone of West Africa, where rainfall ranges between 750 and 1,400 mm annually. Rainfall is highest in the cotton-growing areas of central Côte d'Ivoire and decreases as one moves northward to central Mali and Burkina Faso. Fields are prepared and planted beginning in mid-May to mid-June, and harvested in December and January. The general statistics of cotton production for the three countries are given in table 1.2.

Table 1.2. Seed cotton production, Mali, Burkina Faso, Côte d'Ivoire, 2004/5

Category/Country	Mali	Burkina Faso	Côte d'Ivoire
Number of producers	172,353	200,000	150,000
Area in cotton (ha)	564,971	670,538	270,000
Average yield (kg/ha)	1,042	947	1,300
Total Production (tonnes)	578,000	606,000	350,00

Low-income cotton producers typically apply less than the recommended amount of agricultural inputs to their cotton fields. Rather than three sacks of fertilizer, they might apply two sacks and use the third on a food crop field. Depending on the severity of pest problems, a farmer may only apply insecticides six or seven times, not eight. Relatively poor households will not use herbicides. They are also more likely to use the cheaper but labor-intensive hand-powered pesticide applicator over the battery-powered sprayer. Poorer households will also rely more on family labor and reciprocal labor groups than employ off-farm labor. When one considers these cost-saving but labor-intensive measures, the monetary costs of production for a relatively poor household could decline to FCFA 72,250 ($139) per hectare, or to 36 percent of gross income. In this case, farmers' net income would amount to $244 per hectare.

We can compare these hypothetical costs and incomes with real figures for one village cooperative in Burkina Faso in the Béréba area. In 2004/5 there were approximately seventy members of the cooperative that produced a total of 260 metric tons of seed cotton for a gross income of FCFA 54,658,800. The cooperative had a credit of FCFA 24,277,028 for insecticides, herbicides, fertilizers, and insecticide sprayers. These costs amounted to nearly 45 percent of gross income. The costs of seeds, batteries, off-farm labor, amortization of oxen, and farm equipment are not included in these expenses.

In summary, cotton growers' incomes are closely tied to the production process and primary marketing stages, at which the costs of growing and marketing cotton are high. Farmers' incomes would be much higher if producer prices were higher, yields per hectare were higher, and the costs of inputs were lower. Basic agricultural inputs to the production process amount to between 35 percent and 45 percent of producers' gross incomes. To minimize these costs and at the same time increase net incomes, cotton growers spread these inputs over a larger area of cotton cultivation. The goal of agricultural extensification is to increase the volume of production by simultaneously expanding the area in cotton and reducing the amount of recommended inputs per hectare (Bassett 2001). Yields per hectare will fall under this strategy but overall output will rise due to the larger area under cultivation. In addition, the cost of chemical inputs for each kilogram of seed cotton produced will be lower than the costs for each kilogram produced following the intensification strategy. In sum, the goal of extensification is to increase overall output with lower production costs and thus achieve stable to higher incomes.[8]

COTTON GINNING AND MARKETING

In this segment of the cotton commodity chain, cotton companies incur costs related to the transportation, ginning, and marketing of cotton (see table 1.3). The FOB cost price is the sum of anticipated costs for buying, transporting, and ginning seed cotton, and transporting and marketing cotton fiber to port.[9] During producer price-setting negotiations, cotton companies compare world market prices with their FOB cost price as the basis for determining the purchase price for a kilogram of seed cotton. It is important to remember that the FOB cost price represents target operating costs (*les coûts objectifs de revient*) and not actual operating expenses. The latter could be lower than those projected in the table. In the event they are lower, cotton companies do not share their hidden profits with producers. For example, if the official FOB reference price is FCFA 685 but the actual operating costs are FCFA 635, the additional fifty-franc profit (multiplied by the tonnage of exported cotton fiber) is not shared with producers. The practice may partly explain why producer purchase prices often stagnate or decline (Campbell 1984).

The case of Mali for 2003/4 gives one reason to believe that such accounting practices can result in cotton companies reaping millions of dollars in profits at the expense of producers. Nicholas Gergely's report on the CMDT's expenses shows operating costs amounting to

Table 1.3. Cotton company costs, Burkina Faso and Mali, 2003/4 (FCFA/kg of cotton fiber)

Cost	Burkina Faso	Mali
Producer price	418.0	478.9
Upstream costs (research, extension, seeds, roads)	12.8	26.3
General operating expenses (administration, technical assistance, interest on loans)	28.6	24.1
Collection and transport to gin (producer group return for collection, interest on loans)	75.8	77.7
Ginning	79.9	99.2
Delivery to port	82.6	67.5
Total costs (FOB)	697.7	773.7

Source: Gergely 2004.

FCFA 773.6 per kilogram of cotton fiber that fiscal year (Gergely 2004, 10). Mariama Walet reports in her analysis of CMDT's costs for the same year that the company's operating expenses amounted to FCFA 737.1 per kilogram of cotton fiber (Walet 2005). If one supposes that this discrepancy of FCFA 36.5 is the difference between target and actual operating expenses, and multiplies that figure by the total tonnage of seed cotton exported that year, then CMDT may have earned an additional profit of $16.6 million in 2003/4 that it did not share with producers.[10]

Ginning companies sell cotton fiber (lint cotton) either to cotton traders who speculate in cotton markets or to commission agents who serve as middlemen between textile mills and cotton companies. Before structural adjustment reforms of the 1990s and early 2000s, much of the three countries' cotton was sold to commission agents. COPACO, the subsidiary of Dagris (formerly CFDT), was the leading commission agent in all three countries. In 2001, COPACO handled 96 percent of Burkina Faso's cotton exports (Résocot 2003a, 21) and 50 percent of Mali's sales (Résocot 2003b, 21). COPACO was the major commission agent of Côte d'Ivoire cotton before partial privatization of the cotton sector in the late 1990s. Privatization of Côte d'Ivoire's cotton sector opened the door to other cotton-trading firms, such as Reinhart, OLAM, CDI, Volcot, and Cargill. Reinhart became a major shareholder in Ivoire Coton, one of the three companies created following the breakup of CIDT. In 2005 Reinhart marketed one-third of Côte d'Ivoire's cotton (Italtrend 2006, annexes, 69). This upstream movement of cotton-trading firms means that intracompany cotton sales are taking place, most likely at the expense of producers' incomes (see below).

Cotton quality greatly influences the prices paid to producers. Cotton is graded in village markets according to two grades, high and low. High quality (first-grade) seed cotton fetches a premium price in comparison to low quality (second-grade) cotton. However, cotton companies distinguish between three to five first grade classes at the gin as opposed to just one in village markets. For example, in Burkina Faso, Sofitex distinguishes four high-quality classes at the gin (Boby/S, Bola/S, Boby, and Bola). The company receives a ten-franc premium for the first two standards (Boby/S and Bola/S) even though that cotton is bought from producers at a fixed first-grade price for which Bola is the reference. Some observers believe that cotton company profits are 10 to 20 percent higher than believed because of the difference between gin and village-level grading differences for top-quality cotton. Others argue that ginning companies do not receive such premiums in world markets.

Among cotton traders and textile companies, West African (francophone) cotton is known for its high quality. It contains little debris (dry leaves, stems, etc.) and has an above-average fiber length (at least 1⅛ in., or 28.6 mm). However, this above-average quality is jeopardized by the contamination of cotton by plastic strings that enter the fiber during the harvest and village-level storage because farmers place handpicked cotton in polyethylene and polypropylene sacks during the harvest (fig. 1.3). Contamination results in a five-cent-per-pound discount for West African cotton (Estur 2005, 4–5).

There is no organized market exchange for West African cotton in which future contracts and options are possible. Instead, cotton is priced in relation to a proxy measure called the Cotton Outlook

FIG. 1.3. Harvesting seed cotton in the Katiali region of northern Côte d'Ivoire.

index, commonly referred to as the Cotlook A price. The index is based on quotes received daily by Cotlook, Ltd., from traders on the prices they would be willing to pay for cotton of specific origins. It also takes into account closing prices on the New York Cotton Exchange, which handles only U.S. cotton, and the results of other cotton transactions, such as public auctions and online trading (Fok 2005; World Bank 2006). The Cotlook index is not tradable; that is, "it is not possible to buy or sell the index spot or forward, and it is susceptible to manipulation" (World Bank 2006).

The Cotlook A indicator is for a cotton type whose characteristics (e.g., fiber length of 1 ³/₃₂ in., or 27.8 mm) are inferior to West African cotton. Nevertheless, when the sales managers of West African cotton companies negotiate with cotton merchants or spinners on a selling price, they use the Cotlook A price as the base price. Premiums and discounts are added to or subtracted from this price based on the quality of the product, the reputation of the gin, and the relationship between the gin and trader or spinner. The forward contract that is finally negotiated typically sets a fixed FOB price in euros or

U.S. dollars per kilogram of cotton fiber. More than 80 percent of West African cotton is sold as fixed-price forward contracts (World Bank 2006).

The number of firms involved in the global cotton trade is not as concentrated as in the grain trade, in which just five companies control 85 to 90 percent of global food markets (Murphy 2002). In 2003 there were nineteen cotton merchants that accounted for 38 percent of world cotton production (ICAC 2004, 2). In West Africa there are seventeen traders that are active in the cotton trade. However, just five handle 70 percent of production (table 1.4) (Estur 2004, 11). This trade oligopoly means that cotton-trading firms are more likely to be price setters than price takers. When these powerful traders become owners of newly privatized cotton-ginning companies, their market power is strengthened by their monopsonistic control over cotton markets within their company's geographical zones.

As on the global scale, the privatization and liberalization of Africa's cotton sectors is leading to the substitution of private for government trading organizations. Half of the largest cotton traders active in West Africa (table 1.4) are now major investors in Côte d'Ivoire (Reinhart,

Table 1.4. The major cotton-trading companies of West Africa , 2003/4

Company	Headquarters
Major (more than 100,000 tonnes)	
1. Compagnie Cotonnière SA (COPACO)	Paris
2. Louis Dreyfus Group International Cotton NV	Antwerp
3. Paul Reinhart AG	Winterthur, Switz.
4. L'Aiglon SA	Geneva
5. Dunavant Enterprises Inc.	Geneva
Large (50,000 to 100,000 tonnes)	
6. Plexus Cotton Ltd.	Liverpool
7. Société Cotonnière de Distribution (CDI)	Lausanne
8. Mambo Commodities	Paris

Note: Companies are ranked by estimated volume of FCFA-zone cotton purchased in 2003/04.

Source: Estur 2004, 11.

Dreyfus, L'Aiglon), Mali (COPACO), and Burkina Faso (COPACO, Reinhart). The implications of this entry of the largest international cotton traders for cotton growers' share of cotton incomes has been absent in the heated discussions taking place at WTO conferences over the past five years. As Sophia Murphy notes, "Unfortunately, debate at the WTO has overwhelmingly emphasized governments, farmers and, to a lesser extent, consumers. Companies are nowhere mentioned . . . [but] companies trade—not farmers or countries" (2002, 8, 11). As the largest cotton traders assume more power within the vertically integrated commodity chains and geographical monopolies that are currently multiplying in the World Bank's spaces of (partial) privatization and liberalization, there is reason to believe that market distortions linked to market power concentration will occur, even if all domestic and export cotton subsidies are eliminated.

Cotton is traded on world markets in U.S. dollars, but cotton growers are paid in West African francs (FCFA)—a currency that is tied to the euro. Thus, the exchange rate between the dollar and euro is a key variable in the competitiveness of African cotton in world markets (Estur 2005). When the dollar is strong, the costs of producing a kilogram of cotton are relatively low in dollar terms. When the euro is strong, these same costs are higher in dollar terms. The effects of exchange rates on price formation is illustrated in the following example. Between August 2002 and January 2004 the world price for cotton rose by 54 percent. However, due to the depreciation of the dollar vis-à-vis the euro, there was only a 19 percent price increase in terms of FCFA.

Producers' Share of the World Market Price

The goal of the fair trade movement is to increase the producer's share of the world market price. When it comes to cotton, this is a tricky calculation because the daily quoted price (Cotlook A) is not based on actual market transactions. An alternative indicator of "world price" is the average FOB price received by cotton companies in a given year. This price more accurately reflects real market prices received by a cotton gin. However, since cotton-ginning companies make money on the difference between their declared cost price for a kilogram of cotton fiber and the FOB price they receive from cotton traders, they are reluctant to divulge these actual numbers. It is because of this difficulty in obtaining accurate sale price data that the Cotlook A indicator is used in determining "world price" for cotton.

But to calculate cotton growers' share of world market prices, we need to know more than just the world price of cotton. We also need to know the price that cotton growers receive for their crop in village-level markets. In most West African countries, cotton companies buy seed cotton in these primary markets at either one of two grades. First-grade cotton is bright white, relatively dry, and contains little plant debris. Second-grade cotton is gray or yellow, more humid, and includes some stems and leaves. Most cotton analysts use the first-grade seed cotton price to indicate cotton grower prices (Goreux 2003; MacRae and Marmignon 2004).[11] However, not all seed cotton sold by producers to cotton companies is first grade. A proportion is sold as second and even third grade in a given country. Thus, one needs to know *the average market price of seed cotton* based on the proportion of cotton sold at these different grades in any given year. In sum, any estimate of producer share of world market prices must specify both the world price indicator (FOB price or Cotlook A) and the average market price of seed cotton. Different measures will yield different results.

If we use the Cotlook A indicator (converted from U.S. cents per pound to West African Francs (FCFA) per kilogram of cotton fiber) and the first grade price received by producers, we find that cotton growers received just 48 percent of the world market price. If we use the average annual FOB price obtained by West African cotton companies as the world market price, the producer's share increases to 56 percent. The Cotlook A (CIF) gives a higher "world price" since it includes shipping costs to the recipient country. It thus gives a relatively lower producer share. The FOB average sale price of African cotton companies results in a lower "world price" because shipping costs are lower. They only include the costs of transporting cotton fiber to a West African port, not to the recipient country. It thus gives a relatively higher producer share.

When we compare producer prices (first grade only) with the Cotlook A measure, two trends stand out (fig. 1.4). In years when cotton prices are high, the producer's share is low. When world cotton prices are low, the producer's share is higher. For example, the top three years in which producer prices were high correspond to the three years of lowest world market prices (1998, 1999, 2001). A second trend evident in figure 1.4 is the relative stability of producer prices despite fluctuating world market prices. Although cotton growers receive a relatively low share of the world market price, administered prices buffer them from the boom-and-bust nature of cotton export markets. A key factor that explains this price stability is the guaranteed price that is set annually in each country by committees composed of representatives of ginning companies, cotton growers, and governments.

The producer price–setting mechanism varies from country to country but typically contains two components: (1) a floor price that is set in relationship to cotton company and producer costs and the projected world market price (Cotlook A), and (2) a supplemental payment (*la ristourne*) if world market prices (Cotlook A) turn out to be higher than the one projected during price-setting negotiations earlier in the season. This price-setting mechanism ensures that

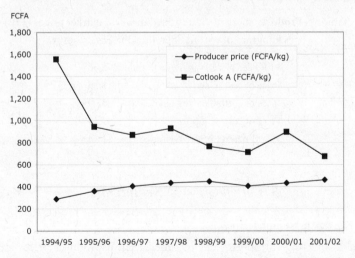

FIG. 1.4. Trends in producer price and world market price (Cotlook A) for a kilogram of cotton fiber.

producer prices are the same throughout the national territory and do not drop below the guaranteed price in the event that world market prices drop.[12] These pan-seasonal and pan-territorial dimensions of the guaranteed price effectively reduce market risks for producers (Estur 2004, 25). The administered price also means that ginning companies are positioned to take a larger slice of the cotton cake when world market prices are high. However, the supplemental payment mechanism (la ristourne) ensures that some of these profits are shared with producers. Thus, although the graph in figure 1.4 lends support to the World Bank's position that there is little relationship between world market prices and producer prices, there is a connection via the role of the Cotlook A index in the price-setting mechanism. As noted earlier, the recourse to the Cotlook A indicator rather than the average FOB price is due to the difficulty in obtaining reliable sale price figures from cotton companies. Notwithstanding these data problems, table 1.5 uses cost price and FOB sale price figures collected by Gergely (2004) to calculate the value added in world market prices for a kilogram of cotton fiber for Burkina Faso. The data show that cotton growers captured 58 percent of the FOB world price between 2001 and 2003, which is close to the average (56 percent) noted above.

Table 1.5. Producer share of value added in world market price (FOB) per kilogram of cotton fiber, Burkina Faso, 2001/3

Producer price	$.66
Price of cotton arriving at gin	$.86
Price of cotton leaving gin	$.99
Price of cotton at port	$1.11
World market price	$1.14

Cotton Growers' Net Incomes

The producers' share of the world market price is not the only variable affecting cotton growers' incomes. Even if producer prices are stable, the high costs of fertilizers and pesticides will affect farmers' net incomes. As noted above, the agrochemical costs of growing cotton can amount to 45 percent of gross cotton revenues. Cotton growers have repeatedly boycotted cotton markets in Côte d'Ivoire and Mali over the past decade because of the high price of inputs.

Another factor affecting farmers' incomes is indebtedness (Bassett 2001; Gray this volume). In the past, if a farmer failed to repay the cooperative for cotton input loans at harvest time, the debt would be carried forward to the following year's harvest. Indeed, many cotton growers found themselves ensnared in debt for years. Some of these loans were never repaid. To ensure repayment, cotton companies now hold the cooperative responsible for covering the debts of all its members. This collective responsibility for outstanding debts means that the income of successful farmers is often reduced to pay off the debts of their less successful neighbors. This practice produces tensions within communities and reduces the attractiveness of cotton growing even when world market and producer prices are high.

Finally, cotton growers' incomes and the entire cotton economy ultimately depend on cotton companies paying farmers for their crop in a timely manner. Yet, delayed payments are increasingly common, especially in Côte d'Ivoire. Following the privatization of the Ivorian cotton sector, some companies (LCCI, CIDT) and producer cooperatives (URECOS-CI) did not pay producers for months, and sometimes for years. In the past, cotton growers received payment within the month of selling their crop. In 2006 cotton-ginning companies owed producers $38 million for seed cotton deliveries made between 2001 and 2005 (Italtrend 2006). Low world market prices and poor company management combined to produce these catastrophic conditions. Desperate cotton growers began to sell their crop outside their designated zone to companies that were paying their producers. They also sold cotton to itinerant merchants known as *pisteurs*, who offered cash to farmers for their crop but at half the official price. These clandestine sales in Côte d'Ivoire resulted in the trafficking of up to seventy thousand metric tons of seed cotton to neighboring Mali and Burkina Faso (USDA 2006).

The analytical approach of the global commodity chain allows one to investigate the upstream and downstream processes shaping prices as seed cotton is produced and transformed into cotton fiber and sold on world markets. This study investigates the segments beginning with the supply of farm inputs to the sale of cotton fiber to cotton traders. The objective is to determine if cotton growers are positioned to capture any increase in world market prices in the event that the U.S. cotton subsidy programs end. The following findings emerge from this analysis.

First, producers' incomes are shaped as much by the costs of production as they are by world market prices. Cotton is an input-intensive crop, which means that any increase in fertilizer and pesticide prices will result in lower incomes if yields and seed cotton prices remain constant. This agronomic dimension is often missing from fair trade value chain studies (e.g., Fitter and Kaplinsky 2001). In contrast to other fair trade crops, such as coffee, that do not require large amounts of agrochemical inputs (Fend 2005, 43; Ponte 2001, 27), cotton is input intensive. Cotton growers must obtain credit from cotton companies, agribusiness firms, or other institutions to successfully grow cotton (Larsen 2003; Bourdet 2004). Cotton growers will benefit from this upstream improvement in their farming system as much as from higher seed cotton prices.

Second, hidden profit taking by cotton companies and traders in the ginning and marketing links of the cotton chain systematically erodes cotton growers' incomes. The interfirm ties linking various segments of value chain raise questions about conflicts of interests, cooked books, and backroom deals that are more likely to occur in vertically integrated industries.

Third, since cotton is traded in U.S. dollars in world markets, a strong euro reduces the value of cotton in local currencies (Estur 2004). Devaluing the FCFA is a double-edged sword. On the positive side, a strong dollar would increase the amount of CFA francs earned on international cotton markets. However, devaluation would also increase cotton growers' costs for imported agricultural inputs.

Fourth, cotton growers operate on an uneven playing field in which prices are shaped by national cotton companies and international cotton traders as well as by U.S. agricultural subsidies. The vertically integrated structure of the cotton sector remains strong despite reforms aimed at increasing competition via privatization and liberalization. The World Bank's zoning model of privatization and liberalization has likely strengthened the hands of the largest international cotton companies in setting market prices.

The question remains: In the event that world cotton prices increase as a result of the elimination of trade-distorting subsidies in the United States and the European Union, will African cotton growers' incomes increase? The answer in the short term is yes. There are two reasons for being guardedly optimistic. First, producer prices are set in all three countries according to a formula that is tied to the average world market price (Cotlook A). *If* world market prices increase, even in the short term, producer prices should correspondingly increase. Second, cotton growers have secured a seat at the price-setting table in all three countries thanks to the growing clout of producer organizations. Their voices are clear and their collective actions (e.g., market boycotts) are highly effective in their struggle for a fair share of the cotton cake. For these two reasons alone, we have cause to be optimistic. However, any price increase related to subsidy suppression will likely be short term, as competitive cotton-growing countries will boost their production leading to a leveling off of world market prices. This analysis highlights the many links in the commodity chain where market prices are formed to the detriment of producers. Cotton producers and their supporters must struggle in both local and global arenas to increase their share of world market price as a step toward improving rural livelihoods in West Africa.

Notes

The epigraphs to this chapter are drawn from speeches at the Center for Strategic and International Studies, Washington, DC, June 14, 2004, in Charles Cobb Jr., "Uganda's President Calls Extending African Import Law Urgent," http://allafrica.com/stories/200406150034.html; and at the swearing-in ceremony for Secretary of Agriculture Ann Veneman, Washington, DC, March 2, 2001, http://www.whitehouse.gov/news/releases/2001/03/20010302–6.html.

1. The 2005 WTO Hong Kong meetings ended with an agreement that committed the United States to ending its cotton export subsidies in 2006. However, this agreement was not a concession since the WTO had already required the United States to end its export subsidies in its appellate body ruling of March 2005. At the end of the Hong Kong meetings, Mamadou Ouattara, secretary of the Association of African Cotton Producers, pointed out that 90 percent of U.S. cotton subsidies are domestic subsidies. "It [the agreement] is deceptive; we wanted the end of all subsidies but we obtained nothing." Agence France Presse, "OMC: Semi-défaite pour l'Afrique dans la bataille du coton," December 18, 2005.

2. There is some debate about the impact of U.S. cotton subsidies on world cotton prices. For a useful summary of the different projections, see FAO 2004.

3. Economic Research Service, USDA. Costs were calculated from the table in http://risk.cotton.org/CotBudgets/us.htm.

4. The notion that agricultural subsidies sustain low-income farmers is clearly a myth (Thompson 2005, 4). It is the wealthiest farmers and exporters that mainly benefit. The Environmental Working Group's analysis of the distribution of agricultural subsidies shows that they are highly skewed in favor of a small number of large farms and states. There are just twenty-five thousand cotton growers in the United States, in comparison to more than half a million producers in Mali, Burkina, and Côte d'Ivoire. Just 10 percent of U.S. cotton growers received 79 percent of all payments. An astonishing 1 percent received 25 percent of all payments (Environmental Working Group 2005).

5. CIDT (La Compagnie Ivoirien pour le Développement des Fibres Textiles), Sofitex (Société Burkinabè des Fibres Textiles), CMDT (Compagnie Malienne pour le Développement des Textiles).

6. FCFA refers to Francs de la Communauté Financière Africaine. The CFA franc has a fixed exchange rate of FCFA 656 to one euro.

7. Supplier credits are normally offered for a thirty-to-sixty-day period.

8. Studies conducted in Mali and Guinea show that despite lower yields per hectare, the extensfication strategy results in higher production levels than if farmers simply applied the same inputs to the recommended area. However, whether incomes increase, remain stable, or fall depends on the relationship between market prices for cotton, prices of inputs, and overall total production levels. If cotton prices fall faster than the output per farmer rises, then incomes will decline. Total production levels dropped in Côte d'Ivoire in the early 1990s because of the introduction of a high

input–demanding variety of cotton known as GL7. The variety did not respond well to lower input levels and production plummeted.

9. In a free on board (FOB) situation, the seller pays all costs necessary to deliver cotton to the port of export.

10. To arrive at this figure one multiplies the difference between the target and actual costs (FCFA 36.542) by the tonnage of cotton fiber exported that year (FOB) (251,700,000 kg) and then divides that additional profit (FCFA 9,197,621,400) by the average exchange rate that year (FCFA 555 per dollar).

11. To convert seed cotton to cotton fiber, one needs to know the average gin yield of a country. If the producer price for first-grade seed cotton is FCFA 170 per kilogram and the gin yield is 43 percent, then the producer price for a kilogram of seedless or cotton fiber is FCFA 395.

12. Under pressure from the World Bank to expose the Malian cotton sector to market forces, the CMDT, the Malian government, and producers agreed in 2005 to remove the floor price. According to the new price-setting mechanism, if the average world market price (Cotlook A) falls below the average market price forecasted during price-setting negotiations, producer prices will also fall (Rép. du Mali 2005).

References

Agence France Press. 2005. "OMC: Semi-défaite pour l'Afrique dans la bataille du coton." December 18.

Bair, J. 2005. "Global Capitalism and Commodity Chains: Looking Back, Going Forward. *Competition and Change* 9 (2): 153–80.

Bassett, T. J. 2001. *The Peasant Cotton Revolution in West Africa: Côte d'Ivoire, 1880–1995*. Cambridge: Cambridge University Press.

———. 2003. *Le coton des paysans: Une révolution agricole (Côte d'Ivoire, 1880–1999)*. Paris: Institut de Recherche pour le Développement.

Bingen, J. 1994. "Agricultural Development Policy and Grassroots Democracy in Mali: The Emergence of Mali's Farmer Movement." *African Rural and Urban Studies* 1:57–72.

Bourdet, Y. 2004. "A Tale of Three Countries: Structure, Reform, and Performance of the Cotton Sector in Mali, Burkina Faso, and Benin." Swedish International Development Cooperation Agency (SIDA) Country Economic Report 2, Stockholm.

Bradsher, K. 2005. "Trade Officials Agree to End Subsidies for Agricultural Exports." *New York Times,* December 19.

Campbell, Bonnie K. 1984. "Inside the Miracle: Cotton in the Ivory Coast." In *The Politics of Agriculture in Tropical Africa*, ed. Jonathan Barker, 143–71. Beverly Hills: Sage.

Environmental Working Group. 2005. "After Hong Kong, Redraw America's Farm Subsidy Map." http://www.ewg.org:16080/farm/redraw/index.php.

Estur, G. 2004. "Commodity Risk Management Approaches for Cotton in West Africa." Washington, D.C.: International Cotton Advisory Committee.

———. 2005. "Is West Africa Competitive with the U.S. on the World Cotton Market?" Paper presented to the Beltwide Cotton Economics and Marketing Conference, New Orleans, January 7.

FAO (Food and Agricultural Organization of the United Nations). 2004. "Cotton: Impact of Support Policies on Developing Countries—Why Do the Numbers Vary?" FAO Trade Policy Brief on issues related to the WTO negotiations on agriculture, no. 1.

Fend, R. 2005. "The Fair Trade Response to the Coffee Crisis: Achievements, Limitations, and Prospects of a Voluntary Certification Scheme." MA thesis, Fletcher School of Law and Diplomacy, Tufts University.

Fitter, R., and R. Kaplinsky. 2001. "Who Gains from Product Rents as the Coffee Market Becomes More Differentiated? A Value Chain Analysis." *IDS Bulletin* 32 (3): 69–82.

Fok, M. 2005. "Coton africain sur le marché mondial: Défis pour un juste prix." Paper presented at the conference on West and Central Africa Cotton, Cotonou, May 10–12, 2005.

Fok, M., and Taze, S. 2003. "Rapport de synthèse régionale: Dispositif de suivi des filières cotonnières au Bénin, Burkina Faso, Cameroun, Côte d'Ivoire, Ghana, et Mali: Évolution institutionnelle, approche statique et dynamique de la performance en relation avec les objectifs de développement." Montpellier: CIRAD.

Gereffi, Gary, and Miguel Korzeniewicz, eds. 1994. *Commodity Chains and Global Capitalism*. Westport, CT: Praeger.

Gereffi, G., J. Humphrey, and T. Sturgeon. 2005. "The Governance of Global Value Chains." *Review of International Political Economy* 12 (1): 78–104.

Gergely, Nicholas. 2004. "Étude comparative sur les coûts de production des sociétés cotonnières au Mali, au Burkina Faso et au Cameroun." Agence Française de Développement, Paris.

Goreux, L. 2003. "Réformes des filières cotonnières en Afrique subsaharienne." Washington, DC: World Bank; Paris: Ministère des Affaires Étrangères.

ICAC (International Cotton Advisory Committee). 2004. *Structure of World Trade*. Vol. 1. Washington, DC: ICAC.

IFDC (International Fertilizer Development Center). 2002. *Marchés, systèmes de distribution, associations professionnelles, et systèmes d'information des intrants agricoles au Mali, au Burkina Faso, et au Ghana*.

Italtrend Spa. 2006. "Côte d'Ivoire: Élaboration d'une stratégie sectorielle coton: Perspectives à moyen et long termes, rapport provisoire de première étape." European Commission, Contrat cadre Europaid/ 49860/C/SV/multi.

Larsen, M. N. 2003. "Quality Standard-Setting in the Global Cotton Chain and Cotton Sector Reforms in Sub-Saharan Africa." IS/Gl, Kongevej Working Paper 03.7, Institute for International Studies, Copenhagen.

MacRae, J., and C. Marmignon. 2004 "Côte d'Ivoire: Étude des measures d'urgence pour l'amélioration de la performance de la filière coton." Final report, Commission Européenne.

Murphy, Sophia. 2002. *Managing the Invisible Hand: Markets, Farmers and International Trade*. Minneapolis: Institute for Agriculture and Trade Policy.

National Cotton Council. 2005. "U.S. Cotton Economic Situation and Issues Update." March. http://www.cotton.org/issues/2005/upload/ EconOutlookIssues.pdf.

Oxfam. 2003. "Cultivating Poverty: The Impact of U.S. Cotton Subsidies on Africa." Oxfam Briefing Paper 30.

Pfeifer, K. 2005. "No Fluff, Just Cotton: The Strategic Importance of Cotton Production to Development in West Africa." Paper presented at the ICAC meetings, London.

Ponte, S. 2001. "The 'Latte Revolution'? Winners and Losers in the Restructuring of the Global Coffee Marketing Chain." CDR Working Paper 01, Centre for Development Research, Copenhagen.

Raikes, P., M. Friis Jensen, and S. Ponte. 2000. "Global Commodity Chain Analysis and the French Filière Approach: Comparison and Critique." *Economy and Society* 29 (3): 390–417.

République du Mali. 2005. *Protocole d'Accord Etat-CMDT-Producteurs sur le mécanisme de détermination du prix d'achat du coton grain*. Bamako.

Résocot. 2003a. "Filière cotonnière du Burkina Faso: Modes d'organisation et performance au regard des objectifs de développement." Rapport de synthèse nationale, CIRAD, Montpellier.

———. 2003b. "Filière cotonnière malienne: Modes d'organisation et performance au regard des objectifs de développement." Rapport de synthèse nationale, CIRAD, Montpellier.

Ricard, P. 2005. "L'OMC bute sur le coton et la banane." *Le Monde*, December 16.

Thompson, R. 2005. "Essentials for the 2007 Farm Bill in a Global Context." *Trade Policy Analysis* 7 (6): 1–30.

UNDP (United Nations Development Program). 2005. *Human Development Report—2005*. New York: United Nations.

USDA (United States Department of Agriculture). 2006. "Cotton and Products: West Africa Region: Benin, Burkina Faso, Côte d'Ivoire, and Mali." USDA Foreign Agricultural Service, GAIN Report IV5010, March 16.

Walet, Mariama. 2005. "Analyse des coûts du coton fibre de la CMDT." Memoire de Maîtrise, Université de Bamako.

Wescott, P. C., C. E. Young, and J. M. Price. 2002. "The 2002 Farm Act: Provisions and Implications for Commodity Markets." USDA, Agricultural Information Bulletin 778. http://www.ers.usda.gov/publications/aib778, accessed December 18, 2005.

World Bank. 2006. "Strategies for Cotton in West and Central Africa: Enhancing Competitiveness in the 'Cotton 4.'" Preliminary report, Washington, DC, May.

WTO (World Trade Organization). 2001. "Doha WTO Ministerial 2001: Ministerial Declaration." http://www.wto.org/English/thewto_e/minist_e/min01_e/mindecl_e.htm.

2

Cotton Production in Burkina Faso

International Rhetoric versus Local Realities

Leslie C. Gray

VOICES RANGING FROM the editorial page of the *New York Times* to organizations such as Oxfam and the presidents of Burkina Faso and Mali have argued that U.S. cotton subsidies depress world cotton prices and hurt African farmers. These policies deny West African countries their comparative advantage in cotton, which they can produce more cheaply and with lower environmental impacts than farmers in the United States. Some have gone as far as phrasing this as a national security issue; editorials in the *New York Times* and the *Wall Street Journal* have suggested that removing subsidies would have a strong auxiliary benefit by defusing a potential source of "feverish anti-Americanism."[1]

Unlike the United States, where large corporate farmers dominate production, small farmers grow cotton in West Africa. Small changes in cotton prices have significant implications for poverty rates in a region that is consistently ranked as the world's poorest. A study undertaken by International Food Policy Research Institute researchers in Benin indicates that reductions in farm-level prices result in increases in rural poverty (Minot and Daniels 2002). The International Cotton Advisory Committee predicts that if the United States removed subsidies, cotton prices would increase between 6 and 11 cents per pound (ICAC, cited in Baffes 2004).

While debates about international pricing policies and subsidies are extremely important for farmers in West Africa, they are not the only relevant debates regarding cotton production there. Local farmers in Burkina Faso have a distinctly different view of cotton affairs.[2] Instead of concern over international battles over cotton prices, their concerns are decidedly local. For many farmers in Burkina Faso, cotton is the only way to become wealthy. While they would favor increases in world prices, they are troubled by how cotton policy is being implemented in Burkina Faso, particularly about government determinations of cotton prices, high levels of corruption in cotton marketing and transport, high levels of indebtedness and late payments to farmers. Farmers also highlighted the difficulty of fitting cotton—a crop that requires high levels of inputs, both chemical and labor—into a production system where labor is constrained and access to fertile land is declining. Finally, farmers are concerned about pesticide use. Pesticides, while used at nowhere near the levels typical of wealthier countries, affect environmental health in Burkina Faso because of how they are applied.

The Evolution of Cotton Production in Burkina Faso

Despite recent fluctuations in world cotton prices and controversies over agricultural subsidies, cotton production has taken off in West Africa in the past twenty years. The share of world production by four West Africa countries—Burkina Faso, Benin, Côte d'Ivoire and Mali—has increased from 2.4 percent in the early 1980s to 9.4 percent in the period from 2000 to 2003. Burkina alone saw its share of world cotton exports increase from 0.5 percent to 2.3 percent during this same twenty-year period (Baffes 2004).

In Burkina Faso most cotton production occurs in the southwestern part of the country in an area referred to as the *zone cotonnière*. Cotton is extremely important to Burkina Faso, accounting for 40 percent of exports in Burkina Faso and 5 percent of GNP. Since the 1980s, cotton fiber production, area under cotton production, and cotton yield per hectare have all increased. Figure 2.1 shows how total

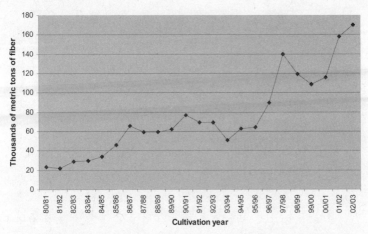

FIG. 2.1. Total cotton fiber production, Burkina Faso. (World Bank, 2003)

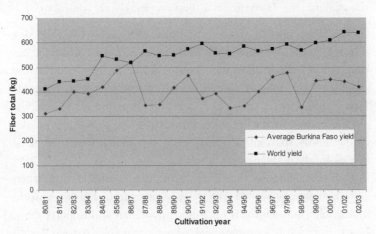

FIG. 2.2. Yield of cotton fiber per hectare. (World Bank, 2003)

cotton fiber production has increased in Burkina Faso, rising from 23,000 metric tons in 1981 to 170,000 tonnes in 2003. However, figure 2.2 demonstrates that yields per hectare have not increased at the same magnitude, increasing by only 35.5 percent during the same period. Thus, most of the increase in Burkina is coming from an expansion of the area under production (fig. 2.3), which increased from 74,000 hectares in 1981 to 406,000 hectares in 2003.

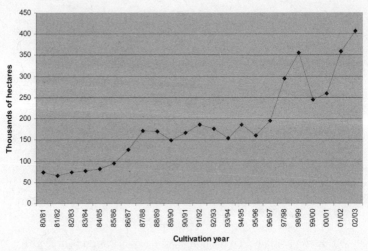

FIG. 2.3. Total area planted in cotton, Burkina Faso. (World Bank, 2003)

This recent growth in cotton production does not reflect the long history of cotton production in Burkina Faso. In the precolonial period, cotton was an important local crop. It was grown on a very small scale, generally by women, who grew cotton in fields alongside "sauce" condiments, such as peppers and okra, and other modern-day cash crops such as tobacco. Production was low and primarily used at home, spun into strips of cotton thread that were then made into clothing and blankets (Capron 1973).

Cotton production increased during the colonial period, when cotton became associated with colonial plans to fuel growing world industrialization with African cotton (Isaacman and Roberts 1995). Isaacman and Roberts argue that African farmers failed to heed the call to grow more cotton and generally did not produce cotton in sufficient quantity or quality, partly because cotton production required large amounts of backbreaking household labor, but also because the colonial powers never provided the inputs or the right price signals to increase production. Bassett (2001) illustrates how the colonial state failed to capture local production in Côte d'Ivoire, where most of the cotton was sold on the more lucrative local market. Colonial powers in Côte d'Ivoire did not use forced labor but instead relied on a host of indirect yet coercive measures, such as taxes and field surveillance, to increase production. Cotton exports would wax and wane in direct relation to the amount of coercion used.

More coercive means of producing cotton were found in other French colonies. In 1924, in colonial Haute-Volta, now Burkina Faso, the area under cotton production was very low. French colonial authorities attempted to increase production by forcing peasants to cultivate cotton in village fields. The policy was a complete failure. Not only was production extremely low, but the policy played an important role in a general subsistence crisis that came to a head in 1930 (Schwartz 1993). Roberts (1995) paints a similar picture of cotton production in colonial Mali.

Cotton production remained minimal during much of the post-colonial period, due partially to associations of forced labor and famine that remained with cotton in many peasant farmers' eyes but also due more fundamentally to the lack of inputs, infrastructure, and sufficiently high prices. This began to change during the 1970s when the French cotton development organization CFDT (Compagnie Française pour le Développement des Fibres Textiles) organized the production, processing, and exportation of cotton. In 1979, the CFDT partnered with the government of Burkina Faso to create Sofitex, which then became the main organization responsible for cotton production. With the creation of Sofitex, resources began to pour into the cotton sector and agricultural extension, financial and marketing services became available. This resulted in a rapid increase in cotton production (Schwartz 1991).

Schwartz (1991) attributes the success of cotton in the late 1980s to the GVs (*groupements villageoises*), grower cooperative associations that linked individual farmers to the different agencies that provide inputs and financing. Through the village GV, a farmer could apply for short-term loans for fertilizer, seeds, and herbicides from a regional CRPA (*centre régional de promotion agro-pastorale*) and for medium-term loans for equipment and oxen for animal traction through the CNCA (Caisse Nationale de Crédit Agricole). The GV also operated *marchés auto-gérés*, village-run marketing cooperatives that manage the weighing and selling of cotton to Sofitex (Tersignel 1992).

Despite the success of the GVs in getting inputs to farmers, by the mid-1990s the GVs were in crisis. Debts accrued as farmers not growing cotton were allowed to borrow inputs on credit, even though cotton production was the main way of getting enough money to pay back the credits at the end of the season. There was also a free-rider problem. Individual farmers would take inputs on credit, sell them in the market and assume the rest of the growers would pay back their loan. This problem was exacerbated by general downturns in the cotton market. In the early 1990s, cotton prices dropped. The situation, for cotton producers, worsened in January 1994, when the French devalued the CFA franc (FCFA) to 50 percent of its previous value. While prices had rebounded by this time, the devaluation meant that inputs became much more expensive. Farmers responded by applying less fertilizers and pesticides to their cotton fields. The reduced use of inputs was complicated by the introduction of a new variety of cotton, a glandless variety, GL7, that many farmers felt was much less resistant to pests and more drought prone. Indeed, the harvest of 1996/97 was badly affected by a caterpillar infestation against which pesticides were largely ineffective.

These production downturns in the 1990s, combined with the poor management of the GVs, led to a problem of widespread indebtedness in the cotton-growing region. The government responded harshly, putting villagers in prison for failure to pay their outstanding cotton debts. Facing these constraints, many farmers complained that they could no longer afford to produce cotton and abandoned cotton production. Because of their widespread indebtedness, the GVs were eventually replaced by GPCs (*groupements des producteurs de coton*) that were based on group lending models that had tighter membership and payback requirements. These smaller groups gave inputs only on credit for cotton production; they also exhibited stronger peer pressures to pay back loans over time (Goreux 2003). GPCs could also choose their members, thus allowing them to exclude farmers who might not farm responsibly. If a farmer were not able to pay back a loan, then the entire group would need to make up the shortfall in order to receive inputs the next year. This system has worked out much better than the GV system, but there is still a problem of widespread indebtedness. The blow of indebtedness has been somewhat softened as Sofitex has let go of coercive means to force repayment, such as imprisoning people, and allowed indebted GPCs to work out payment plans whereby they could repay debts over a number of years.

One cause for optimism in the cotton sector is the increased role of the Union Nationale des Producteurs de Coton du Burkina (Union of Cotton-Growing Farmers), the union that represents all cotton farmers in Burkina and has acquired a 30 percent share in Sofitex in that country. Farmers now have a seat on the Sofitex board and are instrumental in deciding producer and input prices. This has given rural producers much more power in changing policy. Cotton prices increased in the 2004/5 season, likely to due to the negotiating power of this national union.

Local Farmer Perceptions of Cotton Production

While much of the media and international focus on cotton production in West Africa has been on declining prices and American subsidies, local farmers in Burkina Faso have a different perspective of cotton production. When I first started asking questions about cotton in September 2005, many local farmers were largely unaware of the international debates surrounding cotton production. In February 2005, though, their knowledge of international affairs had increased after the government announced that cotton prices for the 2005/6 season would be reduced from FCFA 210 per kilogram to FCFA 175. This change in prices was directly blamed on declines in the world price. Most farmers, however, were unaware of the role that agricultural subsidies played in price declines. When I explained American policy of supporting farmers through subsidies, many farmers thought it seemed unfair and welcomed any effort to increase the prices they received for their crops. However, their primary concerns were overwhelmingly local. Instead of U.S. subsidies, they were much more focused on issues that they perceived as local, such as how governments set pricing policy on cotton grain and agricultural inputs, indebtedness, labor shortages, drought, declining access to fertile soil and the effects of pesticide use on human health.

The following discussion comes from research with farmers in three villages, Sara, Dohoun, and Dimikuy, villages in the Province of Tui, the country's largest cotton-producing province. Figure 2.4 is a map of the study area. These three villages are fairly similar in demographic terms: they are evenly split between migrant Mossi farmers and local Bwa farmers. They all grow cotton, although one village, Dohoun, stands out as being much more successful in cotton production than the other two.

COTTON PRICING

While world prices affect how much farmers get for their cotton in Burkina Faso, the government's own pricing is also a large factor. The national governments of West Africa give a much lower share of world market prices to their farmers than do other countries (Bassett 2001). In the mid-1990s Burkina farmers received on average 39 percent of the world market price; they now receive about 51 percent of the world price. The rest goes to operating costs of the cotton companies, subsidies offered to cotton parastatals, and the provision of public services

FIG. 2.4. Map of study area.

(Badiane et al. 2002). While some infrastructure costs are expected, there are also concerns about corruption and misuse of funds, particularly as these cotton companies are state-managed enterprises with no external competition (Baffes 2004). Farmer perception of low prices reflects this lack of competition—they feel they are being short-changed by their own governments.

Since Sofitex has become partially owned by the Union of Cotton-Growing Farmers, prices have increased for local farmers—indeed, the 2004/5 season saw cotton prices increase significantly, with no change in input prices. Interestingly, many local farmers also felt that the union was corrupt and working with government leaders to take advantage of farmers. This, however, is not borne out by prices that have generally risen to their highest recent levels since the partnership between the union and Sofitex. The power of the union is limited, though, as prices for the 2005/6 season have decreased by 17 percent, a decrease the government blames on declining world prices. In any case, this decrease in price means that the margin of error for producing cotton will be reduced and the risk of falling into debt significantly increased.

INDEBTEDNESS

Cotton production in Burkina Faso is full of contradictions. On the one hand it is the only way to make money; any farmer who has become wealthy in the Province of Tui has likely done so because of cotton. On the other hand, it is a risky crop. Farmers carry much of the burden of risk for a crop failure. They take their inputs on credit from Sofitex and then what they owe is subtracted from their cotton payment after harvest. But producing a good harvest is a complicated process. It depends on sufficient labor for plowing, seeding, weeding, judicious and timely application of fertilizer and pesticides, and early harvest. It also depends on the correct amount of rainfall; either too much or too little can reduce cotton yields. If any one of these elements is missing, debt can occur as a farmer can have borrowed inputs on credit and be unable to pay them back.

It is not surprising, therefore, that one of the largest problems facing cotton farmers is debt. Of the eighty-two farm households I interviewed, thirty-seven have been indebted during one point in the last five years. In the village of Sara, where debt is a very serious problem, seventeen of the twenty-three farmers who are currently growing cotton had experienced debt in the past five years. Many farmers in the sample are no longer growing cotton at all, either because they had been indebted or were afraid of becoming indebted. Indebtedness means that it is very difficult to get inputs on credit, reducing both the chance that the farmer will grow cotton and his ability to pay back debts. One farmer in Dimikuy explained that he has not grown cotton in the last five years because he had been indebted and did not have the oxen or the financial means to grow cotton or pay back his debts. It is not uncommon for farmers to sell their productive assets such as oxen to pay back their debts. This creates a cycle of debt whereby farmers in debt lose the productive assets that will get them out of debt.

Debt can be at both the individual level and the level of the GPC. Individuals can be indebted, but in order for the GPC to remain solvent it must pay back the debts of its members. Many GPCs have folded under the weight of collective debt. In the village of Sara, only six out of fourteen GPCs remained functioning in 2004. The indebted GPCs had not received inputs from Sofitex since 1999 but were allocated half the inputs needed on credit this past season, in the hopes that they could start paying off their debts. The payment period has been spread out over three years, but many indebted farmers are simply growing cotton to pay off debts and will not see any profit.

How GPCs decide to repay their debt is a matter of internal decision making. Most GPCs share the debt of their indebted members among the group as a whole and then try to collect the money—only sometimes successfully—at some later point. One particularly successful GPC in Dohoun had a much more severe internal rule; they collected the debts of farmers by taking the proceeds of the cotton harvest from their closest relative. One farmer in this situation stated that he was "not cultivating cotton this year because my cotton money is still serving to pay the debt of my little brother." Another GPC in Sara collected the productive assets—oxen, plows, and bicycles—of their indebted group members.

Reasons for an entire GPC falling into debt vary. Some GPCs are indebted because of the actions of individual farmers, who either sell their inputs on the market to gain cash or for some other reason are not able to harvest enough cotton to pay off their loans. In these cases, the GPC can generally survive, as other members will pay off the indebted member's debt. However, a general natural disaster can put an entire GPC into debt. For example, 1999 stood out as the year when most of the GPCs in the village of Sara became indebted, because of flooding and an infestation of white flies. Many farmers told me that the insecticides they used were largely ineffective against white flies that year. One farmer who is the secretary of the Union of Cotton-Growing Farmers at the provincial level confirmed these concerns, explaining that it was the fault of the insecticide manufacturer, who omitted a key ingredient in the production of a third, generally effective insecticide used against white flies. Whatever the reason, debt remains an extremely serious concern for growers in Burkina.

CORRUPTION, TRANSPORTATION, AND LATE PAYMENTS

Another very large concern of farmers was corruption in either getting their cotton transported or graded. In informal interviews, eleven farmers mentioned that they needed to give the driver of the cotton truck a bribe to pick up cotton early. Corruption is a very sensitive topic to ask farmers directly about, but many farmers listed it as one of their top three concerns about cotton production. Interviews with officials from the Farmers' Union also yielded many discussions of the corruption of truck drivers. As the head of one village's farmers' union put it, "Sofitex [including its truckers] is rotten."

There are several reasons why farmers are concerned about getting cotton transported on time. Paramount among them is the reduction of cotton quality. Many things can reduce the quality of a cotton crop that sits in open air. A late rain can rot the fibers. Debris can make its way into cotton that is sitting on the ground, reducing quality. Animals can trample cotton, introducing debris. The water content of cotton fiber diminishes as cotton sits in the sun, leading to weight reduction and, as payments are given on weight, less money. In fact, much of the village of Dohoun's cotton was downgraded last year because water was put in it to boost weight. Farmers explained that they did this because the cotton had been sitting in the sun for a long time, losing weight in the process.

Also, the earlier cotton is transported, the earlier a farmer will get paid. All these things mean that farmers are very concerned about when their cotton is picked up. This has led to a system of bribery; basically, to ensure that cotton is shipped earlier, a farmer must bribe a driver with a sack of maize. Farmers also complained that they needed to bribe the people who grade cotton in order to make sure that their cotton was rated first quality.

Approximately two-thirds of the farmers mentioned the lateness of cotton payments as a major concern. Many explained that they would have their cotton weighed and graded in December but would not get paid until April or in many cases May. This delay in payment is a real problem for farmers, who must sell their grain if they do not have their cotton payments. One farmer complained that he sold his maize because he had not received his cotton money; when it came time to repurchase maize, the price had gone up significantly. One of the poorest farmers in the village of Dimikuy, who had not received his cotton money until fairly late last year, explained how "cotton cultivation is tiring and there is not much benefit because you will sell your cotton to be able to buy things but you can wait months before receiving money and you will be obliged to sell your cereal crops." This year, late payments have proven to be very difficult for poor farmers who have sold their maize crop in anticipation of their cotton payments. A drought and the resulting shortage of maize has led to maize prices going from FCFA 5,000 per sack after the 2004 harvest to FCFA 15,000 per sack at the beginning of the 2005 planting season. This has put poorer farmers, who have sold their cereal crops while waiting for their cotton payments, in a tenuous position in terms of household food security.

INPUTS: ANIMAL TRACTION, LABOR, AND CHEMICALS

Almost two-thirds of farmers interviewed mentioned animal traction, household labor, and chemical inputs as major constraints to successful cotton production. Farmers explained the difficult nature of cotton production. Farmers without oxen are severely limited in their ability to cultivate cotton early enough. Farmers also need to apply inputs at the right moment to insure good production. Cotton requires fertilizer during its vegetative growth cycle and insecticides at crucial moments such as seed setting and fiber development. Lack of labor or resources during these stages can seriously lower yields. It is not uncommon to put a significant amount of labor and money into cotton and then have a poor yield due to either resource constraints or natural disaster. Because so many farmers are experiencing indebtedness, many cannot get inputs on credit. Therefore farmers are putting much less than the recommended dose of either fertilizer or insecticides on crops. This lack of sufficient inputs is probably the reason that yields in Burkina Faso are generally lower than the world average, as illustrated in figure 2.2.

In the 2004/5 season, the rain came early but then stopped. Many farmers had to replant their cotton due to insufficient rains at planting. Furthermore, there was a slight drought at flowering time. Farmers stressed how important getting cotton in the ground early was to have a good crop. In the village of Dohoun, where many farmers either own or hire tractors, they were able to take advantage of early rains because they had plowed their fields before the rains even started, something that oxen-drawn plows cannot do. This was particularly beneficial during the 2004/5 season because after the first rains came in May, there was a short drought, which meant that farmers without access to tractors did not get their cotton in the ground until early June. Farmers without oxen did not get their cotton planted until late June, which turned out to be disastrous for them because the rains ended early, resulting in very low yields. A Sara farmer said this about the risks of late cotton cultivation: you have to cultivate early because when cotton is planted late, the yields are low and can cause you to be indebted. Late planting also means that the crop can be destroyed by fire or animals. One of the most difficult periods is the harvest. Cotton matures later than other crops, and the harvest is labor intensive. Those who can afford to do so will hire extra labor to insure an early harvest. Weeding can be quite labor intensive as well. If a farmer does not have the right equipment, then the job will not be done in time, resulting in loss of yield.

ACCESS TO FERTILE LAND

In all three villages, farmers have become increasingly concerned that quality land is no longer available. This region is an area of high demographic pressure. Population in southwestern Burkina Faso has increased rapidly due to migration of Mossi farmers from their drought-stricken homeland. Initially, Mossi migrants were greeted with open arms by local Bwa farmers and were given land to cultivate in return for ritual gifts of grain and poultry. Today, many young Bwa complain that their ancestors gave away their heritage for a chicken or kola nuts. The result is that most farmers, particularly migrants but also local farmers, have little access to fallow land or land of good quality (Gray and Kevane 2001). It is not uncommon to find farmers who have been cultivating the same field for thirty or forty years and cannot leave the field fallow because they have nowhere else to cultivate. Farmers who own livestock are able to improve their land with manure applications, but poorer farmers complain that they have few means to improve their soil and that this affects the yields of crops such as cotton (Gray 2005).

The land situation is acute in the village of Sara, which has almost no land left that is uncultivated (Gray 1999). Many Mossi migrants have since left the village because of a lack of good land. The effect of land quality on yield is apparent in this village where not only are new lands not available but the soil in cultivated fields is poor. Most of the soil is sandy, which farmers believe to be the worst type of soil for cotton. Lack of fertile land is tied to debt. As noted earlier, the village of Sara has particular problems with debt while the village of Dohoun—generally acknowledged to have some of the most fertile land in the region—has generally experienced low levels of debt.

PESTICIDE USE

Kutting (2003) highlights the ironic situation in West Africa, where poverty is actually good for the environment. Cotton in Burkina Faso is produced with far fewer inputs than in the developed world, where large amounts of agrochemicals are used to produce cotton. Researchers, therefore, have tended to laud West African cotton production as much more environmentally friendly. There are no huge problems with pesticide drift, though studies of the effects of pesticides on nonhuman health are few. Kutting argues that farmers are "too poor to pollute."

Despite this lower pesticide use, insecticides are damaging to the health of farmers who apply them. Farmers highlighted insecticide use as a risk. The application method has a significant effect on human health. Farmers apply pesticides using small backpack sprayers that frequently leak pesticides. Some farmers are aware of the side effects of pesticides; for example, farmers in the village of Sara, who tend to be better educated than other farmers, do wear masks. But this is not sufficient to completely protect people, who are advised to wear not only masks but also gloves, boots, and goggles, and to cover their entire bodies. In the heat of the tropical sun, it is not surprising that few follow that advice.

Of the cotton-growing farm families I interviewed, forty-four (about 55 percent) experienced negative health effects after pesticide application. Few farmers wore the recommended protective gear; approximately 40 percent wore masks but nothing else. Some farmers were not aware of the dangers of pesticide application, others felt that it was too hot to wear the appropriate gear, and others further argued that the gear cost too much money.

This is particularly worrisome, as many of the pesticides used on cotton production are quite toxic, particularly the endosulfans and organophosphates, which are both used extensively. These main insecticides are nerve toxins and carcinogens. In the past agricultural season, many farmers reported short-term negative effects after pesticide application (see table 2.1). The most frequent symptom is headache, followed by flulike symptoms, but there were also some more worrying symptoms, such as paralysis. The nurse in Sara, a village of about fifteen hundred people, reported four cases of acute pesticide poisoning in the last year.

Cotton production in Burkina Faso is problematic at both the global and local scales. At the global scale, the agricultural subsidies

Table 2.1. Effects of pesticide application

Symptoms	Farmers (N = 71)
Never ill	27
Headache	23
Flulike symptoms	9
Skin problems	6
Vomiting	3
Paralysis	2
Eye problems	1

of wealthy countries such as the United States push down cotton prices, squeezing the profit margin of farmers. The most recent declines in world prices have led to declines in cotton prices in the coming agricultural season, a situation that will surely increase the debt load carried by farmers.

At the local scale, though, even if subsidies were removed and cotton prices increased, cotton production would still be problematic for resource-poor farmers. The ability to produce cotton without incurring debt varies widely with farmers' wealth. Most farmers concurred with this, indicating that poor farmers cannot effectively cultivate cotton. Particularly important is access to oxen and a plow, which allows a farmer to plow, seed, and weed early. As one farmer in the village of Sara put it, "cotton is for people who are at ease financially; the poor can't cultivate early enough, especially if you don't have oxen."

One of the problems for farmers is that they bear much of the risk of crop failure; there are no mechanisms such as crop insurance that might protect them from the outcomes of a poor agricultural season or a natural disaster. And cotton appears to be particularly risky for the farmers of Burkina Faso; reduced yields due to unforeseen events are not uncommon. Thus, the farmers in Burkina Faso are doubly disadvantaged, both from the effects of cotton production by the wealthiest countries of the world, and by the fact that there are few safety nets to protect them when production does turn bad.

Notes

1. "The Long Reach of King Cotton," *New York Times*, August 5, 2003; "Hanging by a Thread," *Wall Street Journal*, June 26 2002.

2. The research I conducted in Burkina Faso was part of a larger project looking at farmer perceptions and practices surrounding cotton production that I undertook with eighty-two heads of farm households in September 2004 and February 2005, but also reflects a broader field research project that began in 1995. This research was made possible with funding from the National Science Foundation.

References

Badiane, Ousmane, Dhaneshwar Ghura, Louis Goreux, and Paul Masson. 2002. "Cotton Sector Strategies in West and Central Africa." World Bank Policy Research Working Paper 2867. Washington, DC: World Bank.

Baffes, John. 2004. "Cotton: Market Setting, Trade Policies and Issues." World Bank Policy Research Working Paper, February. Washington, DC: World Bank.

Bassett, Tom. 2001. *The Peasant Cotton Revolution in West Africa: Côte d'Ivoire, 1880–1995.* Cambridge: Cambridge University Press.

Capron, Jean. 1973. *Communautés villageoises bwa: Mali, Haute Volta.* Paris: Institut d'Ethnologie.

Gray, Leslie C. 1999. "Is Land Being Degraded? A Multi-scale Examination of Landscape Change in Southwestern Burkina Faso." *Land Degradation and Development* 10:329–43.

———. 2005. "What Kind of Intensification? Agricultural Practice, Soil Fertility and Socioeconomic Differentiation in Rural Burkina Faso." *Geographical Journal* 171 (1): 70–82.

Gray, Leslie C., and Michael Kevane. 2001. "Evolving Tenure Rights and Agricultural Intensification in Southwestern Burkina Faso." *World Development* 29 (4): 573–87.

Isaacman, Allen, and Richard Roberts, eds. 1995. *Cotton, Colonialism, and Social History in Sub-Saharan Africa.* Portsmouth, NH: Heinemann.

Kutting, G. 2003. "Globalization, Poverty and the Environment in West Africa: Too Poor to Pollute?" *Global Environmental Politics*, 3 (4): 42–60.

Minot, Nicholas, and Lisa Daniels. 2005. "Impact of Global Cotton Markets on Rural Poverty in Benin." *Agricultural Economics* 33 (3): 453–66.

Oxfam. 2003. "Cultivating Poverty." Oxfam Briefing Paper no. 30.

———. 2004. "Finding the Moral Fiber: Why Reform Is Urgently Needed for a Fair Cotton Trade." Oxfam Briefing Paper no. 69.

Roberts, Richard. 1995. "The Coercion of Free Markets: Cotton, Peasants, and the Colonial State in the French Soudan, 1924–1932." In *Cotton, Colonialism, and Social History in Sub-Saharan Africa,* ed. Allen Isaacman and Richard Roberts. Portsmouth, NH: Heinemann.

Schwartz, A. 1991. "L'exploitation agricole de l'aire cotonnière Burkinabé: Caractéristiques sociologiques, démographiques, économiques." Document de travail, ORSTOM, Ouagadougou, 88pp.

———. 1993. "Brève histoire de la culture du coton au Burkina Faso." In *Découvertes du Burkina,* ed. Jean-Baptiste Kethiega et al. Ouagadougou: SEPIA-A.D.D.B.

Tersignel. 1992. "Boho-Kari, village bwa: Les effets de la mécanisation dans l'aire cotonnière du Burkina Faso." Doctoral thesis, Université de Paris X.

World Trade Organization. 2003. *Brief from West African Countries.* Geneva: World Trade Organization.

3

Mali's Cotton Conundrum

Commodity Production and Development on the Periphery

William G. Moseley

COMMENTATORS FROM ALL SIDES of the political spectrum have asserted that American and European agricultural subsidies inhibit prosperity in the developing world, particularly Africa (e.g., Bhagwati 2002; Oxfam 2002). Critics have argued that the club of rich nations aggressively dismantled trade barriers on industrial goods yet shamelessly refused to do so for agricultural goods, an area where many African nations would have a comparative advantage. If Americans and Europeans were to reduce subsidies to their own farmers, then global production of certain crops would likely decline and global prices would rise. These higher prices would benefit African farmers of the same crop. In the Sudanean zones of West Africa, cotton production by smallholders is inhibited by trade-distorting subsidies from the global North (Oxfam 2002). In 2003, the presidents of Mali and Burkina Faso argued in a *New York Times* op-ed piece that American cotton subsidies were stymieing their poverty reduction efforts (Touré and Compaoré 2003). A similar argument was made by the editorial team at the *New York Times* in a running series entitled "Harvesting Poverty" (NYT 2003a, b).

At the World Trade Organization meetings held in Cancun, Mexico, in September 2003, the price of cotton in world markets made it on to the agenda. A delegation from Benin, Chad, Burkina Faso, and Mali asked the WTO to scrap U.S. cotton subsidy programs. In the summer of 2004, an agreement was reached in Geneva (part of the Doha round of trade negotiations) to reduce European and American agricultural subsidies. In March 2005 the WTO declared U.S. cotton subsidies illegal. In a rare moment, the neoliberal economists (pushing for freer trade) and the neostructuralists (pushing for fairness in global trading regimes) seem to have come together on an issue.

In Mali the World Bank has long encouraged the government to further develop its exports (mainly cotton) as part of its structural adjustment program. With over 228,000 metric tons of cotton lint produced in 2004/5, and an average of 200,000 tonnes of production per annum between 1998 and 2005, Mali is the largest cotton exporter in Africa (FAO 2006). With cotton accounting for the largest share of GDP and government revenues, the Malian state is interested in maintaining and increasing cotton-related exports and revenues. With cotton holding such a prominent position in the Malian national economy, it has sometimes been referred to as white gold or *l'or blanc* (Moseley 2001; Tefft 2004). Others note that "*coton est le moteur du développement*" (cotton is the motor for development) (Mali 1998). Government officials argue not only that cotton promotes economic growth but that it enhances food security and promotes environmental stewardship. When interacting with farmers, for example, agricultural extension agents often assert that *kori tigi ye nyo tigi ye* (successful cotton farmers are successful millet farmers) (Moseley 1993). In a variety of interviews with mid- and high-level government and donor officials in 2000, these persons suggested that poverty is a major source of environmental degradation. Cotton, they argued, provided the wealth necessary for farmers to be good stewards of the land.

Objective and Research Questions

While I agree that American cotton subsidies are bad for Malian cotton producers in the short run, the notion that removing such subsidies will resolve Mali's development woes is problematic. A long-term development strategy for Mali based on continued increases in cotton production is fraught with problems for local ecologies and livelihoods. My objective is to investigate the social, economic, and ecological dynamics of cotton production at the village level in southern Mali—as well as the political-economic interests at broader scales vested in the continued and expanded production of this commodity. More specifically, I will attempt to answer two interrelated questions: (1) how, if at all, does cotton production influence household-scale natural resource management practices and community-scale dynamics; and (2) what broader-scale political and economic processes are linked to the factors that influence local-level cotton management decisions?

Background on Mali and Research Sites

Cotton production in Mali for the external market dates to the early 1900s, but it really began to expand in the 1950s when the French shifted their focus to the promotion of rain-fed cotton (as opposed to irrigated varieties) in southern Mali (Roberts 1995, 1996). The French Company for the Development of Textile Fibers (CFDT) was responsible for facilitating cotton production in this area. The CFDT was active directly in Mali from 1950 through 1974. In 1974 the Malian government and the CFDT agreed to create the Malian Company for Textile Development (CMDT), with 60 percent of the capital coming from the government and 40 percent from the CFDT. Malian cotton lint production averaged 200,000 tonnes between 1998 and 2005, making Mali the leading producer in Africa (USDA 2001; FAO 2006). Mali's relatively high cotton production is supported by a number of policies, namely guaranteed purchase, a fixed floor price, and credit for agricultural inputs.

I undertook fieldwork for this study in 1999, 2000, and 2003 in eight villages split between two sites in southern Mali: Siwaa and Djitoumou (see fig. 3.1), where rain-fed cotton production for the external market has been occurring for different lengths of time. I chose the Siwaa research location because it falls within the oldest rain-fed cotton-growing zone in Mali (also known as the old cotton basin), where

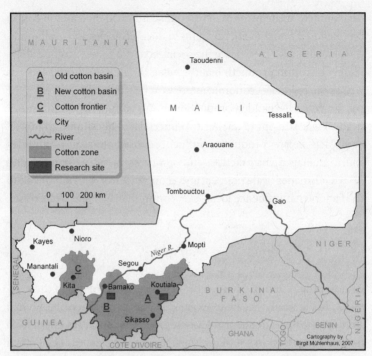

FIG. 3.1. Research sites and cotton-growing areas of southern Mali.

production for the external market has been occurring since the 1950s. Remotely sensed vegetation measures and soil sampling also suggested that this area has stable to decreasing biomass and declining soil conditions (Moseley 2001). I chose the second research location, Djitoumou, because it falls within the new cotton basin, where cotton production for the external market has been occurring since the late 1960s. Remotely sensed vegetation measures and soil sampling also indicated stable to moderately increasing biomass and stable soil conditions in this area (Moseley 2001).

Methods

Much of the fieldwork for this study was originally undertaken to examine the relationship between household wealth, vulnerability, and environmental management (Moseley 2001). In the original study, a random sample of 133 households was taken from the aforementioned eight villages in the two research areas. Households were interviewed (semistructured format) to determine asset levels, how their wealth had evolved over the past twenty years, and how they were managing their agricultural soils. Households were then placed into three groups (poor, intermediate, and rich) depending on local definitions of wealth. More specifically, household wealth was based on an inventory of animals, farming equipment, and major consumer goods identified by community members as indicative of wealth. What I soon learned, however, was that there is a strong positive correlation between wealth and cotton cultivation in southern Mali (see table 3.1). At the local level in Siwaa and Djitoumou, the rich are clearly more involved in cotton production than the poor. In Siwaa the rich have three times as much land in cotton as the poor, as well as a greater proportion of their total cultivated area devoted to the crop. This disparity is even more accentuated in Djitoumou, where the rich have over four times as many hectares in cotton as the poor, and a much larger proportion of their cultivated area devoted to the crop. While there is a greater disparity between rich and poor in cotton production in Djitoumou than in Siwaa, the average household in Siwaa produces more cotton and devotes more land resources to

Table 3.1. Cotton by wealth group, Siwaa and Djitoumou, 1997–99

Zone	Wealth group	Household production (kg)	Households farming cotton (%)	Hectares/ household in cotton	Cultivated area in cotton (%)
Siwaa	Poor	2,242	93.5	2.0	23.8
	Intermediate	5,024	100	4.4	33.1
	Rich	6,141	100	6.2	32.2
	Mean	4,066	97.1	3.7	28.7
Djitoumou	Poor	2,036	82.5	1.9	22.4
	Intermediate	3,226	100	3.8	29.4
	Rich	8,464	100	8.5	39.1
	Mean	3,181	89.2	3.1	26.1

the crop than its counterpart in Djitoumou. The greater involvement of the average Siwaa farmer in cotton production is related, most probably, to the longer history of export-oriented cotton production in the area, which began in the 1950s (as compared to the late 1960s in Djitoumou).

I also conducted soil analysis on the farm fields of a subset of the 133 households (twenty-six farms, eight samples per farm, as well as unfarmed areas as a control). The tests performed were infiltration, bulk density, pH, and aggregate stability. Soil quality was chosen as an environmental variable because soil degradation was said to be a major problem in southern Mali (World Bank 1997; Mali 1998). Soil quality variables could also be linked to a specific farm field and household. For the purposes of this chapter, it is also a set of variables that should reflect the positive or negative consequences of cotton production.

A number of village-level group conversations were also undertaken to explore interhousehold dynamics and village-level themes. Finally, roughly forty interviews were undertaken with government, donor, and NGO officials to understand their perspective on cotton production, poverty alleviation, and natural resource management.

Cotton Impacts

Does cotton production influence household-scale natural resource management practices and community-scale dynamics? If so, how? Even though cotton production has increased more rapidly in Djitoumou over the last twenty years than in Siwaa, producers in Siwaa still produce more on average than those in Djitoumou (4,066 kg versus 3,181 kg), although large producers in Djitoumou produce more than their counterparts in Siwaa (8,464 kg versus 6,141 kg). Figure 3.2 presents data on the distribution of household cotton production in Siwaa and Djitoumou in the 1982–84 versus the 1997–99 periods . As reflected by the movement of curves for each area, average household production in Djitoumou has risen between the two periods (from an average of 2,125 to 3,181 kg/household), while it has

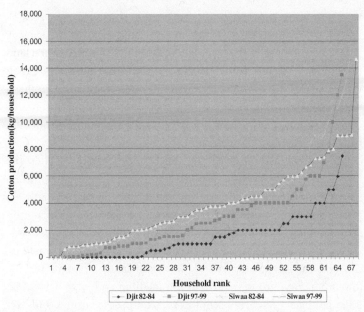

FIG. 3.2. Distribution of cotton production, Siwaa and Djitoumou, 1982–84 and 1997–99.

dropped slightly in Siwaa (from 4,191 to 4,065 kg/household). Production gains in Djitoumou are largely related to more extensive farming, as average cotton yields in the area have declined by 17 percent, yet land devoted to cotton has more than doubled between the two periods. In Siwaa, cotton yields declined by 16 percent, but land devoted to cotton increased by only 19 percent (leading to the slight loss in average household production).

In particular, the large producers in Siwaa have experienced a fall in production as their yields have declined. From 1982 to 1984, the top Siwaa cotton farmers (those with over five metric tons of annual cotton production) produced an average of eight tonnes on 5.5 hectares at a yield of 1,546 kilograms per hectare. The situation had changed such that by 1997–99, the top cotton farmers now only produced an average of 7.3 tonnes on 6.6 hectares at a yield of 1,214 kilograms per hectare. There has been a 21.5 percent decline in yield for the rich in Siwaa versus 16 percent decline on average in Siwaa. Given these declining yields, the argument has been that soil degradation is not linked to cotton farming per se, but to poverty—a situation aggravated by low global cotton prices (which in turn are linked to the subsidy issue). Wealthier farmers, it is argued, are better stewards of the land (Gray 1999). Yet, given that yields have declined more for rich than for average cotton farmers in Siwaa, it is clear that this hypothesis needs to be tested. If poverty is responsible for declining cotton production in the oldest production areas of Mali, then one should expect to see wealthier farmers taking better care of the land.

One of the assertions of the state cotton agency in Mali, the CMDT, is that large cotton farmers are not only wealthier than those who farm little or no cotton, but better land managers. Table 3.2 presents soil management data for small, medium, and large cotton farmers in the Siwaa area. Using the Mann-Whitney mean rank nonparametric statistical test, it was found that a number of characteristics and management practices are significantly different for the low-production group relative to the medium and large producers. As might be expected, household size, wealth, area farmed, and percent of area in cotton, increase in step with the level of cotton production. Differences in management practices between groups are even more interesting. Both inorganic fertilizer and insecticide use are significantly lower for those who farm less cotton. Use of inorganic fertilizers (especially when used to excess) and pesticides could be considered to be environmentally problematic. For example, Camara, Haidara, and Traoré (2000) found that pesticide resistance was

Table 3.2. Characteristics, management practices by size of cotton producer, Siwaa, 1997–99

Size of producer	Wealth (US$)	Household size	Cult. area (ha) cotton (%)	Cult. area in (carts)	Org. fert./ha (kg)	Inorg. fert./ha	%Area intercrop	% Area no-till	% Area insecticide
Low (0–1,999 kg)	$849*	9.2*	5.6*	18.1*	6.3	64.3*	16.3	31.1	16.5*
Medium (2,000–4,999 kg)	$3,436	15.7	14.5	30.7	10.9	95.4	16.2	23.5	30.7
High (5,000+ kg)	$6,678	32.1	19.3	35	10.4	115.8	23.2	22.0	36.0

* Significantly different from the medium- and high-production groups at the .01 level.

a growing problem in Mali. The conventional wisdom, as articulated in interviews with government, donor, and NGO representatives, is that one of the main ways that large and wealthier cotton farmers take better care of the land is by applying more manure and compost to their fields. This difference in management practices is not supported by the data.

Given the assertion that large, wealthy cotton farmers take better care of their soil than poorer, smaller-scale cotton farmers, I examined four soil quality measures to test this hypothesis: infiltration (higher better), pH (higher better in this case, as soils run acidic), bulk density (lower better; indicates less compaction), aggregate stability (higher better; indicates more organic matter). Tables 3.3 and 3.4 present soil data for the Siwaa and Djitoumou areas. A dummy regression model was run on the soil data for Siwaa (a simple linear regression model with soil classified by rich, intermediate, or poor farmer) in which no significant relationship was found between the wealth/cotton group variable and any of the soil quality measures. In other words, there is no significant difference in the data between cotton/wealth groups. Given the smaller sample size in Djitoumou, a nonparametric test (Mann-Whitney mean rank) was used to assess the potential difference of means for the Djitoumou soil data. This analysis suggests that the mean rank of infiltration measures was significantly better for the intermediate group than the rich; aggregate stability worse for the poor than the rich; and bulk density better for the poor and intermediate than the rich. This mixed result suggests that there is no clear difference between the rich (large cotton producers) and poor (small cotton producers) in Djitoumou. The results for Siwaa and Djitoumou call into question the assertion that wealthy, large cotton farmers are better managers of the land.

Indirect Effects of Cotton Production

The management practices of any individual cotton farmer cannot be fully understood without also examining its situation within the context of a community of farmers. Not only are the large, wealthy

Table 3.3. Integrity measures for loamy sand soils by wealth stratum, Siwaa

Wealth stratum group	Statistic	Final infiltration (cm/hr)	pH-KCl*	Bulk density (g/cm3)	Water-stable aggregates (%)
Poor	Mean	20.46	5.55	2.20	12.7
	SD	15.91	0.54	0.18	8.3
	CV	.778	.097	.082	.654
	N/farms	41/6	43/6	43/6	43/6
Intermediate	Mean	15.24	5.49	2.12	14.1
	SD	11.94	0.58	0.22	7.7
	CV	.783	.106	.104	.546
	N/farms	30/4	32/4	32/4	29/4
Rich	Mean	16.52	5.53	2.13	9.8
	SD	11.35	0.54	0.14	5.3
	CV	.687	.098	.066	.541
	N/farms	31/4	32/4	32/4	32/4
Average	Mean	17.73	5.52	2.15	12.2
	SD	13.59	0.55	0.19	7.4
	CV	.766	.100	.088	.607
	N/farms	102/14	107/14	107/14	104/14
Control	Mean	30.68	5.74	1.84	21.9
	SD	22.50	0.38	0.16	10.8
	CV	.733	.066	.087	.493
	N	9	5	8	5

CV = coefficient of variation
SD = standard deviation
Note: Using a dummy regression model, no significant relationship was found between the wealth group variable and any of the soil quality measures.
* The figures for pH-KCl are roughly comparable to those found by Vos (1991) for Try (one of the Siwaa study villages). Vos (1991) found pH-KCl values of 6.0 under natural vegetation and 4.8 to 5.6 in farm fields. These are averages for all soil texture classes.

cotton farmers not clearly better stewards of the land, but interviews with farm households and large groups at the community level suggest that cotton farming often generates a number of side effects that are transmitted between households. To be more specific, it is possible that some of the social and environmental impacts of cotton production are being externalized or transmitted from large, wealthy cotton-farming households to poorer, more limited cotton-farming households.

First, cotton is an extremely labor-intensive crop (see fig. 3.3). Interviews revealed that at key junctures in the agricultural calendar

Table 3.4. Integrity measures for sandy clay loam soils by wealth stratum, Djitoumou area

Wealth stratum group	Statistic	Final infiltration (cm/hr)	pH-KCl*	Bulk density (g/cm3)	Water-stable aggregates (%)
Poor	Mean	7.48	6.23	1.56*	34.5*
	SD	6.38	0.45	0.17	16.3
	CV	.853	.072	.109	.472
	N/farms	23/4	16/4	24/4	24/4
Intermediate	Mean	9.25**	5.93	1.55*	43.4
	SD	6.81	0.40	0.16	12.6
	CV	.736	.067	.103	.290
	N/farms	17/2	8/2	18/2	14/2
Rich	Mean	3.72	6.32	1.70	48.9
	SD	2.10	0.41	0.16	18.5
	CV	.565	.065	.094	.378
	N/farms	9/2	5/2	9/2	9/2
Average	Mean	7.41	6.16	1.58	39.9
	SD	6.21	0.45	0.17	16.5
	CV	.838	.073	.108	.414
	N/farms	49/8	29/8	51/8	47/8
Control	Mean	33.00	6.52	1.53	48.4
	SD	38.13	0.39	0.31	13.9
	CV	1.155	.060	.203	.287
	N	8	6	9	9

CV = coefficient of variation
SD = standard deviation
* = Significantly different than the rich, using Mann-Whitney mean rank test ($p < .05$)
** = Significantly different than the rich, using Mann-Whitney mean rank test ($p < .01$)

(planting, weeding, harvesting) male heads of household call upon the labor resources of their women. Wealthier households also often draw upon the labor of poorer households. While poorer households gain wages, food, or access to equipment from these labor exchanges, and women may see some benefit from cotton receipts that accrue to their male heads of household, the timing of these labor exchanges is often highly problematic. At issue is the fact that these labor demands often constrain the agricultural production of women (who typically have their own fields) and poorer households.

Second, it was found that farmers often seek to expand their cotton hectarage during years of high prices. In Djitoumou it was reported

FIG. 3.3. Family members take a break during the cotton harvest. (Photo by author)

that the rich (whose land resources are often fully exploited) frequently borrow land from the poor in such circumstances. The resulting constraints on the fallow rotation systems of the poor are likely to result in lower average soil fertility for this group.

Third, the plow was introduced by the French along with cotton. However, large, wealthy farmers received the plow first (Jonckers 1987, 1995). This disparity gave the wealthy an edge in expanding cultivated area and was particularly advantageous under a traditional tenure system in which usufruct rights (or use rights) were awarded based on land tilled by current and past household members. This helps explain why some households hold the usufruct rights to much larger areas (see fig. 3.4).

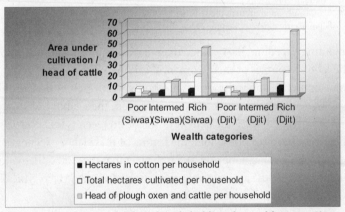

FIG. 3.4. Cotton farming, land, and cattle holdings by wealth group, Siwaa and Djitoumou.

Finally, wealthy cotton-farming households hold much more cattle than poor households on average. In Djitoumou the rich have an average of 60.3 head of cattle per household versus 13.3 head for the poor. In Siwaa the rich have an average of 45.3 head of cattle versus 3 head for the poor (see fig. 3.4). When these cattle are near the village, they tend to be herded on common lands. While common property resources in the villages were historically regulated by traditional rules and authorities, that traditional power has been weakened in the face of wealthy households that wield considerable economic power at the local level. In addition to certain activities (e.g., shea nut collection) suffering directly from the reduction of biomass on common lands that may come from grazing, the position of most common property in the landscape means that any degradation affects neighboring parcels of land. Village common land is spatially located at the bottom and the top of the toposequence in many cases—that is, on elevated plateaus where marginal soils are located and along seasonal stream beds (see fig. 3.5). Overgrazing at the top of the toposequence often leads to reduced infiltration and increased runoff. This may lead to increased erosion in the mid- to lower sections of the toposequence, where the majority of farms are located (a cost borne by the entire community).

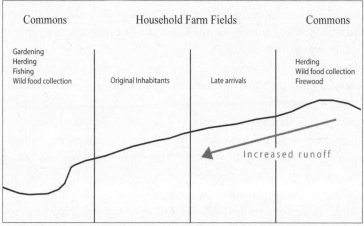

FIG. 3.5. Generalized location of common property in the toposequence and increased runoff from overgrazing.

Broader-Scale Considerations

The government of Mali has been very reluctant to recognize ecological problems associated with cotton cultivation. Part of the government's reluctance to focus on the ecological consequences may be explained by the fact that it depends on cotton for more of its revenues than any other source. This is reflected in popular discourse. It is not uncommon to hear "*grace à la CMDT, nos fonctionnaires sont payées* (because of the state cotton company, our civil servants are paid)." (Keeley and Scoones 2003) Rather than seeking to temper production while searching for more sustainable alternatives, the government is hoping to nearly double cotton production over the next few years (Chaka Berthe, director of CMDT, pers. comm., 2000). While cotton has long been an important source of revenue for the government, this source of income is increasingly important in light of agreements with the World Bank and IMF to implement policies of structural adjustment that put added pressure on the government to balance the budget. The government and the CMDT's strategy for increasing production has been to move into new areas rather than pushing for sustainability in older production zones, moving from the old cotton basin, to the new cotton basin, to the cotton frontier (see fig. 3.1). In other words, as yields have declined in the old cotton basin, production has moved steadily west into the new cotton basin and the cotton frontier (production in the latter area is discussed by Koenig in chapter 7 of this volume).

A convenient development at the level of international environment-development discourse has been the notion that poverty is both the cause and effect of environmental degradation. The World Bank has been especially fond of the poverty-induced environmental degradation thesis, as it allows the bank to push on with its structural adjustment package focused on increased export earnings (of which cotton is important) and leaner government services. This international discourse has now pervaded the national policymaking apparatus in Mali. Donors, government officials, and NGO representatives routinely suggest that poverty is at the root of many of Mali environmental problems. This focus on poverty in environmental discussions has precluded serious debate on the sustainability of cotton production. In fact, since poverty alleviation or wealth generation is now the name of the game, some have even suggested that more cotton cultivation will help bring a resolution to southern Mali's environmental problems. More recently, the rhetoric of poverty and environmental degradation at the national level has been supplemented with a condemnation of American subsidies, arguing that their removal would enhance wealth and environmental sustainability in Mali.

Not only does the government narrative of wealthy cotton farmers being food secure and good stewards of the environment seem problematic at the household scale, this study's data suggests that there is more of a boom-and-bust cycle that manifests itself at the basin scale. Changes in cotton production for different socioeconomic groups in either area help explain, in part, changes in wealth distribution over the past fifteen years. Siwaa has seen its wealth become more evenly distributed over that time while in Djitoumou the distribution of wealth has remained more or less the same (see table 3.5). While not previously the case, wealth is now more evenly distributed in Siwaa than in Djitoumou. The Gini coefficients for the two areas have changed from .410 to .364 in Siwaa and from .388 to .386 in Djitoumou between 1982–84 and 1997–99.

The more equal distribution of wealth in Siwaa is largely related to the fact that the wealthiest quintile has a smaller share of the sample's total wealth than in the past, declining from 58.1 to 48.5 percent. For the most part, this decline is not due to the first four quintiles in Siwaa increasing their wealth, but rather to declines in absolute wealth for

Table 3.5. Change in share of wealth,
Siwaa and Djitoumou, 1982–84 to 1997–99

Area	Period	Population quintile				
		1	2	3	4	5
Siwaa	1982–84	1.8	6.1	13.3	20.7	58.1
	1997–99	3.0	6.6	15.9	26.0	48.5
	Change	+1.2	+0.5	+2.6	+5.3	-9.6
Djitoumou	1982–84	2.0	6.6	13.1	21.7	56.7
	1997–99	2.4	7.5	12.2	21.6	56.3
	Change	+0.4	+0.9	-0.9	-0.1	-0.4

the wealthiest quintile. More specifically, the cumulative wealth for the wealthiest quintile dropped from 80.5 million CFA francs (FCFA) to FCFA 69.8 million (measured in constant 1999 francs) between 1982–84 and 1997–99, while cumulative wealth for the sample as a whole in Siwaa rose from FCFA 120.2 million to FCFA 165.9 million over the same period. This change in wealth distribution, particularly the declining wealth of the rich in Siwaa, is in part due to changes in cotton production.

When changes in wealth and cotton production are viewed together, some interesting lessons may be drawn about the cycle of wealth creation, environmental change, and wealth deterioration in cotton-farming communities. Together the two areas potentially represent different time segments in a trajectory of cotton-induced social and environmental change. Djitoumou is an example of an area in the earlier stages of cotton farming, while Siwaa is a more advanced case. In the early stages of cotton farming, the crop generates wealth for those most involved (often the rich). Even if cotton farming leads to declining soil fertility, such declines have little effect on total production if farmers are able to expand the area devoted to cotton (facilitated by the plow). Gains in cotton induced wealth may lead to growing inequality between households (although this was not clearly evident in the twenty-year period studied in Djitoumou). Growing inequality may not have occurred in Djitoumou because the poor have become involved in other activities, such as shea butter production, that have allowed them to keep pace with the rich. A number of studies suggest that growing inequality was the norm in Siwaa before 1982–84 (e.g., Jonckers 1987, 1995; Steenhuisjen 1989; Vos 1991). However, at some point farmers eventually claim all available land, forcing those who farm cotton the most to address declining yields through more inputs or face lower production. When adequate inputs are not applied, lower production for the rich leads to a leveling effect between households, and an improvement in wealth distribution (as the recent history in Siwaa suggests). Rather than the rising tide of economic growth lifting all boats, this appears to be a case of the wealthy prodigal son returning to the fold after expending his natural-resource capital on a cotton scheme that could not be sustained.

Policy Implications

There is a growing consensus among commentators from all sides of the political spectrum that American and European agricultural subsidies inhibit prosperity in the developing world. The plight of West African cotton producers has, in particular, received considerable coverage in the media. The underlying assumption of these arguments is that a global system of free trade would be advantageous for African nations if only the industrialized nations would commit to an across-the-board reduction in subsidies and tariffs. While I agree that American cotton subsidies are bad for African cotton producers in the short run, I use this case study of Malian cotton producers to problematize the notion that removing such subsidies will resolve the development woes of some African nations.

The problems with commodity-crop production number at least two. First, there are a lot of commodity-crop producers, which leads to increasingly small profit margins. A national economy dominated by the production of one or two commodity crops (the case for many African nations) is subject to violent upswings and downturns as global prices for these crops rise and fall. The long-term downward trend in the prices for these goods also suggests a similar fate for the economies overly dependent on them. As estimated by UNCTAD (reported in FAO 2004), the terms of trade for African agricultural commodities declined by 119 percent between 1970 and 1997. For the specific case of cotton, the world price has gone from US$3.48 per kilograms between 1971 and 1973 to $0.88 per kilogram in 2001/2 (adjusted for inflation using 1995 U.S. dollars). As a result, the six West African countries that depend on cotton for more than 20 percent of their total revenues (Central African Republic, Togo, Mali, Benin, Chad, and Burkina Faso) saw their cotton-related export revenues drop by 4 percent during the 1990s, while their export volumes increased by more than 40 percent during the same period (FAO 2004). While removing agricultural subsidies may improve prices in the short term (average estimates suggest a 4 percent increase), such a change seems less significant against a backdrop of long-term steady decline.

Second, the environmental sustainability of commodity-crop production, particularly cotton, is highly questionable in many instances. Cotton accounts for more pesticide use than any other crop. It is also notorious for a being highly destructive to the soil if sufficient organic inputs are not employed in its cultivation. In Mali cotton production is declining most rapidly in its oldest production area, centered around Koutiala. This is because of declining yields and little to no possibility for extensification. Despite the narrative of wealthy, large cotton producers being good stewards of the land, there is no real evidence to support this claim.

The government of Mali, under pressure from structural adjustment programs pushed by the World Bank and IMF, has consistently sought to increase cotton production rather than acknowledge that the crop is problematic for the nation's soil resources. As soil fertility has declined in the old production areas, new "virgin" zones are opened up for cultivation of the crop. Continually increasing cotton production seems to be a questionable long-term development strategy for Mali.

Those who are truly concerned about Africa's development prospects need to consider other approaches than working for policy changes that simply encourage African nations to produce more commodity crops—a temporary boost at best. One might consider policy alternatives that stand a better chance of promoting positive macroeconomic change in many African nations. The agricultural sectors of many African nations desperately need a greater diversity of export crops so that there will be other cash crops to fall back on when prices drop precipitously low for some commodities. This may mean abandoning free-trade orthodoxy to allow targeted subsidies for the production of new (highly promising) export crops. Ideally, these new crops would be ones for which sustainable production is possible in the long run. The emerging market for organics appears to be a potential high-value niche that some African nations could exploit. As Dowd discusses in chapter 10 of this volume, there are now a number of organic-cotton initiatives underway in Africa.

References

Bhagwati, Jagdish. 2002. "Trading for Development: The Poor's Best Hope." *Economist,* June 21.

Camara, Mamadou, Fadimata Haïdara, and Abdramane Traoré. 2000. *Étude socio-économique de l'utilisation des pesticides au Mali.* Bamako: Institut du Sahel/FAO.

FAO. 2004. *The State of Agricultural Commodity Markets.* Rome: Food and Agriculture Organization of the United Nations.

————. 2006. FAOSTAT: "Core Production Data." http://faostat.fao.org.

Gray, Leslie. 1999. "Is Land Being Degraded? A Multi-scale Investigation of Landscape Change in Southwestern Burkina Faso." *Land Degradation and Development* 10:329–43.

Jonckers, Danielle. 1987. *La société minyanka du Mali: Traditions communautaires et développement cotonnier.* Paris: L'Harmattan.

————. 1995. "Stratégies alimentaires et développement en région cotonnière du Mali-Sud. In *Alimentations, traditions et développements en Afrique intertropicale,* ed. René Devisch, Filip de Boeck, and Danielle Jonckers. Paris: L'Harmattan.

Keeley, James, and Ian Scoones. 2003. *Understanding Environmental Policy Processes: Cases from Africa.* London: Earthscan.

Mali, Government of. 1998. *Plan national d'action environnementale.* Bamako: Ministry of Environment.

Moseley, William G. 1993. "Indigenous Agroecological Knowledge among the Bambara of Djitoumou Mali: Foundation for a Sustainable Community." Master's thesis, University of Michigan, Ann Arbor.

————. 2001. "Sahelian 'White Gold' and Rural Poverty-Environment Interactions: The Political Ecology of Cotton Production, Environmental Change, and Household Food Economy in Mali." PhD dissertation, Department of Geography, University of Georgia.

New York Times. 2003a. "Cancun Targets Cotton." Sec. A, September 13.

New York Times. 2003b. "The Case against King Cotton." Sec. A, December 7.

Oxfam. 2002. "Cultivating Poverty: The Impact of U.S. Cotton Subsidies on Africa." Oxfam Briefing Paper 30, Oxfam International.

Roberts, Richard L. 1995. "The Coercion of Free Markets: Cotton, Peasants, and the Colonial State in the French Soudan, 1924–1932." In *Cotton, Colonialism, and Social History in Sub-Saharan Africa,* ed. Allen Isaacman and Richard Roberts. London: James Currey.

————. 1996. *Two Worlds of Cotton: Colonialism and the Regional Economy in the French Soudan, 1800–1946*. Stanford: Stanford University Press.

Steenhuisjen, Piters B. de. 1989. *Systèmes de production et culture attelee en zone Mali-Sud*. Vol. 1, *Analyse du système de production agraire du village de Kaniko*. Sikasso: IER and KIT.

Tefft, James. 2004. "Mali's White Revolution: Smallholder Cotton from 1960 to 2003." *Building on Successes in African Agriculture*, ed. Steven Haggblade, focus 12, brief 5. Washington, DC: International Food Policy Research Institute.

Touré, Amadou T., and Blaise Compaoré. 2003. "Your Farm Subsidies Are Strangling Us." *New York Times*, sec. A, July 11.

USDA (U.S. Department of Agriculture, Foreign Agricultural Service). 2001. "Mali's Cotton Production Doubles and Nears Record Levels." FAS online. October 18. http://www.fas.usda.gov/pecad2/highlights/2001/10/mali/mali_cotton_01.htm

Vos, Henk de. 1991. "L'érosion et la degradation des sols dans la zone CMDT: Le cas des villages de Try." Amsterdam: Institut Royal des Tropiques.

World Bank. 1997. *Partenariat Mali–Banque Mondiale, 1997–1998*. Bamako: Bureau de la Banque Mondiale au Mali.

4

The Decline of Bt Cotton in KwaZulu-Natal

Technology and Institutions

Marnus Gouse, Bhavani Shankar, and Colin Thirtle

The Development and Spread of GM Cotton

DEVELOPMENT

Monsanto, Calgene, and Agracetus started developing genetically modified (GM) insect and herbicide resistant cotton varieties in the mid-1980s in the United States. They conducted the first field trials of transgenic varieties in 1989. The agricultural biotechnology companies claim that GM crops offer a range of production benefits. The most important of these are:

> higher yields
> quality increases
> labor savings
> reduction in pesticide use
> healthier environment.

GM cotton was rapidly adopted by U.S. farmers, accounting for three-quarters of the acreage as early as 2000 and its use inevitably spread to other countries. Delta and Pineland Company (DPL), which had the largest share of the U.S. cottonseed market, started negotiating with several companies to have their varieties transformed with insect and herbicide resistance genes in 1988 and 1989. DPL signed non-exclusive agreements with several companies. In 1993 they signed an exclusive agreement with Monsanto to market transgenic cotton internationally except in Australia and India. By 1997 they had approval for commercial use in China and by 2001 over 30 percent of the crop was GM.

South Africa, Zimbabwe, Nigeria, Kenya, and Egypt are the only African countries that have some form of GMO legislation in place, while some countries, including Namibia, Ethiopia, Tanzania, Zambia, Malawi, and Cameroon either have biosafety guidelines being drafted or are entering into discussions regarding legislation. Currently South Africa is the only African country commercially producing transgenic crops. This may mean that the success of genetically modified crops in South Africa will and already has greatly influenced adoption and regulatory decisions in other African countries.

In 1997, South Africa became the first country in Africa to permit the commercial production of a genetically modified crop—insect-resistant, or Bt, cotton. Bt cotton contains the gene, attained from the soil bacterium *Bacillus thuringiensis* (Bt), that controls the production of a natural pesticide that acts specifically on Lepidoptera, including bollworms, and is harmless to all other pests. In 1998 Bt maize (white and yellow) was approved by the South African Department of Agriculture under the Pest Control Act of 1983, following the recommendation of the South African Committee for Genetic Experimentation (SAGENE). The South African Genetically Modified Organisms Act (Act 15 of 1997) was implemented in December 1999, and herbicide-tolerant cotton and soybeans were approved for commercial production in 2001/2. Herbicide-tolerant maize was released in 2003/4, and after an extended review period "stacked-gene" cotton (cotton with insect resistance and herbicide tolerance) was approved in 2005. South Africa is still the only African country that produces transgenic crops, but a small number of countries in West and East Africa have started or are close to starting field trials. Probably the most advanced is a public-sector white maize variety in Kenya and Bt cotton field trails in Burkina Faso (see chapter 9).

In the 1999/2000 cotton production season in South Africa an estimated 51,000 hectares of cotton were planted, compared to the previous season's 99,000 hectares. In 2002 the South African cotton producers' organization (CottonSA) estimated the season's production at about 31,000 hectares, down from the 56,692 hectares in 2000/2001. In the 2003/4 season only 36,000 hectares were planted, and in 2004/5 the area dropped to an estimated 22,000 hectares. In the 2000/2001 season an estimated three hundred large-scale commercial farmers produced 95 percent of South Africa's cotton crop. The other 5 percent was produced by about three thousand smallholders on the Makhathini Flats and a further 312 smallholders in the Tonga area in Mpumalanga (CottonSA 2002). In 2003 less than five hundred farmers planted cotton on the Makhathini Flats. The decline in commercial plantings is due to the deflated cotton world price, the fluctuating exchange rate between the South African rand and the U.S. dollar, and comparatively better prices of competing crops like maize and sunflower. Large-scale commercial farmers can in most instances convert to a different crop or farming system, but for smallholders in dry areas like the Makhathini Flats this is not an option. The massive decline there is due much more to local organizational changes.

The performance of Bt cotton on the Makhathini Flats has been hailed by industry and pro-biotech bodies as the first real example of how genetically modified crops can assist resource poor farmers and better the life of rural households in developing countries. Makhathini Flats is a great example, as in the first couple of seasons insect-resistant cotton outperformed conventional varieties and small-scale farmers benefited despite having to pay more for seed—thus transgenic crops can work for resource-poor farmers in other developing countries. But another crucial lesson developing countries can learn from the Makhathini Flats experience over the past few seasons is that farmers can benefit from technological innovation only if the correct infrastructure is in place.

The Makhathini Flats is in northeastern KwaZulu-Natal (fig. 4.1). The Pongolapoort dam was built in 1972 for the initial purpose of supplying irrigation water to a proposed project for small-scale white farmers planting sugarcane. However, due to decreasing international sugar prices and domestic overproduction of sugarcane in the late 1970s, this scheme never materialized. The major share of land on the Flats belonged to the state, and in 1979 under the old apartheid regime this area was declared a "black area," along with the already existing KwaZulu area. In the early 1980s the government attempted to develop the necessary infrastructure to settle Zulu farmers on small commercial farming units to produce cotton and other crops under irrigation. For a range of reasons that fall outside the scope of this paper this project was essentially a failure and now mainly dryland cotton is produced on the Flats.

During the late 1980s two ginning companies, Clark Cotton and Tongaat Cotton, were active on the Flats, supplying credit and inputs and buying cotton from small-scale farmers. The two companies shared a weighing bridge and there was a positive attitude of cooperation. Even though some farmers borrowed production credit from one company and delivered their harvest under a different name to the other company, losses and gains generally balanced out. Around 1989, Clark and Tongaat formed a partnership called Vunisa (which in isiZulu means "to harvest"). In 1994/95, Lonrho Africa bought the cotton interests of the Tongaat-Hulett group and Tongaat's interest on the Flats was purchased by Clark. From then on Clark Cotton operated under the name of Vunisa in KwaZulu-Natal and Swaziland. The South African Land Bank supplied credit and repayment default risk was shared between the Land Bank and Vunisa. Vunisa administrated production loans from the 1998/99 season and according to Clark Cotton and Vunisa the first few years were very successful for both cotton farmers and the ginning company and the loan recovery rate was close to 90 percent. The crucial point was that Vunisa was the only buyer and, because of this monopsony, could use the forthcoming crop as collateral for input loans.

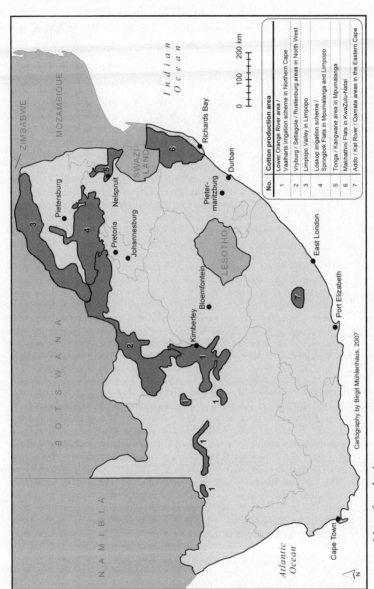

No.	Cotton production area
1	Lower Orange River area / Vaalharts irrigation scheme in Northern Cape
2	Vryburg / Setlagole / Rustenburg areas in North West
3	Limpopo Valley in Limpopo
4	Loskop irrigation scheme / Springbok Flats in Mpumalanga and Limpopo
5	Tonga / Kangwane area in Mpumalanga
6	Makhathini Flats in KwaZulu-Natal
7	Addo / Kat River / Qamata areas in the Eastern Cape

Cartography by Birgit Mühlenhaus, 2007

FIG. 4.1. Map of study sites.

During the 2001/2 production season a new company, Makhathini Cotton (Pty.), Ltd. (MCG) erected a new gin on the Flats, right next to the Vunisa depot. According to their Web site, their vision was "to stimulate rural development and reduce poverty on the Makhathini Flats by creating a world-class cotton agribusiness through construction of a ginnery in the heart of the area." But by opening a competing gin they set in motion a chain of events where farmers borrowed production credit from Vunisa but delivered their harvest to MCG. Due to substantial financial losses to Vunisa and the Land Bank, no credit was made available for 2002/3, with the effect that very few farmers were able to produce cotton. Regardless of the technology, farmers need appropriate upstream and downstream institutional structures—functioning input and output markets that facilitate production and trade.

The Land Bank could probably provide credit but is understandably wary about investing in an area and in a crop where defaults have already cost millions of rand. The South African Development Trust Corporation, the Department for Development and Aid, the KwaZulu Finance and Investment Corporation, and the Development Bank of South Africa have all had roles in failed credit provision programs on the Flats over the years. Thus, the Land Bank and Vunisa are no longer involved and it appears that MCG has decided that it is more profitable to rent land from the farmers to produce cotton themselves than to finance farmers. This approach also seems flawed, as some farmers steal the cotton (produced on their own rented land) to deliver it to MCG under different names. MCG is showing great initiative and determination in trying to establish irrigated units for the production of cotton and maize or wheat with the aim of establishing small-scale farmers on these areas over the longer term. However, unless appropriate institutions can be developed, history is likely to repeat itself and any success will make MCG vulnerable to new entrants, just as Vunisa was, so development, poverty alleviation, and economic progress on the Flats seems unlikely.

CREDIT DEPENDENCE

The majority of farmers on the Flats cannot finance their own cotton production inputs. A study by Hofs and Kirsten (2002) showed that the farmers on the Flats who were able to produce during the seasons when credit was not available were mainly the elderly, who could finance inputs through pension money. The fact is that due to the supply of credit by the South African government through development programs, combined with the inability of financial corporations to enforce repayment of loans, adverse selection is the norm for farmers on the Flats. Borrowing money from one gin and delivering the crop to another gin is hardly a new or a rare occurrence in Africa. Group credit schemes and a good relationship between farmers and companies as well as cooperation between competitors can improve loan repayment rates, but in sub-Saharan Africa communal ownership prevents land being used as collateral. Then, the only collateral is the forthcoming harvest, and the tendency to default is exacerbated by droughts, which make repayment impossible in some years. A farmer who cannot repay is bound to be tempted to deliver his cotton under a different name or to break his contract and deliver his harvest to a different buyer.

APPROPRIATE INSTITUTIONAL SUPPORT

The recent experience of GM cotton production in Makhathini makes it clear that technology alone is not the answer. Without a range of support services and markets—accessible input supplies, technical advice, finance, reliable output markets—many smallhold producers will be either unable or unwilling to adopt new technologies, even if they do promise higher productivity to the user. However, markets are often imperfect or missing in rural sub-Saharan Africa, while the incentives for the provision of support services to poor smallholders are weak. Thus, institutional arrangements need to be developed to provide appropriate incentives for service provision. In the case of cotton, this must take account of the simple fact that most producers cannot operate without credit and that, because it is nearly impossible to enforce contractual compliance, an input supplier has to have monopsony power to be able to use the crop as collateral. Thus, there must be an appropriate balance between competition, collaboration, and coordination among seed cotton buyers (Poulton 2004).

Assessing Bt Technology: Farm Management Accounting

In 1998 the smallholders in the Makhathini Flats began adopting Bt cotton.[1] A Monsanto report (Bennett 2002) shows that in 1998/99, there were 75 adopters, growing less than 200 hectares of Bt cotton. In 1999/2000, this rose to 411 adopters with a little under 700 hectares, and in 2000/2001, to 1,184 adopters with about 1,900 hectares. Thus, in only three years, 40 percent of the producers, representing almost two-thirds of the area planted, had adopted the new technology, and the International Service for the Acquisition of Agri-biotech Applications reported that by 2001/2 over 90 percent had adopted Bt varieties (ISAAA 2004).

Delta Pineland has sole distribution rights to Monsanto's Bt gene in South Africa, which means that all Bt cotton varieties in South Africa belong to DPL and Monsanto receives the additional technology fee. Up to 1999/2000 mainly NuCOTN 37-B (based on Acala 90) was sold, and in 2000/2001 NuOpal (based on the best-performing conventional variety, Opal) was added and was commonly known and marketed as Bollgard cotton. Non-GM varieties were also still available from Vunisa, which also provided support services for farmers through their extension officers, including credit for land preparation, chemicals, and seed.

The main source of information is a survey of one hundred farmers, conducted jointly by the University of Pretoria and the University of Reading, covering the 1998/99 and 1999/2000 seasons. Information was collected on household background, farming practices and problems, reasons for adopting Bt cotton, and input costs and returns. Rather than relying on farmers' recall, most of the crucial information used in evaluating the technology came from farm records supplied by Vunisa.

The smallholders in the survey are all Zulus producing under rainfed conditions; there were no large commercial producers. Cropping land is unfenced, so livestock damage crops due to the communal grazing system. Due to out migration of younger men, 42 percent of the household heads were female and 76 percent were over forty years old. Limited or mixed cropping is the norm, with an assortment of maize, beans, and vegetables grown for subsistence, and cotton, which is usually the only cash crop. As is common in South Africa, most households (75 percent) also kept livestock and almost 30 percent had a source of income other than the farm, such as the police service, truck driving, and mining. Over 60 percent of the farmers "owned" less than five hectares of land, with the largest concentration (37 percent) in the 2.5-to-5-hectare group. Cotton areas varied from one hectare to a single farm of twenty-five hectares.

Evaluating the technology is complicated by two factors. In the first year farmers with less than five hectares had an average yield of 510 kilograms of seed cotton per hectare and only 15 percent adopted the Bt variety. Those with over five hectares produced only 378 kilograms per hectare and 25 percent were adopters. Thus, any simple comparison will be biased by this positive correlation of farm size with adoption and negative correlation with yield. It is also important to note the low yield level, mainly explained by a relatively low rainfall, germination problems, and the fact that none of the farmers used chemical fertilizer or a crop rotation system.

The farm accounting efficiency measures, based on Vunisa's data, are reported in table 4.1, beginning with the first season. The division of the nonadopters between the forty farmers who did not adopt in either year and the forty-two who adopted Bt in the second season allows the innate differences between farms to be separated from the effects of the Bt technology. Neither the forty nonadopters or the forty-two second-year adopters used Bt seed in the first year and they averaged nearly the same production per hectare.

Thus, there is no clear yield advantage to the Bt variety, as the second-year adopters have the highest yields, which are 4 percent higher than the first-year adopters as well as being 16.5 percent higher than the group who never adopted. The lack of advantage may be explained by the correlations noted in the last section and by the seeding rate (seed used per unit of land) of 0.43 bags per ha, which is 22 percent lower than for the full set of nonadopters, probably because of the cost of the seed (197 rand per hectare compared with 119 rand for all the nonadopters). However, pesticide costs are lower for the adopters. The extra cost of seed can be set against the

Table 4.1. Costs and returns for nonadopters and adopters, 1998/99, 1999/2000

| | First season, 1998/99 | | | | Second season, 1999/2000 | | | |
| | Bt cotton | Non-Bt cotton | | | Bt cotton | | | Non-Bt cotton |
Averages per category	*1st-year adopters*	*All nonadopters*	*Adopted neither year*	*2nd-year adopters*	*All adopters*	*1st-year adopters*	*2nd-year adopters*	*Adopted neither year*
Number of farmers	18	82	40	42	60	18	42	40
Yield (kg/ha)	475	457	423	493	425	433	421	304
Bags (25kg) of seed/ha	0.43	0.55	0.55	0.53	0.46	0.46	0.46	0.57
Yield/kg of seed (kg)	50	37	32	42	44	40	46	23
Seed cost/ha (rand)	197	119	124	115	214	211	214	127
Chemical cost/ha (rand)	93	132	145	120	83	83	83	129
Gross margin/ha (rand)	781	791	687	890	675	673	676	428

savings on pesticides and the increase in output, since the gross margin is defined as the value of output minus the costs of intermediate inputs.

However, the gross margins show that the nonadopters were actually ten rand better off, because although the Bt adopters got almost one hundred rand per hectare more than those who never adopt, they are over one hundred rand worse off than the second-year adopters. Thus, neither yields nor gross margins explain why none of the adopters discontinued the Bt variety and a further forty-two adopted it in the next year. The obvious flaw in these commonly used measures of productivity and profitability is that the cost saving in labor used for spraying is not taken into account, and 20 percent of the farmers rated this as the main reason for adoption. Net margins do include labor and land costs, but those costs cannot be calculated since although the survey data includes the quantities of labor and land, neither land nor family labor has a price. However, the quantities alone show that the farmers who had a significant increase in yield did not use less labor, as the increase in harvest labor compensated for the reduction in labor for spraying.

The right side of table 4.1 reports the results for the second season, when the lower yields are attributable to late heavy rains, which were 50 percent above average, compared with the lower-than-average rain at the beginning of the previous year. Whereas the first season was good for the cotton crop, the second was not. The average yield of the nonadopters fell to 304 kilograms per hectare, a decline of 28 percent. The first important outcome is that all adopters had an average yield of 425 kilograms per hectare, which is 40 percent higher than the nonadopters, leaving little doubt that the Bt variety yields better in a wet year, when bollworms are a greater problem, partly because the rain washes the pesticide residue off the plants. But, since by these measures the second-year adopters appear to be the best farmers, what proportion of this 40 percent increase is actually attributable to the Bt variety?

The second year adopters, who had 16.5 percent greater yields than the nonadopters, when using the same seed, now have a 38.5 percent yield advantage after adopting the Bt variety. Thus, the yield benefit due to the Bt variety appears to be 22 percent, or close to 70 kilograms per hectare. The percentage gain is in line with Monsanto's field trials (for the first season, which was a good year), which show a 27 percent yield gain for the Bt variety (Bennett 2002, table 1).

The second result is that the decline for those who used Bt in both years was only from 475 to 433 kilograms per hectare (a 9 percent fall), whereas for those who changed to Bt in the second year, the fall was from 493 to 421 kilograms per hectare (a 15 percent fall). Despite switching to the Bt technology, the second-year adopters now have lower yields than the first-year adopters, which suggests that by the second season there is learning by doing. Average seed costs per hectare were 68 percent higher for adopters in this second season, as the Bt seed costs nearly twice as much. However, chemical costs fell by 36 percent, from 129 rand for nonadopters to 83 rand for adopters. Monsanto's field trials show a reduction from 220 rand per hectare for the non-Bt variety to 23 for Bt cotton, a reduction of almost 90 percent. Therefore, much of the trial plot gains in chemical reduction have not occurred at the farm level in this bad season.

Even so, the second-year results are far clearer and the outcome entirely unambiguous. The yield gain of 40 percent and the lower chemical cost easily offset the extra seed cost, so that the average gross margin for the adopters is 675 rand, which is 58 percent higher than the margin for the nonadopters (428 rand). The share of this that is attributable to the Bt variety can be calculated as it was for yields. The advantage of the second-year adopters was 30 percent when the two groups used the same seed and is now 58 percent, so 28 percent can be attributed to the Bt variety, which is worth 190 rand per hectare. Again, this result can be compared with Monsanto's trial results, which showed a gain of 944 rand per hectare, due to higher trial plot yields and a greater reduction in chemical use.

The yield increase reported in Thirtle et al. (2003) for 1999/2000, which was 40 percent, may not be unreasonable. Studies for developed countries show lower yield gains, but Qaim, Cap, and de Janvry (2003) and Qaim and de Janvry (2005) compare commercial farms and smallholders in Argentina and find that the yield gain to large farms is 19 percent, while the smallholders gain 41 percent. This is remarkably similar to the South African results and we attribute the difference to the financial and human capital constraints that cause smallholders to invest less in chemical pest control, so their crop damage is higher. These reasons also apply to South African smallholders. By the time a small-scale farmer has noticed bollworms, bought pesticides with a limited amount of credit, and started to spray, severe damage has already been done. Many farmers indicated that they were not even able to apply pesticides on their whole field due to a lack of time, backpack sprayers, labor, and the high cost of pesticide. Further, a low education level makes the mixing of pesticides and the calibration of backpack sprayer nozzles problematic; the efficacy and efficiency of pesticide applications is thus questionable for many small-scale farmers.

Econometric Estimation of the Impact of Bt Technology

PRODUCTION EFFICIENCY

Both yields and gross margins are incomplete indictors and say very little about the reasons for any observed differences between farms. Yield is a partial measure of productivity and is of limited use when the levels of nonland inputs used, such as labor and fertilizer, differ between farms. Gross margins take account of intermediate inputs but ignore the efficiency with which the major inputs, labor and land, are used. All inputs are properly accounted for when a production function is estimated.

Whereas simple regressions take the average line of best fit through the observations (and hence are sometimes called mean response functions) and thus tacitly assume that all farms are efficient, this efficiency assumption can be misleading if there are significant differences in efficiency levels. Tests show that the appropriate approach is a production frontier, which will give results that are more accurate and also generate an efficiency level for each farm. Thus, Thirtle et al. (2003) explain how cotton output varies with inputs of land, labor, chemicals, and seed, differentiating between conventional and Bt varieties. The results are unambiguous, even in the first year, when the adopters had a far higher mean efficiency of 88 percent, as compared with the mean of 66 percent for those who did not use Bt cotton. This suggests that when all the inputs are included in the efficiency calculations, the adopters are one-third more efficient. The key point is that this analysis takes full account of the efficiency with which labor and land are used, and these two inputs account for 70 percent (or more) of output in African agriculture. For 1999/2000, 73 percent of the variance in output was explained and the mean efficiency for the nonadopters was 48 percent and for the adopters, 74 percent. The efficiency advantage of the adopters has now risen to 54 percent, compared with 33 percent in the first season. Finally, the only variable that was significant in explaining the efficiency levels, in both years, was adoption of the Bt variety.

PESTICIDE PRODUCTIVITY: WHY YIELDS INCREASE SO MUCH IN MAKHATHINI FLATS

The estimation techniques above treat pesticide in exactly the same manner as the other inputs, but it actually adds nothing to output if there are no pests. When there are, it controls damage, keeping yields closer to what they would have been without pests. Thus, in parallel with Huang et al. (2002) (for China) and Qaim, Cap, and de Janvry (2003) and Qaim and de Janvry (2005) (for Argentina), Shankar and Thirtle (2005) take a "damage control" approach to estimating the role of pesticides and Bt technology.

The results for the conventional part of the model add nothing to those above, but the damage control parameters are highly significant, with signs that conform to expectations. Particularly, increasing pesticide use does reduce damage and the Bt dummy variable is positive, which confirms that adoption of Bt varieties is effective in controlling pest damage, with less pesticide. With no pesticide applied, non-Bt producers would realize only about 16 percent of potential output. By shifting to Bt use, about 40 percent of potential output can be recovered, even without application of pesticide. At the current average application rate of 2.2 liters per hectare, a nonadopter attains only about 36 percent of potential output. A Bt user, at the current average application rate of 1.1 liters per hectare (half the nonadopter average), realizes 55 percent of potential output. Almost 9 liters would be required to get close to 100 percent output.

The efficiency of pesticide use can be judged by comparing the financial gain from pesticides with the pesticide price. The computations were done by holding all other inputs constant at the sample average values, while varying the quantity of pesticide. In 1999/2000 an additional liter of pesticide cost approximately 9.3 rand (US$1.40) per hectare and at that price, the correct level is 4.7 liters per hectare, so the reported use of 2.1 liters per hectare is less than 50 percent of the optimum. Thus, whereas Huang et al. (2002) reported overuse of 40 kilograms per hectare in China, African smallholders use far too little pesticide and consequently suffer serious crop losses. Similarly, Qaim, Cap, and de Janvry (2003) found relatively large yield gains to smallholders in Argentina, as compared with commercial farmers. This is why Bt gives impressive gains in yields in Makhathini Flats. There are several factors that could cause this outcome in Makhathini. First, there are financial reasons for underuse. Pesticide purchases often require larger cash outlays than are available to smallholders, particularly mid-season, when reserves are low and other crops and activities compete for available cash. Many complain that they are unable to get sufficient credit. Others who can afford the chemicals do not own a backpack sprayer and would hire someone to perform the task. But labor availability for spraying poses a similar dilemma. Over the Christmas period, an important time in the South African cotton cycle, hired labor is often unavailable (Gouse, Kirsten, and Jenkins 2003).

A similar analysis of the Bt users shows that at the current average application rate of about one liter per hectare, Bt users, like the nonadopters, are using about half the optimal amount of pesticide. Although the Bt gene provides resistance to the bollworm, so that bollworm-specific sprays are no longer needed, Hofs and Kirsten (2002) note that leafhoppers and aphids are causing increasing damage. Clearly, the current applications of pesticides to deal with these other pests are inadequate. With conventional cotton they were killed in the crossfire aimed at the bollworm. With the use of Bt cotton, the "sucking insects" have now become the main problem and farmers still have to apply appropriate pesticides to control them.

For both the adopters and nonadopters, these private optimal application rates take no account of the environmental and health costs of pesticide use. If these negative impacts could be measured, the optimal pesticide application rates reported above would be reduced.

Implications for African Agriculture

The history of Bt cotton in Makhathini Flats shows the technological potential of GM crops in an African smallholder environment. The differences between the two years studied show that a single season sample is not a good basis for generalization. But, in the wet growing season, when bollworm pressure was severe and conventional pesticides were less effective, there is no doubt that Bt was effective in preventing crop losses. Those who had adopted the Bt variety were substantially better off, and 28 percent of the yield advantage could be attributed to Bt. But the continuing problems and the collapse of cotton in the Flats also shows that good governance and institutional structure are required, or the potential gains will not be realized. It is not reasonable to expect the farmers to change their behavior quickly: they have seen a procession of failed schemes and broken promises. As individual farmers have no land rights, the forthcoming crop has to be used as collateral, and this is only feasible if the credit provider is a monopsonist or there is some degree of competitive cooperation. Liberalization may be good as a general principle, but here is a case where competition destroys the whole operation rather than increasing efficiency. Like a number of simple ideas in economics, the belief that competition is always good is blatantly wrong. The Makhathini story again illustrates that in the African context scientific advances really are easier than establishing the social and economic conditions necessary for progress to occur.

Note

1. This section is fully covered in Thirtle et al. 2003 (which superseded earlier work, such as Ismael, Bennett, and Morse 2001 and Beyers et al. 2002).

References

Bennett, Andrew. 2002. "The Impact of Bt-Cotton on Small Holder Production in the Makhatini Flats, South Africa." *Bt Cotton Report*, www.monsantoafrica.com.

Beyers, Lindie, Yousouf Ismaël, Jenifer Piesse, and Colin Thirtle. 2002. "Can GM-Technologies Help the Poor? The Efficiency of Bt Cotton Adopters in the Makhatini Flats of KwaZulu-Natal." *Agrekon* 41 (1): 15–27.

Cotton SA. 2002. Monthly Market Reports. Cotton SA, PO Box 912232, Silverton, RSA. www.cottonsa.org.za.

Gouse, Marnus, Johann Kirsten, and Lindie Jenkins. 2003. "Bt Cotton in South Africa: Adoption and the Impact on Farm Incomes amongst Small-Scale and Large-Scale farmers." *Agrekon* 42 (1): 15–28.

Hofs, Jean-Luc, and Johann Kirsten. 2002. "Genetically Modified Cotton in South Africa: The Solution for Rural Development." CIRAD/University of Pretoria Working Paper.

Huang, Jikun, Raifa Hu, Scott Rozelle, Fangbin Qiao, and Carl Pray. 2002. "Transgenic Varieties and Productivity of Smallholder Cotton Farmers in China." *Australian Journal of Agricultural Economics* 46 (3): 367–87.

ISAAA (International Service for the Acquisition of Agri-biotech Applications). 2004. "Bt Cotton: South Africa Case Study." http://www.isaaa.org.

Ismaël, Yousouf, Richard Bennett, and Stephen Morse. 2001. "Can Farmers in Developing Countries Benefit from Modern Technology? Experience from Makhatini Flats, Republic of South Africa." *CropBiotechNet* 1 (5). http://www.isaaa..org/KC.

Ismaël, Yousouf, Lindie Beyers, Colin Thirtle, and Jenifer Piesse. 2002. "Efficiency Effects of Bt Cotton Adoption by Smallholders in Makathini Flats, KwaZulu-Natal, South Africa." Paper presented at 5th International ICABR Conference, Ravello, Italy, 2001. In *Economic and Social Issues in Agricultural Biotechnology*, ed. Robert Evenson, V. Santaniello, and David Zilberman, 325–50. Wallingford, UK: CABI Publishing.

Poulton, Colin. 2004. "Competition and Coordination in Liberalized African Cotton Market Systems." *World Development* 32 (3): 519–36.

Qaim, Martin, Eugenio Cap, and Alain de Janvry. 2003. "Agronomics and Sustainability of Transgenic Cotton in Argentina." *AgBioForum* 6 (1–2): 41–47.

Qaim, Martin, and Alain de Janvry. 2005. "Bt Cotton and Pesticide Use in Argentina: Economic and Environmental Effects." *Environment and Development Economics* 10 (2): 179–200.

Shankar, Bhavani, and Colin Thirtle. 2005. "Pesticide Productivity and Transgenic Cotton Technology: The South African Smallholder Case." *Journal of Agricultural Economics* 56 (1): 97–116.

Thirtle, Colin, Lindie Beyers, Yousouf Ismaël, and Jenifer Piesse. 2003. "Can GM-Technologies Help the Poor? The Impact of Bt Cotton in the Makhatini Flats of KwaZulu-Natal." *World Development* 31 (4): 717–32.

Part II

Organizing Cotton

National-Level Reforms and Rural Livelihoods

5

The Many Paths of Cotton Sector Reform in East and Southern Africa

Lessons from a Decade of Experience

David Tschirley, Colin Poulton, and Duncan Boughton

COTTON IS A RARE economic success story in sub-Saharan Africa (SSA). While SSA's share of world agricultural trade fell by half from 1980 to 2000, its share of cotton trade rose by 30 percent (FAO 2002), and predictions are that its share will continue to grow. Production grew three times more rapidly in SSA over the period than in the rest of the world (Goreux 2002). Moreover, cotton is predominantly a smallholder crop, with over two million poor rural households in SSA depending on it as their main source of cash income. Among export crops with substantial involvement of smallholders in SSA, cotton ranks second in value only to cocoa, and its production is spread much more widely across the continent. Clearly, the profitability of cotton production and processing in Africa has large and widespread impacts on poverty in the continent.

Because of the need for purchased inputs to achieve economic on-farm yields and high financial returns on quality, processed commodities such as cotton require effective coordination to be produced, processed, and marketed competitively. Since most farmers in SSA require credit to access the needed inputs, two of the key coordination challenges are to ensure timely use of appropriate inputs and to recover the credit. Due to widespread failure of credit and input markets in SSA, most approaches to the input credit problem have featured interlocked transactions, in which a firm wishing to purchase the farm output—typically a ginner in the case of cotton—provides inputs to farmers on credit and attempts to recover the credit upon purchase of the product.

Variously referred to as *contract farming* or *outgrower schemes*, such arrangements have governed production of a wide range of cash crops throughout the developing world for many decades.[1] When effective, they allow smallholders to profit from a crop they might ordinarily not have access to, and allow processors to benefit from these farmers' low costs of production.[2] Yet the conditions under which contract farming can be expected to emerge and persist are relatively restrictive, relating primarily to production and marketing characteristics of the crop and to characteristics of the market into which farmers sell (Delgado 1999; Benfica, Tschirley, and Sambo 2002).[3] Numerous examples exist of failed efforts, primarily related to the inability of processors to recover input credit (Stringfellow 1996, Glover 1990). While cotton often lends itself to contract farming operations, it too has frequently been threatened by acute credit default crises. Over the longer term, cotton systems can be undermined by the inability of participants in the supply chain to agree on and develop financing mechanisms for investments in research, extension, and quality control.

Thus, a fundamental fact is that the performance of cotton input systems in SSA, which is key to the crop's overall performance, is strongly influenced by the structure and behavior of the market for seed cotton. By affecting the prospects for successful collective action, the characteristics of the seed cotton market may also influence the ability of cotton sectors to meet longer-term productivity and quality challenges. This fact has fueled concern that the economic reforms sweeping the continent since the early 1990s may derail this remarkable success story, by undercutting the basis for effective interlocking of transactions and also complicating collective decisions on long-term investment. For example, a major comparative review of cotton sector performance in anglophone and francophone countries of SSA through 1988 concluded that, in West Africa's single channel systems (which to that time had been far more successful than systems in anglophone countries), "privatization of input distribution . . . should be considered only with the greatest caution, due to the need to link distribution with credit and output marketing" (Lele, Van de Walle, and Gbetibouo, 1989). It further cautioned about the potential "collapse of the cotton industry in francophone Africa" if research and extension were moved out of existing single channel systems without viable alternative institutional approaches to ensure the continuity of these activities (for more information on West African cotton systems, see chapter 1).

At the same time, real cotton prices have declined by over 50 percent since 1970–75 (FSRP 2000), putting severe pressure on inefficient production and marketing systems. Much has been made of the role of subsidies to cotton farmers in developed economies in reducing world prices (chapter 1). Indeed, these subsidies are massive and appear to have significantly affected world price levels.[4] Yet the trend in world prices would be strongly negative even without these subsidies.[5] As the International Cotton Advisory Committee notes, "advances in technology, including biotechnology and other pest management techniques, are reducing cotton production costs worldwide, and many producers can cover costs at current (low) prices" (ICAC 2005; parentheses added). Clearly, countries have no choice but to innovate continuously to reduce the cost of production, ginning, and marketing over time.

With cotton sector reform in much of SSA a decade old, it is now possible to review the empirical record and begin drawing lessons from experience. In this chapter we assess the record of five countries in East and southern Africa: Tanzania, Uganda, Zimbabwe, Zambia, and Mozambique (for location of these countries, see fig. 0.1 in the introduction). In four of these countries, cotton is the first- or second-most-important smallholder cash crop; only in Uganda does it substantially lag behind other cash crops.[6]

If they are to generate sustainable increases in value added over time, cotton supply chains need to deal with nine technical challenges:

Support strong varietal research and dissemination. Seed quality has major impacts on yields, ginning ratios, and fiber characteristics. It thus establishes the outer limits of productivity and quality throughout the system.

Maintain the purity of varieties once they are released. This typically requires varietal zoning agreements, which demand some horizontal coordination among players.

Assure sufficient and timely provision of chemically treated seed to farmers. Treated seed reduces disease in a very cost-effective manner.

Assure sufficient and timely provision of appropriate pesticides to farmers. Most cotton varieties currently in use in SSA are highly susceptible to attack by pests, so that in many areas three to five pesticide applications are considered necessary for economical yields.

Manage pesticide use to reduce cost and avoid insect resistance. The "pesticide treadmill"—inappropriate use of chemicals, which increases insect resistance, leading to more use—increases financial costs and environmental and human health externalities.

Manage pesticide use to reduce damage to human health and the environment. This issue has received little attention to date and is becoming increasingly important within several francophone systems; Maumbe and Swinton (2003) note the significant health costs incurred by pesticide-using cotton farmers in Zimbabwe.

Assure appropriate use of fertilizers. The high cost of fertilizers and varieties that do not respond well to fertilizer mean that this input is often not profitable for cotton in SSA. Wider use, which may be a prerequisite for cotton to make major and sustainable contributions to poverty reduction, requires reducing its cost and combining it with improved varieties more responsive to fertilizer.

Control quality from the farm gate through the export of fiber. Quality relates to fiber characteristics and contamination with foreign matter. Countries with a reputation for uniformly high quality will have a ready market and will receive better prices even during the periodic gluts that afflict the world cotton market.

Remunerate farmers sufficiently to ensure their continued and increasing participation in the sector.

Meeting these challenges requires both public and private goods, and hence a great deal of coordination among public and private players. The state is often ill equipped to provide the necessary public goods; if they are to be provided at all, these and the necessary private goods must typically be provided by the cotton companies. This is easier when few companies are involved. On the other hand, cotton farmers want attractive prices, which may more likely be generated where a large number of companies compete vigorously for seed cotton. This reasoning suggests that there may be a trade-off between competition and coordination in cotton systems (Poulton et al. 2004). More precisely, it suggests that the structure of the cotton market in a producing country may strongly influence which challenges are most difficult to meet, and may thus condition the types of institutions that need to emerge if the system is to be sustainable.

Prereform Institutional Setups

Prereform institutional setups for cotton production and marketing in East and southern Africa can be classified into three groups: cooperative unions working with national cotton marketing parastatals (Tanzania and Uganda), single-channel state marketing monopolies (Zimbabwe and Zambia), and nationalized but quasi-independent units coordinated by a state organization (Mozambique).

TANZANIA'S AND UGANDA'S COOPERATIVE-BASED SYSTEMS

Into the 1960s gins in Tanzania and Uganda were primarily owned by independent Asian businessmen (Baffes 2002; Dorsey 2002). With independence and the rise of the cooperative movement in each country, these ginneries passed into the hands of rural cooperatives. In Tanzania through 1994, primary cooperative societies (PCSs) typically handled the marketing of seed cotton from farmers, while regional cooperative unions (RCUs) handled ginning. Each enjoyed a statutory monopoly in their geographic area of operation. RCUs then returned a share of the ginned cottonseed to the PCSs for distribution to farmers and sold the lint to the cotton board.[7] The cotton board had a monopoly on the export of lint, imported pesticides and distributed them on credit to RCUs, and set pan-territorial and pan-seasonal producer prices.

The system in Tanzania suffered from financial difficulties at least from the early 1970s (Baffes 2002; Gibbon 1999). Overstaffing, poor management, and poor credit recovery led to liquidity crises for the cotton board, which was frequently unable to purchase the crop in a timely manner from the RCUs. These in turn could not advance inputs and operating capital to the PCSs. Producers had to wait one and even two years for payment, which meant that the real value was drastically reduced by inflation. Much cotton was left uncollected or unginned. Production of seed cotton fell from an average of over 200,000 t from 1971 to 1975 to about 130,000 t during the 1980s, while the debt of the cotton board and RCUs exploded (Gibbon 1999).

Uganda's story is similar in many regards, made worse by the intense civil conflict of the Obote and Amin years. Production bottomed-out in late 1980s and early 1990s at less than 20,000 bales, from an average of about 400,000 bales between 1960 and 1973.[8]

ZAMBIA'S AND ZIMBABWE'S SINGLE-CHANNEL SYSTEMS

Similar setups in Zambia and Zimbabwe before reform lead to very different performance. From 1977 to 1994 the state-owned Lint Company of Zambia (LINTCO) provided certified seed, pesticides, sprayers, bags for harvesting, and extension advice to farmers, and purchased seed cotton from them at a fixed price. LINTCO had a near monopsony in buying seed cotton and a monopoly in distributing cotton inputs on credit. Available data suggest that, from 1987 to 1995 (the year immediately following liberalization), production was fluctuating but in secular decline, falling below 20,000 t of seed cotton in the 1995 harvest year. According to the Zambia Privatization Agency, LINTCO was also in serious financial crisis before its sale, having accumulated substantial unpaid debts.

Zimbabwe's Cotton Marketing Board (CMB) was formed in 1967, in the early stages of Rhodesia's unilateral declaration of independence from Great Britain. The CMB exercised monopoly power from the purchase of seed cotton through export of lint and paid fixed prices negotiated between the government and the Rhodesia National Farmers' Union (later renamed the Commercial Farmers' Union; Larsen 2001). At the advent of black majority rule in 1980, the new government progressively reoriented agricultural extension, credit services, and buying depots toward smallholders. One result of this change is that, while over 90 percent of cotton in 1980 was produced by large-scale commercial farmers, by the end of the decade the smallholder sector produced about half.[9] As the number of farmers quadrupled, reflecting the entrance of smallholders, total production boomed, from an average of about 150,000 t of seed cotton between 1980 and 1983 to over 250,000 t between 1988 and 1991. Unlike many parastatals in the region, it does not appear that corruption was a serious problem in the CMB (Government of Zimbabwe 1991). Farm prices continued to be based on strict grading, and smallholders received the highest average prices in East and southern Africa (Boughton et al. 2003; Larsen 2001). A record of strong investment in varietal research continued, and credit was made widely available through the Agricultural Finance Corporation. Partly as a result, smallholder productivity was the highest in the region (average yields of about 700 kilograms per hectare), and the careful quality control that had earned Zimbabwe a ready market and a price premium of about 10 percent in world markets was maintained.

This remarkable success came, however, at the cost of substantial budget deficits, related to a policy of subsidized sales of lint to local spinners (Larsen 2002b) and to the much higher costs of serving large numbers of dispersed smallholders. Though the Cotton Marketing Board's deficit was the smallest of the four statutory boards, by the early 1990s it was becoming increasingly difficult for the country to resist pressures for reform.

From the early twentieth century through the early 1960s, cotton production in colonial Mozambique was based on smallholder production in an outgrower model in which large Portuguese "concession" companies held exclusive rights to the purchase and ginning of cotton in specified geographic areas. State-sanctioned coercion to ensure production by smallholders was a regular feature of the system. Beginning in the mid-1960s, with the rise of the unrest that would eventually topple the regime, colonial authorities began to promote cotton production by commercial settler farmers. This approach succeeded in maintaining total production despite sharply falling smallholder production. Total production of seed cotton averaged about 120,000 t from 1960 to 1974, with a peak of 144,000 mt in 1973. At independence, in 1975, these concession companies were nationalized as quasi-independent units coordinated by the Secretaria do Estado do Algodão. Commercial production collapsed in 1975, and production by both sectors declined steadily into the mid-1980s, driven by the combined effects of civil war and disastrous policies of central planning. By 1985 total production was less than 10,000 t, and the government was ready to begin considering alternative models for the sector.

The Reform Process:
Initial Conditions and Institutional Responses

Table 5.1 summarizes the institutional setup prior to reform, key indicators of performance at the start of reform (primarily production trends and indebtedness in the system), and the timing and key elements of reform in each of our five countries. Table 5.2 highlights the range of institutional approaches used in the countries to ensure input provision and credit repayment. Three points stand out. First, initial conditions (prior institutional setup and performance), and thus the motivation for reform, varied widely across the countries. Second, the reform path in each country shows strong path dependency:

Table 5.1. Cotton sector reform: prior institutional setup and performance; timing and key steps in reform

Country	Prereform institutional setup	Prereform performance	Timing and key elements of reform
Tanzania	Quasi-independent RCUs held local monopolies, sold lint to cotton board, which held national monopoly on exports. Entirely smallholder production in cooperative societies.	Production had declined by about one-third from early 1970s, to about 130,000 t. Massive debt lead to 1- to 2-year delays in paying farmers; much cotton went uncollected or unginned; yet exported cotton received premium on world markets.	Initial steps in 1990 with greater autonomy for RCUs; definitive reform in 1994 with elimination of cotton board monopoly
Uganda	Very similar to Tanzania. Cooperative unions purchased seed cotton from farmers and sold to Lint Marketing Board, which held monopoly on lint marketing and provided all seed to CUs. Entirely smallholder production in cooperative societies.	Production had collapsed to less than 5,000 t, from over 70,000 t from 1960 to 1973. Debt throughout the system. Farmers uninterested in cotton.	1993, with elimination of Lint Marketing Board's monopoly on lint marketing
Zimbabwe	Single-channel system: CMB provided all inputs and extension assistance to smallholder farmers, purchased all seed cotton from them, ginned and exported all lint. Both commercial and smallholder production.	Successful transition from reliance on white commercial farmers to black smallholder farmers. Production increased nearly 70% (to 250,000 t) from independence to late 1980s/early 1990s. High productivity, quality, and farmer prices maintained. Substantial deficits related to higher costs of serving smallholder sector.	Initial steps in early 1990s with "commercialization" of CMB. CMB privatized as Cottco in 1994 and other private firms allowed to compete. Government maintained investment in Cottco until 1997. CMB debts written off as part of privatization process.
Zambia	Single-channel system in hands of LINTCO. Entirely smallholder production.	Production had trended down from about 40,000 t per year in late 1980s to under 20,000 t in 1994. Substantial debt and farmer dissatisfaction with LINTCO.	1994, with sale of LINTCO to two private companies. Each operated in separate areas of the country.
Mozambique	Nationalized and quasi-independent concession companies with local monopolies, coordinated by Secretaria do Estado do Algodão. Roughly equal mix of smallholder and estate production.	Rapid collapse in production from independence, in 1975, to 1985, from about 120,000 t to less than 10,000. Ongoing civil war created insecurity for farmers and high costs for companies.	1986, with establishment of first joint venture company. By 1991 four JVCs responsible for nearly all cotton production in country.

Table 5.2. Selected institutional mechanisms for input delivery to smallholder cotton farmers in five countries of SSA

	Mechanism	Year initiated	Synopsis
Mozamb.	Concession system	1989	Legal geographical monopsonies for seed cotton purchase. Ginning companies responsible for distributing inputs. Wide coverage but low-quality seed and insecticides, no fertilizer. Yields 350 kg/ha. Periodic loan default crises spurred by new entrants. To date, crises resolved by providing new concessions to largest entrants.
	"Open" concession system	2001 (abandoned 2002)	Allowed new entrants to compete for groups of farmers within existing concession areas. Strong opposition from established concession holders. Lack of transparency in mediating claims of new operators.
Zambia	Distributor system	1999	Private (Dunavant). Operates within a liberalized but concentrated cotton sector. "Distributors" contract with company to receive inputs on credit; package includes treated delinted seed, insecticides, foliar spray (micronutrient); Distributors choose which and how many farmers to work with; earnings a function of credit recovery. Credit repayment rates rose from about 60% to 85% by 2001. Yields rose from 450 kg/ha to 600 kg/ha.
	Cotton Outgrower Fund	2002	Public/private. Government credit at low interest to ginning companies to finance input provision. Allocations across companies favored small players in relative sense. High repayment allowed creation of revolving fund.
	Cotton board	2005	Public/private. Statutory body only. Not yet approved. Substantial policing powers to control "poaching" and practices that reduce cotton quality.
Tanzania	Agricultural Inputs Trust Fund	1995 (abolished 1997)	Public/private. Operated in system with many seed cotton buyers. Subsidized credit to input dealers. Low uptake, poor credit repayment.

Tanzania (cont.)	Cotton Development Fund	1998 (abolished 2002)	Public/private. Operated by public sector in system with many seed cotton buyers. Privately financed by levy on ginning activities. Fund imported chemicals and distributed them to local governments for cash sale at below market price. Increased insecticide availability 10x over two years. 95% of cotton inputs purchased through system. Imported unfamiliar chemicals 2001/2, low uptake. Some chemicals diverted to market.
	Passbook system	2002	Public/private. Cotton sellers receive stamp in official passbook entitling them to pesticides sufficient for approximately one spray the following year. Broadens access, may leave more room for private sector and create more accountability in system.
Zimbabwe	Cottco outgrower scheme	1992 (abandoned 2002)	Private (Cottco). Began before reform with soft loan from World Bank; subsequently operated within liberalized but concentrated cotton sector. Borrowers organized into groups. Each farmer must produce at least 800 kg seed cotton. Available inputs include treated seed of proper variety.
	Cottco Gold Club	1992 (abandoned 2002)	Private (Cottco). Upper tier within company's outgrower scheme for loyal (and generally larger) producers. Members can receive larger loans.
	Input voucher program	1995	Private (Cargill). Inputs for next year's crop delivered at time of this year's seed cotton purchase.
Uganda	UCGEA/ CDO input credit scheme	1997 (abolished 1999)	Public/private. Operated in system with many seed cotton buyers. Uganda Ginners and Exporters Association in conjunction with Cotton Development Organization. Supported with loan from World Bank. Inputs distributed on credit to 2–300,000 farmers. Companies competed to purchase seed cotton. Fund replenished by levy on lint exports. Dramatically improved input availability, but suffered from "leakage" to market, required large subsidy. Abandoned after two years. Insecticide use collapsed. No fertilizer use.
	CDO seed scheme	1999	Public/private. Operates in system with many seed cotton buyers. All seed legally belongs to CDO until it has enough to meet anticipated demand. Ginners deliver quota to CDO, which treats and dresses seed, returns to ginners for distribution. Competition from oilseed processors diminishes availability for planting.

historical and prereform institutional setups either reemerge or strongly condition the choice of postreform institutions. Finally, there has been a great deal of institutional "churning" in most countries, centered primarily on the need to ensure input provision and credit recovery.

TANZANIA AND UGANDA: COMPETITIVE SECTORS STRUGGLE TO ENSURE INPUT SUPPLY AND QUALITY

The cooperative-based cotton systems in these two countries lead quickly after reform to highly competitive markets, with twenty to thirty buyers competing for farmers' production. Price competition was intense and farm prices improved, but each country witnessed the collapse of its input supply system and a decline in lint quality.[10] As a result, the two countries that most closely approached the competitive ideal in market structure saw the most direct and persistent state involvement in efforts to ensure input provision to farmers.

Reform in Tanzania has been marked by a succession of institutional approaches to improve input availability and quality. Until recently the country was viewed as a classic illustration of the difficulty of applying a competitive market model to cotton; by 2005, however, new developments provided grounds for guarded optimism that the sector might be finding solutions to its problems.

Reform began in 1990/91, when RCUs were given greater pricing autonomy on seed cotton purchases. In 1991 the Cooperative Act privatized RCUs and PCSs and allowed easier formation of new ones. RCU debt was written off between 1991 and 1995 (Gibbon 1999). Also around this time donors began to provide low interest loans for ginnery rehabilitation and construction. Definitive reform arrived in 1994 with the passage of the Cotton Act, which removed the statutory monopolies held by the cotton board and RCUs and allowed competition at all levels of the system. The cotton board remained as a regulatory body and, in principle, as a buyer of last resort.

The country's prereform setup of relatively autonomous RCUs owning and operating cotton gins strongly influenced the highly competitive market structure that prevails today. Easy finance for rehabilitation and construction of gins reinforced this tendency. Baffes (2002) reports that during the first year following the Cotton Act, twenty-two new private companies began trading seed cotton and eight new ginneries were built. Competition for seed cotton in the main production area of the country was intense (Gibbon 1999). By the 1998/99 production season, RCU market shares had fallen to 44 percent (from over 90 percent), and continued falling to less than 10 percent by 2002, with private ginners and traders handling the rest (Baffes 2002).

The major benefits of increased competition were that farmers received substantially higher prices and were paid on time in cash. Production doubled from 1994 to 1995. The distribution of insecticides, however, collapsed, driven by the heavy competition for seed cotton, which made credit recovery risky at best (Gibbon 1999; Larsen 2002a; Baffes 2002). Even seed distribution faced major problems, as investment in oil mills increased processing capacity in the main production zone by 50 percent and many ginneries decided to sell more seed to the mills. These input supply problems lead to a steady decline in cotton production after the first year of liberalization; during the 1999/2000 and 2000/2001 seasons, production was lower than at any time since at least 1970. Poulton et al. (2005) document the decline of quality control measures at rural buying stations and provide compelling evidence that lint quality declined dramatically.

The Tanzanian government attempted almost immediately upon liberalization to address the input supply problem. The Agricultural Input Trust Fund provided subsidized credit to private input dealers during 1995 and 1996 but was abolished in 1997 due to low use and poor credit recovery (Baffes 2002). The Cotton Development Fund (CDF) was created in 1999, initially financed by a 3 percent levy on cotton exports. Under this arrangement, the cotton board imported chemicals and distributed them to local governments for below-market prices.

The CDF tripled the prereform availability of chemical inputs (Larsen 2002a) but suffered from serious problems. First, the mechanism made it impractical for private input dealers to compete in cotton inputs and may thereby have weakened the broader input distribution system. Second, Baffes (2002) and Larsen (2002a) both report that the fund suffered substantial diversion of product to the market. Third, in 2001/2 the fund abruptly switched to importing water-based insecticides rather than the traditional oil-based products. The former are significantly cheaper and can be as effective as the oil-based products when used properly. However, insufficient efforts were made to prepare farmers for the new products or to ensure availability of water-based sprayers. Farmers took up only about 15 percent of the chemicals; some of the chemicals were still being used during the 2003/4 season (Poulton et al. 2004). Initial attempts to improve quality control were similarly ineffective (Maro and Poulton 2004).

Thus, until at least 2003, thirteen years after the onset of reform and nearly a decade after the entrance of private companies, cotton sector performance in Tanzania on the key dimensions of input supply and quality control provided cause for real concern about the sector's long-term prospects. Three developments since that time, however, suggest reasons for guarded optimism. First, the CDF in 2002/3 switched to a passbook system for input supply. Under this system, cotton sellers receive a stamp in an official passbook entitling them to chemical inputs from the CDF at the start of the next season. On average, the entitlement amounts to enough insecticides for about one application. Poulton et al. (2004) argue that the system has at least three advantages over the old mode of CDF input supply. First, it broadens access to chemical inputs, since all farmers now have a claim on at least a minimal supply of chemicals; previously, half of farmers did not use chemicals despite the subsidized prices charged by the CDF. Second, they argue that the system "has in-built accountability for its financial management" since, if "money leaks out of the system, it should become immediately apparent when farmers are unable to claim the chemicals to which they are entitled." Finally, by providing enough for only one chemical treatment, the system leaves room for private input dealers to grow; in the past, 50 percent of farmers applied an average of two to three insecticide treatments per season, and many of these can be expected to want to continue making more than one application.

The second reason for guarded optimism in Tanzania relates to proposals for a cotton auction system at rural buying posts. Quality deterioration since liberalization has been related primarily to purposeful but hidden spoilage of seed cotton, for example by adding water, soil, and rocks in the bags being sold. By concentrating seed cotton sales in fewer posts and providing independent quality control at those posts in the context of the auction, there is some hope that the quality control problem may begin to be dealt with more effectively. Finally, production reached an all-time high in 2004, driven by high prices paid in 2003, good weather, and increased input availability related to the passbook system.

A deeper reason for the improved performance of the Tanzanian sector may be the concerted action of the cotton board, in collaboration with leading ginners within the Tanzania Cotton Association, to tackle the problems facing the sector. This action has been based on a strengthening consensus that, with so many seed cotton buyers and ginners in the sector, some form of sectorwide action is necessary to promote access to inputs and enhance quality control. While the efficiency and effectiveness of some cotton board actions can be questioned, the consensus has grown that the response to inefficiency should be to increase the accountability of the board to sector stakeholders, rather than to pare back its functions.

In Uganda in 1994 the Lint Marketing Board's monopoly was ended, thirty-nine cooperative ginneries were privatized, and the public-sector Cotton Development Organization was formed. Over the next three years, seventeen private ginners entered the market, spurred in part by low-interest loans as in Tanzania, and production tripled to over 20,000 t. Poor weather reduced production to about 6,000 t in 1997. The CDO focused primarily on ensuring quality seed supply to farmers, while the provision of chemical inputs collapsed, as in Tanzania.

In 1998 the Ugandan Ginners and Cotton Exporters' Association (UGCEA) collaborated with the CDO in an innovative attempt to resolve the input supply problem (Gordon and Goodland 2000). A levy on raw cotton financed a fund that the CDO used to supply chemical inputs to between two and three hundred thousand farmers. Given the competitive market structure in the country, it was felt that credit recovery from farmers would be impossible. The responsibility for repayment was therefore placed on ginners, who competed freely for seed cotton and were to pay back to the fund in proportion to their share of the market. Poor weather the first year, however, resulted in production levels about one-half those anticipated, drastically reducing repayments by ginners. Management of the scheme was also suspect, with inputs leaking into the market. After one more year, in which production was much better, the scheme was abandoned. Through about 2003, no comprehensive strategy for input provision emerged (Lundbaek 2002), the output market remained highly competitive with many small buyers, and production stagnated at around 20,000 tonnes. Over the three years to 2005, ginners had been able to collaborate to resuscitate the so-called seed wave system, and the zonal system had been legalized, limiting "pirate buying" and reducing risk for companies promoting the crop. Production recovered by 2005 to about 45,000 tonnes.

ZIMBABWE AND ZAMBIA: CONCENTRATED SECTORS DELIVER GOOD PERFORMANCE

The two countries with single-channel marketing systems before reform maintained relatively concentrated sectors for some years after. Through the early part of this decade, each performed much better on input provision and cotton quality than did Tanzania and Uganda. Perhaps surprisingly, each also paid attractive prices to farmers. Recent developments in Zimbabwe, however, may be undermining some of this success.

Reform in Zimbabwe—southern Africa's star performer for several decades—was characterized until the early 2000s by an orderly process of "commercialization" of the single-channel parastatal, gradual privatization accompanied by probable bureaucratic favoritism to maintain its position, and the perpetuation of a highly concentrated private sector performing well on productivity, quality, and prices paid to farmers. From the early 2000s forward the sector has seen rapid new entry, spurred in part by macroeconomic distortions; since this time, price performance has been mixed, credit default has increased, and productivity and quality have probably fallen.

In September 1994 the government renamed CMB as Cottco but maintained its public ownership while officially allowing private operators to enter at all levels of the system. Yet over the next two years,

only two significant new ginning companies—Cargill and Cotpro—
entered the market, and Cottco continued to dominate. In 1997 government reduced its ownership share in Cottco to 25 percent, and the
company acquired a majority share in Cotpro. During the 1999/2000
and 2000/2001 seasons, the combined company controlled 70 to 80
percent of the market, while Cargill controlled about 20 percent each
year (Hayani-Mlambo, Poulton, and Larsen 2002).

Cottco's dominance through 2000/2001 can be attributed in part
to its history of outstanding technical support to farmers and attention to quality throughout the chain, and to the stability of company
management.[11] Bureaucratic favoritism may also have played a role:
government officials at this time stated that, while "competition is
good," the country should use its existing ginning capacity before new
capacity is built (Larsen, pers. comm.), and several potential competitors indicated that ginning and export licenses were very difficult to
obtain. The privatized Cottco also received financial assistance from
government as late as 2001 (Larsen 2002b).

A distinguishing characteristic of Zimbabwe through 2001 is that
its broader agricultural input system functioned relatively effectively.
Of the country's roughly two hundred fifty thousand smallhold cotton farmers, only sixty to eighty thousand received inputs on credit
from outgrower companies, most from Cottco (Hanyani-Mlambo,
Poulton, and Larsen 2002; Larsen 2002b). The rest purchased seed and
chemicals on the open market. Mean yields of about 600 kilograms
per hectare among self-provisioning farmers suggests that they were
relatively successful in obtaining a sufficient supply of insecticides, if
not fertilizer, for their crop.[12] This fact has important implications
for the types of outgrower schemes that are likely to emerge: since
cotton can be easily purchased on the open market without supporting farmers with inputs and extension advice, the only schemes likely
to emerge are ones that will substantially increase yield and promote
loyalty to the company.

Cottco's outgrower scheme fits this description. It began during
the 1992/93 season with a soft loan from the World Bank to the CMB
to help relaunch smallholder cotton production after the devastating
regional drought of 1992 (Goreux 2002; Larsen 2002b). The company

carefully screens potential farmers into its scheme and expects all borrowers to be part of a joint liability group. It favors those able to achieve total production of at least 2,000 kilograms of seed cotton (Larsen 2002b); that compares to average total production per household of 800 to 900 kilograms in Zambia, and 200 to 300 kilograms in Mozambique. Borrowers are provided with treated delinted seed of high quality, fertilizer, and an effective mix of insecticides. So-called Gold Club membership is a reward for consistently high supplies to the company—production of at least 6,000 kilograms per year—and entitles the borrower to take cash loans as well as receiving inputs on credit. Through 2001 credit repayment rates were 95 percent or higher in most years.

Cargill avoided providing input credit, instead launching an innovative input voucher scheme (table 5.2) in which farmers selling the current season's crop received inputs for the following season and had the value of the inputs deducted from their sales receipts. High inflation in the country made this approach attractive to many farmers.

Between 2001 and 2004, the total number of seed cotton buyers in Zimbabwe rose from five to eleven, spurred by a fall in the real prices paid to farmers. That decline occurred despite a large depreciation of the Zimbabwe dollar, which Cottco and Cargill did not fully pass on to farmers. New players competed heavily on price, driving Cottco's market share from over 70 percent to below 60 percent. Prices to farmers rose 35 percent in real terms over the period, despite little change in world market prices, making it clear that the large players had depressed prices in 2001 through 2003.

Improved price performance, however, was accompanied by a weakening of input distribution and quality control. Cottco progressively scaled back its high-quality input credit schemes. New entrants established their own schemes, but low credit repayment suggests that several of those schemes may not be sustainable, and it is doubtful that their quality matches that of Cottco. Poulton et al. (2005) also report that "new entrants led the abandonment of grading at primary marketing, quickly forcing established players to follow." They suggest that Zimbabwe may be on the verge of losing the price premium it has commanded for at least two decades on world markets.

Thus, by 2005 Zimbabwe's cotton sector was being afflicted by problems similar to those seen in Tanzania, despite much higher concentration in the Zimbabwean system. Under current circumstances, it is unlikely that the sector will be able to maintain its record of high-quality support to farmers, high and rising smallholder productivity, high credit repayment, and top-quality lint exports. Whether the higher farm prices seen since 2003 will be enough to offset these disadvantages for farmers remains to be seen.

The cotton sector in Zambia since reform has passed through three clear phases: reform and rapid expansion, followed by a credit default crisis, which was resolved entirely through private sector innovation. The sector may now be entering a fourth phase, as the government makes its first forays into proactive policy to promote the sector. Reform began with the sale of LINTCO to two companies, Lonrho Cotton and Clark Cotton. Through 1996 competition between the two was minimal, as they operated in different areas of the country. Each company initiated outgrower programs and had little problem with credit repayment. From 1994 through 1998, cotton production increased three to four times, facilitated by very high international prices and aggressive promotion of the crop by Lonrho and Clark.

However, from 1997 the expansion of the cotton production base attracted many new entrants, both in ginning and assembly. At least four new ginning companies emerged and began to compete aggressively in the purchase of cotton. Some ginners contracted agents to recruit farmers on their behalf in addition to the farmers directly recruited by them. There also emerged a group of independent cotton traders who obtained their own inputs, distributed them to farmers, purchased seed cotton, and sold the cotton to any ginner wishing to purchase it.

Government at the time was committed to a liberalized economic policy and made no attempt to limit this competition. As the number of ginners and assemblers expanded, several problems came to the fore. First, ginning capacity expanded to over 150,000 tonnes per year, while production peaked at about 105,000 tonnes in 1998 and then declined for three years. This overcapacity created a competitive "scramble for cotton" among ginners to increase throughput and minimize unit ginning costs. The emergence of agents and independent traders contributed substantially to this scramble for cotton. Outgrower firms experienced increased loan default as competing firms, some of which did not operate outgrower schemes and hence could offer higher prices, purchased cotton from farmers receiving inputs from other firms. These problems were exacerbated by a continual decline in world market prices from their peak in 1995.

Farmers had grown accustomed over several years to increasing prices, and with limited information on world market conditions, they found it difficult to understand the reasons for the price declines. This, together with a lack of transparency in how each buyer determined its prices and deducted input costs, lead many farmers and their representatives to conclude that they were being exploited. Ginners estimate that loan repayment rates dropped from almost 86 percent in 1996 to about 65 percent in 1999.

At the same time, increased default rates created incentives for outgrower firms to capitalize their bad loans into the cost of inputs for those farmers who did repay,[13] resulting in lower net prices for cotton after deducting the cost of inputs. Farmers who repaid their loans were thus penalized, potentially fueling a vicious cycle of further loan defaults or exit from outgrower programs.

The sector reached a crisis point in 1999. Lonrho, the largest buyer, was sold to Dunavant, a privately held U.S. cotton company. Among its reasons for departing, Lonrho cited US$2 million per year in unpaid loans. Other outgrower firms cut back on the number of farmers they supported from the 1999/2000 season, driving production to a postreform low of less than 50,000 tonnes.

Since this nadir, the sector has undergone important structural change and has recovered dramatically. The agents and independent buyers that contributed so much to the credit repayment problems in the late 1990s have largely disappeared. At least one of the new ginners went out of business in late 2002. These developments were associated with two parallel strategies adopted by Dunavant. First, it launched in 1999, and over the next several years it refined, its Distributor System, which dramatically improved credit repayment rates among farmers. Second, Dunavant used this system to aggressively expand its production network. Partly as a result, national production more than tripled between 2000 and 2004, driven by yield growth in addition to area expansion, and credit repayment improved from about 65 percent to over 90 percent. Contamination from polypropylene fibers,[14] which was threatening the country's export market, has been largely eliminated, and the country now receives a premium on world markets. Finally, despite operating in a much more concentrated sector, companies in Zambia have continued to pay prices nearly as high as in Tanzania.

This recovery was driven entirely by private-sector innovation. Key among these innovations is Dunavant's Distributor System for extension assistance and credit recovery; Clark's less well known (and more traditional) system also seems to have been effective. Tschirley and Zulu (2004) provide a detailed discussion of the Distributor System. The approach relies on independent contractors, called distributors, who receive inputs from Dunavant on credit, decide themselves how many and which farmers to support with the inputs, and work to ensure sale of those farmers' cotton to Dunavant. Distributors' remuneration is tied to the amount of credit Dunavant is able to recover, on an increasing scale. The company screens all Distributors and requires that each produce cotton and live in the same area as the farmers to whom they provide services.

The Distributor System greatly diminishes the amount of information that Dunavant needs to manage to ensure adequate credit recovery. The company develops strong relationships with a limited number of Distributors and creates incentives for them to recover as much credit for the company as possible. Thus, the company attempts to substitute the Distributors' local knowledge, social capital, and financial incentives for its own data bases and enforcement mechanisms. Through 2005 the system has been highly successful.

Zambia appears now to be entering a fourth phase in its postreform period, marked by more direct government involvement in the sector. The two key elements of this new approach are the Cotton Outgrower Fund and the proposed cotton board.[15] The Outgrower Fund is part of a broader government effort, launched in 2002, to support export crop production. The fund's stated objectives are to increase production by increasing the availability of inputs on credit and to reduce "pirate buying," in which firms buy cotton from farmers supported by other companies. The fund started with an allocation of about $250,000 from government during the 2002/3 growing season. Effective credit recovery and additional allocations from government increased the fund to $390,000 for the 2004/5 growing season and turned it into a revolving fund. Distribution from the fund favors smaller players in a relative sense: while the share of total credit disbursements received by the two largest companies (Dunavant and Clark) in 2004/5 was less than their share of national production the previous year, two smaller companies received credit shares three to four times greater than their previous year's production share. Disbursements to two ginners with almost no production the previous year seem clearly intended to allow them to become recognizable players in financing of farmers. The total area financed by the program remains small, at about 3 percent of the previous year's harvested area. For the smaller players, however, the financing substantially increases their ability to work with farmers.

To date the scheme has avoided the error of centralizing input procurement and distribution to farmers within itself—a key factor in the demise of Uganda's and Tanzania's immediate postreform input distribution efforts. By channeling credit to private cotton companies already working with farmers and allowing the companies full freedom in using it, the fund essentially becomes a means to increase resources in the system and reduce borrowing costs for the companies. By attempting to involve all major firms in the sector, the fund may create some leverage to discourage pirate buying. A related benefit may be in helping smaller firms remain in the market while giving them a vested interest in playing by the rules. For this benefit to be realized, the fund must impose strict eligibility rules, which it has not done to date.

The proposed cotton board would be a statutory body with public and private membership and no mandate to participate as a buyer or seller in the cotton market. The genesis of the board dates to at least 2000, when the Cotton Development Trust and private stakeholders started developing a regulatory framework for the sector, driven largely by a desire to avoid a repeat of the credit default crisis that nearly destroyed the sector from 1997 through 1999. Perhaps as a result of this starting point, the proposed Cotton Act (which would create the cotton board) grants very broad policing powers to the board, essentially creating a parallel police force. It uses vague language in specifying the conditions under which these powers can be exercised and attempts to insulate decisions of the board from judicial review. It also transfers powers and responsibilities reasonably within the mandate of the Ministry of Agriculture to an agency another step away from political accountability. Such an approach seems at odds with the fact that the sector survived the crisis of the 1990s due in large measure to the institutional innovations and improved management that emerged from competition between the two major players. Tschirley and Zulu (2004) suggest that the Cotton Act needs instead to focus on developing legal bases and operational approaches to improve information on borrowers' credit histories, on promoting collective action to improve cotton quality and productivity, and on improving the monitoring of sector performance beyond credit repayment.

MOZAMBIQUE: STRUGGLING TO UPDATE THE CONCESSION MODEL

In reforming its cotton sector, Mozambique returned to the concession model prevalent during the colonial era, first with public-private joint venture companies (JVCs), and later complemented by fully private companies.[16] Key themes during the postreform era have been the absence of any systematic approach to evaluating and reawarding concession areas, widely divergent performance between early investors within the traditional Cotton Belt and new entrants outside it, and the government's openness to new investment, albeit always within the concession model. Until recently the country clearly lagged behind its neighbors in productivity and quality, but new entrants since the early 2000s may have begun to change that.

The first JVC began operation in 1986 and was joined by two more in 1990. In addition to exclusive buying rights within a geographic "concession area," each company received blocks of land for direct production, and existing gins. In return, the investors rehabilitated the gins and agreed to supply inputs and technical assistance on credit to any smallholder within the concession area wishing to produce cotton. The civil war was ongoing at this time, intensely so in cotton-growing areas. As a result, companies had to pay for private militias to protect gins and to accompany truck convoys bringing seed cotton out of rural areas and taking lint to the port for export. They also had to rehabilitate roads and bridges with their own funds. Companies and government negotiated pan-seasonal and pan-territorial prices, with little direct input from farmers.

JVCs dominated the sector into the early 1990s, when private companies began to appear. By 1995 there were four JVCs and six private companies, with the former concentrated in the Cotton Belt of Nampula and southern Cabo Delgado Provinces and the latter lying primarily outside that area to the south, in the provinces of Zambezia, Sofala, and Manica. This mixed public-private approach drove production to a postindependence peak of 116,000 tonnes of seed cotton in 1999. Production then plunged below 40,000 tonnes in 2000, driven primarily by a collapse in Nampula.

Falling prices after 1995 and the entry of new buyers had put severe stress on the concession model in Nampula. New private companies operating outside the province negotiated concession agreements with the government and largely respected the rules of the game. Others, operating within Nampula, attracted production out of concession areas by offering higher prices while providing few or no inputs to farmers, leading to widespread credit default by these farmers. The first serious instance of pirate buying, as it was called in Mozambique, occurred in 1995. In a pattern that was to be repeated in future years, the pirate buying resulted in strong protests from concession companies, start-and-stop efforts by government to restrict the illegal purchases, farmer protests in favor of the new buyers, and, eventually, resolution of the problem by providing the buyer with his own concession area. The concession system continued to be challenged, however, by new entrants and growing farmer discontent, the latter linked to the lowest yields and prices in the region.

In 1998 the government's Cotton Development Strategy encouraged the formation of farmer groups to deal independently with the cotton company of their choice, even if the group's land lay within a concession area. Such groups had begun to form before the rule change, many of them contracting with cotton companies for higher prices and better support than could be achieved by individual farmers. However, the policy change was exploited by some new buyers, who formed extremely large groupings of farmers with no training and no coherent governing structure, called them associations, and used them to justify cotton purchases within concession areas despite providing little effective support to the groups. Concession companies responded by promoting associations of their own, and the conflict in the region escalated, reaching a crisis in 1998/99.

Faced with persistent illegal buying that it could not control, mounting farmer protests to be allowed to sell to whomever they wished, and donor pressure to allow increased competition, the government in 2000 launched a short-lived attempt to liberalize the sector. In October 2000, during the first national meeting of government and stakeholders, participants adopted an "open-concession" model with a view toward eventual full liberalization. The model allowed communities within concession areas to opt out of their implicit contract with the concession company and deal with a competing company from input provision through sale of the seed cotton. Competing companies in the early years of the transition were to have the burden of demonstrating that communities within concession areas wished to opt out of the concession and work with them. Eventually, the playing field was to be leveled among new entrants and existing concession companies (MADER 2000a, 2000b).

Production under the more open system recovered to about 70,000 tonnes in 2000/2001 (from 35,000 tonnes the previous year). The system was welcomed by new companies and many farmers but was heavily criticized by concession companies as unwieldy. It foundered on information problems in enforcement and on a lack of transparency in the decision process, allowing communities to opt out of the concession. The second annual stakeholders' meeting, in October 2001, was dominated by the established ginners. The government backed away from the open concession system, eliminated the rights of farmer groups to contract with the company of their choice, and once again resolved the pirate buying problem by offering the largest buyer his own concession area. Since that time, production in the Cotton Belt has stagnated, and yields there have remained between 300 and 400 kilograms per hectare, with levels as low as 230 kilograms reported for some concession areas (Horus 2004).

While Nampula went through these disruptions, policymakers remained open to new investment, albeit always under the concession model. This openness over the past several years has created the conditions to potentially transform the sector. The central region of the country, south of Nampula, now has three of the best-performing cotton companies of sub-Saharan Africa: Dunavant, which expanded its operations from Zambia in 2000; Cottco, which entered from Zimbabwe in 2001; and Dagris, historically linked to West Africa, which began operations in Mozambique in 1995 as the Companhia Nacional de Algodão (CNA). In nine years of operation, the CNA has become the largest cotton company in the country, with average smallholder yields above 800 kilograms per hectare for each of the past three years. Dunavant has expanded its area of operation by acquiring an existing concession company. If it meets production targets for 2004/5, it will be the third- or fourth-largest company, with excellent prospects for sustained rapid growth through both area expansion and yield increases. In only two years of operation, Cottco raised its production to nearly 5,000 tonnes, and its yield of 520 kilograms per hectare in 2004 already exceeds those found in Nampula. Each of these companies brought improved seed from other areas of Africa and combined it with more effective extension assistance. Finally, all three have paid higher than the minimum price in recent years (though the CNA returned to the minimum in 2004), a practice that has been exceedingly rare among established concession holders in Nampula.

Plexus, which took over the Lonrho/Mozambique's cotton concession in Cabo Delgado province (called LOMACO), also shows promise. It has taken advantage of earlier technical work done by LOMACO to raise yields to 480 kilograms per hectare, and intends to raise them to 700 kilograms in two years. The company reports ginning outturn ratios of 40.5 percent, close to the best in Africa and far above Mozambique's recent average of 33 to 35 percent.[17] Plexus has also remained committed to LOMACO's vision of developing farmer organizations, which are a key element in eventually providing a way out of the concession model.

Additional optimism for the sector stems from the more constructive role now being played by the Instituto do Algodão de Moçambique (IAM), the sector's public regulatory body. From its formation in 1991 through the early 2000s, IAM was preoccupied resolving conflicts over price setting and credit default. Since about 2002 it has used between $400,000 and $500,000 generated annually by a 2.5 percent export levy, combined with donor funds to begin a process of institutional strengthening and reform and to play a more active coordinating role in the sector. It has focused on proposals for yearly evaluations of concession holders and rewarding decisions every five years, and for increased transparency of price setting by linking it explicitly to world markets. Outside funding, complemented by sustainable mechanisms for self-financing, will be needed for some time to build technical and managerial capacity within IAM to carry out these functions. Stakeholders have proposed that these tasks be passed eventually to a multistakeholder ("interprofessional") body, but no such body exists at this time.

Lessons for Pragmatic Reformers

Table 5.3 summarizes the status of our five cotton sectors as of 2005. In three of the five countries—Tanzania, Zambia, and Mozambique—there is some cause for optimism. Each brought a very different history into its reform process, and each has used different approaches to solve common problems of input distribution, credit recovery, and quality control. Tanzania, with the most competitive system among the five countries, has paid some of the most remunerative prices to farmers since reform and may now be finding an approach to public-private coordination that will allow it to reverse the sharp postreform declines in input availability (and perhaps lint quality). Zambia has the most concentrated sector yet has also paid attractive prices to

Table 5.3. Status of cotton sectors in southern and East Africa, 2005

Country	Market structure and firm behavior	Input provision and credit recovery	Lint quality	Production and productivity trends	Future challenges
Tanzania	• Many firms compete heavily in output market • High seed cotton prices despite high burden of taxes and levies	• Little progress on seed qual. • Some chemical provision through passbook system • Leaves room for development of independent private input system	• Declining before reform; decline has continued since • Auction system offers hope for improvement, but still awaiting pilot phase	• Record production 2004 after slump of several years • Limited input provision on credit makes production more responsive than in neighboring countries • Increase farm productivity	• Maintain (and expand?) passbook system • Develop auction system for quality control
Uganda	• Many very small firms compete heavily in output market • Cottco left sector in 2005	• Little or no provision by cotton buyers as of 2003; some progress since	• Declined since reform	• Rose to 45,000t in 2005 from 20,000 • Individual farmers produce very small quantities (100–200 kg)	• Public/private cooperation to improve input provision • Increase scale of production at farm level
Zimbabwe	• Concentration declining, with heavy competition from new firms • Cottco's market share <60% • Prices rival Tanzania after brief decline	• Share of farmers receiving input credit steady at 35–38% • Quality of assistance has declined and sustainability open to question	• Indications of decline, as farm-level quality control has diminished	• Yields probably falling, based on Cottco ending its input schemes • Production remains > 200,000 t, near record levels	• Develop sector coordination strategies in a more competitive environment to reinvigorate input and extension assistance and stem decline in quality
Zambia	• Highly concentrated, CR2 > 85% • High prices, rivaling Tanzania	• Effective among top two players, though indications in 2005 of more credit default • More provision by smaller players due to Cotton Outgrower Fund	• Polypropylene contamination controlled since 2003; lint now receives premium on world markets	• Production booming • Yields appear to be rising steadily	• Strengthen effective competition while avoiding credit default crises • Rework Cotton Act to stress coordination overpolicing • Introduce new germplasm
Mozambique	• At least 10 companies, each with geographic concession • Prices to farmers remain lowest in region • Proposals on table for evaluation and rewarding of concessions	• Both effective outside Nampula • New seed available in most of country, including Nampula • Credit default recurring problem in Nampula	• Remains generally poor, with 3% discount on world markets; exceptions for some companies	• Production rising since 2000, but well below 1999 peak • Nampula losing share • Yields outside Nampula rival best in region; among lowest in region w/in Nampula	• Extend performance seen outside Nampula into the province • Operationalize plan to regularly evaluate and reward concessions

farmers and seen steady rises in production, yields, and quality. It is now attempting to use the Cotton Outgrower Fund to ensure some level of effective competition among firms while providing smaller actors with a reason to follow the "rules of the game." Mozambique has, along with Uganda, been the region's poor performer over the past fifteen years. Yet by remaining open to new investment, and by choosing well which new investors to accept, the country has unleashed a positive dynamic that may remake the sector over the next five years.

Political unrest and macroeconomic instability in Zimbabwe complicate assessment of its prospects. Long the star performer of the region, it is now threatened by problems similar to those that afflicted Tanzania for more than a decade after its reform—heavy competition in the seed cotton market, which undermines input provision and quality control. Because its broader input and credit markets work better than those in Tanzania, and because Cottco and Cargill are strong companies, the country's prospects have to be considered good if the political and macroeconomic situation can be stabilized in reasonable time.

Uganda, with a history and market structure similar to Tanzania's, showed little cause for optimism as late as 2003, as repeated failures to solve the input supply and credit repayment problems had led to low and stagnant production. Yet the past two to three years have seen some progress on the sector's key institutional challenges, with an associated doubling of production. It remains to be seen whether this progress will continue.

Overall, the picture that emerges is relatively positive. The fears alluded to at the beginning of this chapter, that reform would undercut the basis for effective interlocking of transactions and also complicate collective decisions on long-term investment, have often proved well founded. Yet predictable benefits of reform, such as higher prices and more timely payment, have also been realized; state budgets have also generally benefited from reduced support to parastatals or cooperatives. It also seems clear that analysts at the outset of reform underestimated the persistence and ability of sector participants—both public and private—to innovate in pursuit of workable solutions to the specific problems unleashed by reform in their countries. Dunavant's

Distributor System, Cottco's outgrower scheme, and, perhaps, Tanzania's passbook system stand out in this regard.

We draw several lessons from this experience. First, though cotton sectors face common technical challenges, workable solutions must be responsive to local conditions. Sector structure is heavily influenced by history and is a key variable in determining what is and is not likely to be appropriate for a given sector. The recent experience of Tanzania (and, arguably, Mozambique) should encourage policymakers to work with sectors as they are, rather than to try to radically influence sector structure or to impose a textbook solution on a particular problem.

Second, institutional innovation is the key to improving performance in cash-crop sectors; large injections of public capital are not needed. Where governance and accountability are tolerably effective, levies on cotton marketing, ginning, or export activities can generate all the funding required for cotton-related research, quality control, and perhaps input supply.[18]

Third, the failure of the CDO scheme in Uganda, and the Agricultural Inputs Trust and Cotton Development Fund in Tanzania, suggest that direct state management of the funds from such levies is problematic. Vesting regulatory and coordination functions within multistakeholder bodies, where the state is one stakeholder among several, may be the most promising approach for many sectors. This perspective suggests that it may be important to transform Mozambique's IAM fairly quickly into a multistakeholder organization, as has been proposed by stakeholders there.

Fourth, the principal objective for institutional innovation, and the appropriate role for public agencies in promoting innovation, varies with the structure of the market for seed cotton. In sectors where many firms compete, the main objective should be to ensure effective and efficient coordination, so as to enable the provision of public/collective goods and to provide assurance for asset specific investment. This may require that the state—or a multistakeholder authority vested with authority by the state—oblige participants to agree to codes of conduct (concerning respect for others' contracts, quality control practices, and seed varietal zoning, for example) as a condition for holding a license to operate in the sector. This is the approach proposed by Zimbabwean stakeholders in response to the sector's recent difficulties.[19] In addition, it may require that the state and private actors collaborate to introduce new sectorwide coordination mechanisms, as has occurred in Tanzania.

In sectors with less direct competition among firms, the main objective should be to provide incentives for strong performance in pricing and service provision. Where limited competition is due to a concentrated market structure, as in Zambia, the focus should be on assuring effective competition for the major players while providing those competitors with reasons to avoid promoting credit default. The Cotton Outgrower Fund has been used for this purpose in Zambia, and seems a potentially more promising approach than giving the cotton board (or any other regulatory authority) exaggerated powers to police the sector. Where the lack of competition is policy induced, as in Mozambique, the challenge is to provide incentives for strong performance, even among firms whose internal culture may not reward such performance. In Mozambique this is being tackled by revisions to the regulations governing cotton concessions. Confidence in the new system will depend on transparency and fairness in the decision-making process for extending or terminating concessions.

Finally, regular "deliberative fora" are invaluable for building trust between stakeholders and seeking innovative solutions to sectorwide problems. It is easier for small numbers of key stakeholders, rather than large numbers, to chart a common course. In some cases stakeholder associations (such as the Tanzania Cotton Association) can partially overcome this numbers problem, but where there are major divisions within stakeholder groups (e.g., among ginners in Mozambique or between established and newer firms in Zimbabwe), progress may depend on the ability of the state to play an evenhanded but strategic role.

Notes

Funding for this research came from the UK Department for International Development (DFID) and from the Food Security III Cooperative Agreement (CDG-A-00–000021–00) between Michigan State University and the U.S. Agency for International Development. USAID Missions in Mozambique and Zambia have also supported this work. The views and opinions expressed are those of the authors alone. We thank colleagues in Tanzania, Zimbabwe, Zambia, and Mozambique who have contributed to this work, especially Benjamine Hayani-Mlambo, Wilbald Maro, Ballard Zulu, Afonso Osorio, Higino De Marrule, and Norberto Mahalambe.

1. For a review of experience in East and southern Africa through the late 1980s, see Glover 1990.

2. These low costs of production are related primarily to the very low price at which many smallholders are willing to "sell" their labor in production of the crop, and to the low supervisory costs inherent in using primarily family labor. See Binswanger and McIntire 1987.

3. For an empirical review of the widely varying circumstances under which contract farming has emerged and for examples of failure where external conditions seemed favorable, see Jaffee 1994.

4. The ICAC estimates that subsidies are equivalent to 50 percent of world prices in the United States, 20 percent in China, and over 100 percent in the European Union. Elimination of U.S. subsidies alone would raise world prices in the short run by as much as twelve cents per pound.

5. The decline in cotton prices is not unusual when compared to other commodities: over the same period, real prices have fallen approximately 45 percent for cocoa and coffee, over 50 percent for maize, and nearly 70 percent for sugar.

6. Based on FAOStat data on the export values of cashew, coffee, cocoa, cotton, tea, and tobacco (http://faostat.fao.org/). In Uganda in 2003 cotton lint's export share among these crops was 6 percent; it was 20 percent in Tanzania, 33 percent in Mozambique, 58 percent in Zambia, and 77 percent in Zimbabwe. Tobacco was excluded from calculations in Zimbabwe because it is primarily produced by large-scale farmers.

7. Gibbon (1999) notes that the board in Tanzania changed names frequently; we will follow him and refer to it simply as the cotton board.

8. Production in Uganda is quoted in 185-kilogram bales of lint. Thus 20,000 bales represent 3,700 tonnes of lint, equivalent to about 10,000 tonnes of seed cotton. The peak of 400,000 bales represented nearly 200,000 tonnes of seed cotton.

9. By 2000 the smallholder share exceeded 80 percent.

10. In 2001 Ugandan and Tanzanian lint (along with Mozambican) were among the most contaminated in the world (Poulton et al. 2004).

11. The managing director and marketing director have been with the company for seventeen and twenty-nine years, respectively (http://www.thecottoncompany.com/about/html/index.html).

12. The figure of 600 kilograms per hectare is calculated from the estimated outgrower yield of 900 kilograms per hectare and a reported national average of 700 kilograms, with approximately one-third of farmers in outgrower schemes. The fact that Zimbabwean cotton continued to earn a 10 percent premium on world markets is further evidence that non-outgrower households have been able to obtain sufficient and appropriate insecticides, since staining is a key quality problem generated by poor control of insect pests.

13. One outgrower company states that in 1999 it attempted to offset its loan defaults by adding a 50 percent markup to the price of inputs.

14. This contamination comes from using polypropylene bags for cotton harvest and results in large price discounts on world markets.

15. Tschirley and Zulu (2004) provide a detailed discussion of each.

16. This section draws heavily from Tschirley, Ofiço, and Boughton (2005).

17. The ginning output ratio represents the amount of lint obtained from one kilogram of seed cotton. The CNA reports a ratio of 41 percent, meaning it obtains 0.41 kilogram of lint for every kilogram of seed cotton.

18. However, it is hard to see African cotton sectors providing anything more than very modest net financial transfers to the remainder of the economy, particularly while international lint prices remain depressed. Instead, their contribution to growth should occur primarily through income/consumption and other multipliers.

19. It is also part of the approach embodied in Zambia's proposed Cotton Act, perhaps in anticipation of more ginning firms arising in the country.

References

Baffes, John. 2002. "Tanzania's Cotton Sector: Constraints and Challenges in a Global Environment." World Bank, Washington, DC. Mimeo.

Benfica, Rui, David Tschirley, and Liria Sambo. 2002. "The Impact of Alternative Agro-Industrial Investments on Poverty Reduction in Rural Mozambique." Research Report 51E, Directorate of Economics, Ministry of Agriculture of Mozambique. http://www.aec.msu.edu/agecon/fs2/mozambique/wps51e.pdf.

Bingen, James. 1998. "Cotton, Democracy, and Development." *Journal of Modern African Studies* 36 (2): 265–85.

Binswanger, Hans, and John McIntire. 1987. "Behavioral and Material Determinants of Production Relations in Land Abundant Tropical Agriculture." *Economic Development and Cultural Change* 36 (1): 73–99.

Boughton, Duncan, David Tschirley, Ballard Zulu, Afonso Osorio Ofiço, and Higino Marrule. 2003. "Cotton Sector Policies and Performance in Sub-Saharan Africa: Lessons behind the Numbers in Mozambique and Zambia." Paper presented at the 25th International Conference of Agricultural Economists, August 16–22, Durban, South Africa.

Delgado, Christopher. 1999. "Sources of Growth in Smallholder Agriculture in Sub-Saharan Africa: The Role of Vertical Integration of Smallholders with Processors and Marketers of High Value-Added Items." *Agrekon* 38:165–89.

Dorsey, Jeff. 2002. "Potential Agricultural Market Opportunities and Enterprise Development for the Teso and Lango Regions, Uganda." Draft report for NARO/DID Client-Oriented Agricultural Research and Dissemination Project (COARD).

FAO. 2002. FAOSTAT. http://faostat.fao.org/site/535/default.aspx.

FSRP (Food Security Resource Project). 2000. "Improving Smallholder and Agri-Business Opportunities in Zambia's Cotton Sector: Key Challenges and Options." FSRP Working Paper 1, Lusaka.

Gibbon, Peter, 1999. "Free Competition without Sustainable Development? Tanzanian Cotton Sector Liberalization, 1994/95 to 1997/98." *Journal of Development Studies* 36 (1): 128–50.

Glover, David. 1990. "Contract Farming and Outgrower Schemes in East and Southern Africa." *Journal of Agricultural Economics* 41:303–15.

Gordon, Ann, and Andrew Goodland. 2000. "Production Credit for African Smallholders: Conditions for Private Provision." *Savings and Development* 24:55–82

Goreux, Louis, and John Macrae. 2002. "Liberalizing the Cotton Sector in SSA: Part 1: Main Issues." World Bank, Washington, DC. Mimeo.

Hall, Peter, and David Soskice. 2001. Introduction to *Varieties of Capitalism: The Institutional Foundations of Comparative Advantage*, ed. Hall and Soskice, 1–68. Oxford: Oxford University Press.

Hanyani-Mlambo, Benjamine, Colin Poulton, and Marianne Larsen. 2002. "System Overview Report for Zimbabwe." Prepared as part of the DfID-funded project Competition and Coordination in Liberalized African Cotton Market Systems.

Hoffmeyer, Martin, and Jörg-Volker Schrader. 2004. *A Medium Term Outlook for Agricultural Commodities*. Rome: Food and Agriculture Organization of the United Nations.

Horus Enterprises. 2004. "Estudo complementar para o melhoramento da estratégia no sector do algodão em Moçambique." Consulting report. Paris.

Jaffee, Steven. 1994. "Contract Farming in the Shadow of Competitive Markets: The Experience of Kenyan Horticulture." In *Living under Contract: Contract Farming and Agrarian Transformation in Sub-Saharan Africa*, ed. Peter Little and Michael Watts. Madison: University of Wisconsin Press.

Larsen, Marianne. 2001. "Zimbabwean Cotton Sector Liberalisation: A Case of Successful Private Coordination?" Working Paper, Centre for Development Research, Copenhagen.

————. 2002a. "Bringing the State Back In? The Tanzanian Cotton Sector in a Post-liberalized Era." Working Paper, Centre for Development Research, Copenhagen.

————. 2002b. "Is Oligopoly a Condition of Successful Privatization? The Case of Cotton in Zimbabwe." *Journal of Agrarian Change* 2 (2): 185–205.

Lele, Uma, Nicolas Van de Walle, and Mathurin Gbetibouo. 1989. *Cotton in Africa: An Analysis of Differences in Performance*. MADIA Discussion Paper 7. Washington, DC: World Bank.

Lundbaek, J. 2002. *Privatisation of the Cotton Sector in Uganda: Market Failure and Institutional Mechanisms to Overcome It*. Department of Economics and Natural Resources. Copenhagen: Royal Veterinary and Agricultural University.

Maro, Wilbald, and Colin Poulton. 2004. "Tanzania Country Report: 2001/02 Production Season." Prepared as part of the DfID-funded project Competition and Coordination in Liberalized African Cotton Market Systems. Imperial College London.

Maumbe, Blessing, and Scott Swinton. 2003. "Hidden Health Costs of Pesticide Use in Zimbabwe's Smallholder Cotton Growers." *Social Science and Medicine* 57 (November): 1559–71.

Poulton, Colin, Peter Gibbon, Benjamine Hayani-Mlambo, Jonathan Kydd, Marianne Larsen, Wilbald Maro, David Tschirley, and Balard Zulu. 2004. "Competition and Coordination in Liberalized African Cotton Market Systems." *World Development* 32 (3): 519–36.

Poulton, Colin, Peter Gibbon, Benjamine Hayani-Mlambo, Jonathan Kydd, Wilbald Maro, Marianne Nylandsted-Larsen, David Tschirley,

Ballard Zulu. 2005. "Research Report: Project R8080." Competition and Coordination in Cotton Market Systems of Southern and Eastern Africa. Imperial College London.

Stringfellow, Rachel. 1996. "Smallholder Outgrower Schemes in Zambia." Natural Resources Institute, Chatham, England.

Tschirley, David, and Ballard Zulu. 2004. "Cotton in Zambia: An Assessment of Its Organization, Performance, Current Policy Initiatives, and Challenges for the Future." FSRP Working Paper 11, Lusaka.

Tschirley, David, Alfonso Osorio Ofiço, and Duncan Boughton. 2005. "Mozambique Country Study." Prepared as part of the DfID-funded project Competition and Coordination in Liberalized African Cotton Market Systems. Imperial College London.

Zimbabwe, Government of, Ministry of Lands. 1991. "Cotton Sub-sector Study." Hertfordshire: Hunting Technical Services Limited.

6

Cotton Production, Poverty, and Inequality in Rural Benin

Evidence from the 1990s

Corinne Siaens and Quentin Wodon

COTTON PRODUCTION IS IMPORTANT for many West African countries. Many rural households in countries such as Benin, Burkina Faso, or Mali derive most of their cash earnings from cotton, and cotton represents more than half, and in several cases more than three-fourths, of the exports of these countries. The 1990s in Benin was a decade marked by two important events for cotton producers: a drop in world cotton prices in the second half of the decade and some difficulties in the reorganization of the cotton sector through the privatization of input supply and ginning as of the early 1990s.

Consider first the drop in world cotton prices. Several factors combined to put downward pressure on prices (e.g., Goreux 2003; Badiane, Goreux, and Masson 2002; Minot and Daniels 2002). While world consumption per capita of synthetic fibers increased fivefold between 1960 to 2000, cotton consumption per capita remained flat. Given that cotton production increased more than consumption, stocks have accumulated, leading to a reduction in world prices. Since the mid-1990s, nominal world cotton prices have been reduced by half, from an average of about US$90 per metric ton in 1994 and 1995 to around

$45 in 2002 and 2003. In real terms, prices have been reduced by about two-thirds, reaching historic lows.

Much of the increase in cotton production can be attributed to the United States and China, two countries that provide large subsidies to their producers, thereby making these producers artificially competitive (especially in the United States) versus lower cost producers in sub-Saharan Africa. This situation has prompted observers to call for a reduction in cotton subsidies in these countries, among others, in order to facilitate poverty reduction in Africa. The fact that subsidies in industrialized countries have not been reduced contributed to the collapse of the 2003 trade negotiations in Cancun.

While there is no doubt that cotton subsidies in the United States and China are hurting West African producers, it is not clear that poverty (and inequality) among African producers have actually increased since the mid-1990s due to the fall of world cotton prices. At least three reasons help explain this apparent paradox. First, in Benin, as in much of West Africa, producers have to some extent been protected from the collapse in world cotton prices through the combination of the 1994 devaluation of the CFA franc (FCFA), which made world prices more attractive in local currency because they facilitated the maintenance of relatively high local purchase prices guaranteed by governments. Second, in part as a result of these high guaranteed prices, but possibly also in part due to reforms of the cotton sector in many countries aiming to dismantle state monopolies in order to empower local producers, there is some evidence from Goreux (2003) that in recent years, the share of the world price of cotton obtained by local producers has increased over time. Third, production increased in Benin, as in many other countries, enabling many producers to weather the recent fall in the real value of guaranteed prices. Finally, from the point of view of inequality, it is unclear whether changes in cotton prices should affect the distribution of income at the margin, because this will essentially depend on the correlation between income from cotton and other sources of income.

Consider next the privatization of the cotton sector. As in many other francophone African countries, Benin's cotton industry was originally a so-called *filière intégrée,* in which a single parastatal company—SONAPRA (National Corporation for Agricultural Promotion)—was responsible for the management of all the steps in the production process, from the provision of seeds and other inputs to farmers to the purchase of their crop at the end of each campaign and the transformation of raw cotton in ginneries for the exportation of cotton lint. Today, the structure of the sector is very different. Input provision and ginning have been partially privatized, and a complex "interprofessional" system of interaction and negotiation between stakeholders of the filière has been put in place for coordination purposes.

The reforms in the cotton sector have had three distinct phases (Coulter and McKenzie 2003). As of the early 1980s, following the renunciation of Marxism by Benin's government, the sector was modernized in order to improve its efficiency. This led to a large increase in production as it became easier for cotton farmers than for other farmers to gain access to input and credit, while also benefiting from guaranteed prices for their crop. The second phase of the reforms is often referred to as the Structural Adjustment Period, during which the input supply function was privatized (starting in 1992) and ginneries were also partially privatized (starting in 1995). In a third phase, starting in 1999, a new interprofessional structure was put in place to govern the sector, with the participation of the various stakeholders but still under the control of the government in key sensitive areas such as the setting of annual guaranteed prices to be paid to producers.

According to Coulter and McKenzie, the reforms of the Structural Adjustment Period were not implemented very well. The quality of the input distribution system was weakened for a few years, generating a decrease in yields for cotton producers in the second half of the 1990s. Preferential treatment was given to the first set of privatized ginneries (namely, a guarantee of operation at full capacity despite subsequent excess ginning capacity at the national level), which contributed to inefficiencies in the sector as a whole. More recently, debt issues have threatened the survival capacity of some local producer organizations, as some of the operators refused to observe the rules of the game set out through the interprofessional management structure.

At face value, the combination of lower world prices and at least some dysfunctions in the privatization process could have led to an increase in poverty among cotton producers, and possibly also to an increase in inequality if richer farmers were to gain more than smaller farmers from cotton production. However, there seems to be no evidence pointing to a deterioration of the living standards of cotton producers during the 1990s. In fact cotton producers may have fared slightly better than other rural households over the period under review, but at the end of the 1990s, the level of well-being of a cotton producer was virtually the same as that of a similar household not producing cotton. And we find that because cotton revenues in rural areas are distributed in a way fairly similar to total per capita consumption, they do not affect inequality much at the margin.

Cotton Production, Prices, and Poverty

Despite the reduction in world cotton prices in the second half of the 1990s, there are good reasons to believe that cotton producers in Benin have fared relatively well over the decade as a whole. First, cotton production has almost tripled in the country over the last dozen years, enabling Benin to become the second-largest producer in Africa, after Mali. As shown in figure 6.1, production increased from 146,000 t (metric tons) in the 1990/91 campaign to 415,000 t in 2001/2. Most of the gains in production were achieved through an extension of the areas cultivated, from 123,000 hectares in 1990/91 to more than 400,000 hectares in 2001/2 (yields have oscillated between 950 and 1,200 kilograms per hectare).

Second, the prices paid to local producers have also increased. As shown in figure 6.2, up to the 1994 devaluation of the CFA franc, local producer prices remained almost constant, at FCFA 95 to FCFA 100 per kilogram for first-choice seed cotton (seed cotton production is classified as first or second choice depending on quality; the trends in prices for both levels of quality are very similar). But thereafter, nominal prices doubled, reaching FCFA 200 per kilogram in 1996/97. Since inflation was relatively low over the same period, this represented a

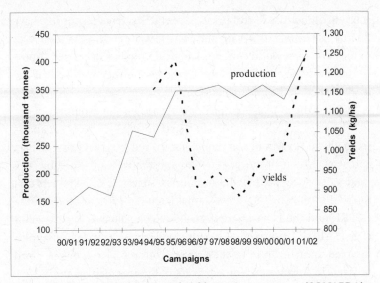

Fig. 6.1. Seed cotton production and yields, Benin, 1990–2002. (SONAPRA)

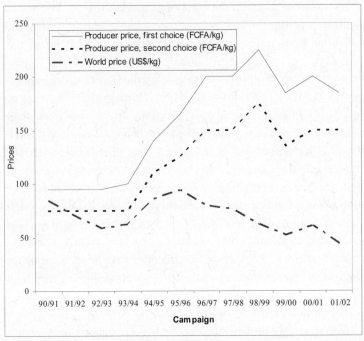

Fig. 6.2. Local and world seed cotton prices, Benin, 1990–2002. (SONAPRA)

substantial increase in real prices. Over the last few years, prices have fluctuated between FCFA 185 and FCFA 225. By contrast, after a peak in 1994 and 1995, world cotton prices in U.S. dollars decreased almost continuously, so that by the end of the period they were at half the level reached in the mid-1990s.

What is the available empirical evidence on the evolution of the well-being of cotton producers in Benin during the 1990s? An analysis conducted by Minot and Daniels (2003) suggests that between 1992 and 1998, cotton producers enjoyed substantive gains in subjective welfare. The data used by the authors is a survey of smallholders carried out in 1998 by the International Food Policy Research Institute (IFPRI) and the Laboratoire d'Analyse Régionale et d'Expertise Sociale (LARES), covering one hundred villages, with nine households sampled in each village. In the data set, cotton is grown by one-third of farmers and accounts for 18 percent of the area planted and 22 percent of the gross value of crop production.

As shown in table 6.1, the questions on subjective perceptions of well-being in the IFPRI/LARES survey suggest that approximately half of all households (52 percent) felt they were better off at the time of the survey in 1998, as compared to 1992, which is the starting point of the reforms implemented during the structural adjustment period. Poorer households—those in the bottom three quintiles of the distribution of consumption per capita—were more likely than richer households to say that their welfare had improved. Less than a third (28 percent) of the households said that their living conditions had deteriorated. The households attributed their improvement in well-being to changes in crop prices, changes in the price of food or its availability, and changes in off-farm production. According to the survey's authors, these results suggest a "strong link between market-oriented policies and cotton expansion on the one hand and the living conditions of farmers in Benin on the other hand," although it could of course also be argued that the gain in well-being may have been related to the devaluation and the increase in the prices paid to cotton producers by SONAPRA.

In table 6.2, we provide new data on poverty trends among cotton producers and other rural households in Benin, using data from the

Table 6.1. Perceived change in well-being among cotton producers, Benin, 1992–98 (percent)

	Poorest quintile	2	3	4	Richest quintile	Total
Improvement	50	59	59	49	44	52
No change	20	15	9	15	15	15
Deterioration	27	18	29	32	31	28
No opinion	2	7	2	4	11	5

Reasons for change from the improvements, by department, 1998

	Atacora	Atlantique	Borgou	Mono	Ouémé	Zou	Total
Crop prices	36	4	20	47	33	16	27
Prices or food availability	6	68	46	2	21	27	25
Off-farm income	42	13	9	15	21	15	20
Cash crop production	5	3	5	—	—	27	7
Household health	8	—	12	—	11	3	6
Seeds and inputs	1	—	—	23	—	5	5
Soil fertility	—	—	0	—	—	2	1
Access to land	—	—	—	—	2	2	1
Weather	—	—	—	2	—	1	0
Access to credit	—	2	—	2	—	—	0
Other	3	10	8	10	12	2	7

Note: Due to rounding, percentages may not total 100.
Source: Minot and Daniels 2002.

Enquète sur les Conditions de Vie en milieu Rural (ECVR) surveys for 1995/95 and 1999/2000. Some households in the samples were interviewed in both years, which provides us with panel data. The households who are identified as cotton producers in the table are those who were producing cotton in 1999/2000 (we do not have the same information for 1994/95). The first part of the table suggests that in 1999/2000, the households who were producing cotton were slightly more likely to be poor than households who were not producing cotton, whether the methodology used for measurement relies on the assumption used in Benin's Poverty Reduction Strategy Paper, or whether we adopt a relative poverty methodology according to which

Table 6.2. Relative poverty trends among rural households, Benin, 1994/95, 1999/2000

	All households	Non-cotton producers	Cotton producers
Number of observations in 1999/2000 survey	1,909	1,554	355
Incidence of poverty according to PRSP measurement methodology	34.8%	34.2%	36.6%
Incidence of poverty according to relative methodology (bottom 3 deciles)	30.0%	29.2%	33.0%
Number of observations in panel, 1994/95 and 1999/2000	747	580	136
Share of panel that emerged out of poverty (A)	17.7%	17.4%	17.6%
Share of panel that became poor (B)	19.0%	18.8%	16.2%
Share of panel that was poor in both periods (C)	12.0%	10.5%	19.1%
Share of panel that was never poor (D)	51.3%	53.3%	47.1%
Poverty incidence in first period, 1994/95 (C+B)	29.7%	27.9%	36.8%
Poverty incidence in second period, 1999/2000 (A+D)	31.1%	29.3%	35.3%

Source: Authors' estimation, using ECVR surveys for 1994/95 and 1999/2000.

we simply consider as poor those households who are in the bottom three deciles of the distribution of consumption.

The more interesting results are those presented in the second part of table 6.2, which relies on the subset of data that consists of a panel and on the relative poverty measurement approach (this enables us to avoid issues related to the comparability of the consumption aggregates and thereby absolute poverty estimates between the two periods). Between 1994/95 and 1999/2000, relative poverty decreased slightly among households identified as cotton producers, while relative poverty increased slightly among households who were not producing cotton. Given the small sample sizes, we should be careful in the interpretation of these results. Still, the results suggest that cotton producers may have fared slightly better over the period as a whole than rural households who were not producing cotton. This could be considered as indirect evidence of a positive impact of the reforms as a whole on producers, although the gains could be due in part to the impact of the devaluation, and the data have severe limits (including the fact that we do not know which households were producing cotton in the first year of data, 1994/95).

Another way to assess how well cotton producers are doing versus other rural households is to ask whether, controlling for a wide range of household characteristics, producing cotton helps households to emerge from poverty. To answer that question, regression analysis is necessary. Table 6.3 reports the results of regressions for the determinants of the logarithm of per capita income and consumption using the 1999/2000 ECVR survey. The mean values in the sample of the variables are given in the first column. The results of the regressions are in the next two columns. All the results that are statistically significant are as expected.

For example, a larger number of infants and children in the household reduces both consumption and income per capita. Households belonging to the Fon, Peulh, and Other ethnic groups have lower levels of income or consumption, as do households with a head working in agriculture. By contrast, households with a head or spouse working as a wage earner, as a self-employed person, as an employer, or as an *exploitant agricole* (a farmer employing others) have higher levels of income or consumption (or both). Households cultivating a larger amount of land are better off, as are households living in villages with a better standard of living and easier access to various resources (e.g., households in villages that are larger, with a smaller share of the population in agriculture, with more primary schools, with a smaller distance to water, with easier access by light vehicles, with more financial services associations, cooperatives, food banks, and tontines, and with fewer self-help groups).

Table 6.3. Determinants of per capita consumption and income, rural Benin, 1999/2000

	Sample mean	Consumption	Income
Number of babies	1.356	-0.094	-0.089
		[5.35]***	[1.69]*
Number of babies squared	3.914	0.009	0.011
		[2.85]***	[1.15]
Number of children	2.166	-0.128	-0.227
		[9.24]***	[5.64]***
Number of children squared	8.542	0.008	0.019
		[4.52]***	[3.69]***
Number of adults	3.194	0.006	0.090
		[0.37]	[1.73]*
Number of adults squared	14.747	0.000	-0.006
		[0.28]	[1.20]
Age of head	48.523	-0.002	-0.004
		[0.44]	[0.30]
Age of head squared	2,598.864	0.000	0.000
		[0.26]	[0.32]
Head female	50.0%	-0.082	0.210
		[1.56]	[1.34]
No spouse	21.0%	0.129	0.090
		[2.25]**	[0.52]
Bariba ethnicity	17.3%	-0.179	-0.230
		[1.50]	[0.60]
Dendi ethnicity	8.5%	-0.143	-0.516
		[1.11]	[1.19]
Fon ethnicity	34.6%	-0.160	-0.256
		[2.17]**	[1.32]
Yoa Lokpa ethnicity	4.1%	-0.149	-0.246
		[1.04]	[0.57]
Peulh ethnicity	4.4%	-0.312	-0.727
		[2.45]**	[1.76]*
Yoruba ethnicity	10.6%	-0.014	-0.051
		[0.15]	[0.19]
Other ethnicity	7.7%	-0.299	-1.256
		[2.41]**	[3.11]***
Head primary education	18.3%	0.047	0.061
		[1.53]	[0.67]
Head secondary/superior	6.7%	0.149	0.254
		[3.05]***	[1.85]*
Spouse literate	1.8%	0.014	0.247
		[0.17]	[1.13]

	Sample mean	Consumption	Income
Head in agriculture	83.0%	-0.039	-0.418
		[0.96]	[3.66]***
Head wage earner	2.3%	0.234	-0.148
		[2.38]**	[0.56]
Head family worker	0.6%	-0.038	0.304
		[0.26]	[0.57]
Head independent/employer or agricultural exploitant	92.6%	0.074	0.290
		[1.21]	[1.68]*
Spouse in agriculture	69.1%	-0.046	-0.120
		[1.17]	[1.01]
Spouse wage earner	0.2%	0.448	2.197
		[1.01]	[2.13]**
Spouse family worker	54.7%	0.081	0.061
		[1.64]	[0.41]
Spouse independent/employer or agricultural exploitant	14.0%	0.082	0.314
		[1.71]*	[2.25]**
Cotton producer	18.6%	0.060	0.159
		[1.76]*	[1.49]
Number of hectares cultivated	0.006	7.425	15.778
		[5.79]***	[4.13]***
Alibori department	18.9%	-0.037	0.786
		[0.29]	[1.96]*
Atacora department	10.8%	0.077	0.254
		[0.60]	[0.62]
Atlantique department	9.9%	-0.004	0.072
		[0.05]	[0.33]
Borgou department	9.0%	-0.121	0.040
		[0.97]	[0.10]
Collines department	7.6%	0.093	-0.108
		[0.95]	[0.39]
Donga department	4.8%	-0.043	0.133
		[0.30]	[0.30]
Oueme department	8.8%	0.149	0.290
		[1.63]	[1.17]
Plateau department	6.7%	-0.099	0.033
		[0.95]	[0.11]
Zou department	11.0%	0.263	0.358
		[2.98]***	[1.52]

(continued)

Table 6.3. (*cont.*) Determinants of per capita consumption and income, rural Benin, 1999/2000

Village characteristics

	Sample mean	Consumption	Income
Number of households (10,000)	0.023	0.427	8.100
		[0.42]	[2.38]**
Share of households in agriculture	85.6%	0.114	-0.593
		[1.47]	[2.66]***
Number of primary schools	1.122	0.079	-0.020
		[4.05]***	[0.31]
Presence of health center	43.3%	-0.015	0.006
		[0.53]	[0.07]
Distance to water	1.439	-0.009	-0.011
		[3.85]***	[1.59]
Electricity	6.3%	0.052	-0.047
		[1.01]	[0.35]
Permanent access with light vehicle	72.3%	-0.005	0.186
		[0.18]	[2.05]**
Number of financial services associations	0.215	0.072	0.183
		[4.31]***	[3.88]***
Number of food banks	0.229	0.045	-0.049
		[2.45]**	[0.78]
Presence of credit/saving bank	13.2%	-0.016	-0.169
		[0.41]	[1.43]
Number of cooperatives	0.922	0.009	0.032
		[1.38]	[1.82]*
Number of stores stocking inputs	0.592	0.027	0.012
		[1.56]	[0.22]
Number of "tontines" (informal credit mechanisms)	3.796	0.007	0.000
		[2.88]***	[0.01]
Number of functional help groups	2.758	-0.007	0.001
		[3.13]***	[0.10]
Constant		11.145	11.243
		[72.25]***	[23.31]***

Source: Authors' estimate, using 1999/2000 ECVR survey. Omitted variables: Couffo, Mono, and 8th department; Adja Ethnie; head and spouse employed in nonagricultural activities; head without education; head and spouse paid by the task. R-squared of 0.31 for consumption (1,646 observations) and 0.28 for income (988 observations).

For our purpose, the key result in table 6.3 is the fact that producing cotton does not bring a statistically significant gain (nor a loss) in per capita income versus other activities once we control for a wide range of other household characteristics. Cotton producers have a level of per capita consumption 6 percent higher than other similar households on average, but this result is only marginally statistically significant, at the 10 percent level.

The estimates presented in table 6.3 could be challenged on the ground that the decision of producing cotton may itself be influenced by a household's initial level of consumption or income. If this were the case, we would face an endogeneity problem, and the coefficient of the cotton dummy variable in the regression would be biased. An alternative empirical procedure to assess how well cotton producers are doing in comparison with households who do not produce cotton but have similar characteristics is to rely on matching techniques (Rosenbaum and Rubin 1983, 1985). In traditional matching techniques, the idea is to compare each household producing cotton with one or more households not producing cotton but having a similar probability of producing cotton (for example, according to a logit regression). The matching is done "one on one" by comparing each producer with one (or a few) household(s) that do not produce cotton. Here, we rely instead on smoothed weighted matching estimators such as those proposed by Heckman, Ichimura, and Todd (1997, 1998), which take the whole sample into account when implementing the matching. This was done for per capita consumption and for the probability of being poor according to the consumption metric using the stata routines provided by Sianesi (2003), who uses an Epanechnikov specification for the kernels.

The detailed results of the matching procedure are available on request. The findings are fairly similar to the results presented in table 6.3. There is a 2 percent gain in per capita consumption among cotton producers and their comparison group, but this difference is not statistically significant, even at the 10 percent level. There is also a 7 percent reduction in the probability of being poor, from 43 percent for the comparison group to 36 percent among cotton producers, but this result is statistically significant only at the 10 percent level. Thus, we again obtained only fairly weak evidence that cotton producers are better off than similar households not producing cotton, but we certainly do not obtain evidence that they are worse off.

Cotton Production, Prices, and Inequality

To examine the contribution of revenues from cotton to the inequality in per capita income in Benin, we used the information on various income sources available in the 1999/2000 ECVR survey and then applied a standard decomposition by source of the Gini index of inequality, as proposed by Lerman and Yitzhaki (1985, 1994).[1] That decomposition tells us what the impact on the overall index of inequality would be of an increase or a reduction in any income source. In the case of cotton, it tells us, for example, what will happen at the margin to income inequality if the price paid to producers were to increase or decrease.

The key parameter in the decomposition is the Gini income elasticity (GIE). A GIE of one means that income from a given source is distributed in the same way as total per capita income, so that an increase or reduction in the income from that source would not affect inequality in total per capita income. A GIE below one indicates an income source for which a reduction in revenues would be inequality increasing at the margin. A GIE above one indicates the reverse, namely an income source for which an increase in revenues would be increasing at the margin. Any income source with a positive GIE is itself positively correlated with total per capita income. That is, a GIE would have to be negative for an income source to accrue on average more to poorer households than to richer households.

The income shares and GIEs of the various income sources that can be identified in the 1999/2000 ECVR survey are provided in table 6.4. It can be seen that cotton revenues account for 19 percent of total per capita income in rural Benin, which is fairly large. Only incomes from nonagricultural activities are larger, at half the total per capita income. The third-largest income source is from livestock, at 8 percent of total income. The key parameter of interest is the GIE, which

Table 6.4. Decomposition of Gini index of per capita income by source in rural areas, Benin, 1999

	Share (percent)	GIE
Cash crops		
Cotton	19.15	0.97
Ananas	0.17	1.18
Cashews	1.69	0.66
Palm oil	3.65	1.14
Other	2.08	0.86
Other crops		
Maize	3.96	1.11
Sorgho/Mill	0.24	0.75
Manioc	1.72	0.85
Igname	0.64	0.93
Sweet potatoes	0.05	0.58
Niebe	0.55	0.58
Peanuts	1.92	0.48
Vegetables	0.63	0.88
Other crops	4.11	0.82
Other income sources		
Livestock	8.13	0.90
Wages	0.74	0.60
Nonagricultural income	46.99	1.12
Private transfers	2.15	0.42
Public transfers	1.08	0.74
Property rents	0.36	0.72

Source: Authors' estimation, using 1999 ECVR survey. Number of observations: 1,256.

is very close to one for cotton. This means that revenues from cotton are distributed in the same way as total income, so that at the margin, a change in revenues from cotton (for example through a higher or lower price paid to producers) would not affect income inequality. A few sources of income, including income from bananas, palm oil, nonagricultural sources, and maize would have inequality increasing at the margin, albeit mildly (the GIEs are not large). All other sources of income tend to have inequality decreasing at the margin.

There is a perception in Benin that the reduction in world cotton prices and the privatization of the cotton sector have been detrimental to cotton producers in the 1990s. On the poverty side, we found that cotton producers fared relatively well over the decade as a whole. Specifically, our panel analysis of data on relative poverty from Benin's rural household surveys for 1994/95 and 1999/2000 suggests that cotton producers fared slightly better over that period than rural households who were not producing cotton. In addition, data on subjective perceptions of welfare from a 1998 survey of cotton farmers implemented by Minot and Daniels (2003) suggests that cotton producers felt better in 1998 than in 1992. Finally, we found that cotton producers in 1999 were as well off as other households with similar characteristics but who were not producing cotton. Looking at the decade as a whole, however, it remains difficult to disentangle the impact of the cotton sector reforms themselves from the positive impact of the 1994 devaluation of the CFA franc which, together with high guaranteed cotton purchase prices for local producers, made the production of cotton more attractive for farmers despite falling world cotton prices during the second half of the 1990s.

On the inequality side, using data from the 1999/2000 rural survey, we found that while cotton revenues represent a large share of total income in rural areas, they tend at the margin to inequality neutral. More precisely, because cotton revenues tend to be relatively highly correlated to income, small changes in prices tend to have a limited impact on income inequality. However, the fact that cotton revenues are distributed in line with total income in rural areas suggests that at the national level, an increase in cotton revenues would probably be inequality decreasing (and certainly poverty reducing), since urban households are typically richer than rural households. This would then mean that apart from providing a stable source of income for many rural households, the growth of the cotton sector in Benin has probably helped decrease inequality nationwide, or at least to ensure that inequality did not increase too much over time.

Notes

This chapter was originally prepared as a contribution to a Poverty and Social Impact Analysis of Cotton Sector Reforms in Benin prepared by the World Bank. Our work benefited from support from the Belgian Partnership for Poverty Reduction under the project Poverty Reduction Strategies, Targets, and Costs. The views expressed here are those of the authors and do not necessarily represent those of the World Bank, its executive directors, or the countries they represent, nor do they necessarily represent the views of the donor agency that helped fund this work.

1. For a review of various applications of the decomposition, see Wodon and Yitzhaki 2002.

References

Badiane, Ousmane, Dhaneshwar Ghura, Louis Goreux, and Paul Masson. 2002. "Cotton Sector Strategies in West and Central Africa." World Bank Policy Working Paper 2867, Washington, DC.

Coulter, Jonathan, and C. McKenzie. 2003. "Benin Cotton Sector: A Poverty and Social Impact Analysis of Past and Present Reforms, 1981–2006." Natural Resources Institute, Chatham Maritime, UK. Mimeo.

Goreux, Louis. 2003. "Reforming the Cotton Sector in Sub-Saharan Africa (SSA)." Africa Region Working Paper Series, no. 62, World Bank, Washington, DC.

Heckman, James J., Hidehiko Ichimura, and Petra E. Todd. 1997. "Matching as an Econometric Evaluation Estimator: Evidence from Evaluating a Job Training Programme." *Review of Economic Studies* 64:605–54.

———. 1998. "Matching as an Econometric Evaluation Estimator." *Review of Economic Studies* 65:261–94.

Lerman, Robert I., and Shlomo Yitzhaki. 1985. "Income Inequality Effects by Income Sources: A New Approach and Applications to the U.S." *Review of Economics and Statistics* 67:151–56.

———. 1994. "Effect of Marginal Changes in Income Sources on U.S. Income Inequality." *Public Finance Quarterly* 22:403–17.

Minot, Nicholas, and Lisa Daniels. 2002. "Impact of Global Cotton Markets on Rural Poverty in Benin." International Food Policy Research Institute MSSD Discussion Paper 48, Washington, DC. Mimeo.

Rosenbaum, Paul R., and Donald B. Rubin. 1983. "The Central Role of the Propensity Score in Observational Studies for Causal Effects." *Biometrika* 70 (1): 41–55.

———. 1985. "Constructing a Control Group Using Multivariate Matched Sampling Methods That Incorporate the Propensity Score." *American Statistician* 39:35–39.

Sianesi, Barbara. 2003. "Implementing Propensity Score Matching Estimators with STATA." University College London. Mimeo.

Wodon, Quentin, and Shlomo Yitzhaki. 2002. "Inequality and Social Welfare." In *A Sourcebook for Poverty Reduction Strategies,* vol. 1, *Core Techniques and Cross-Cutting Issues,* ed. J. Klugman. Washington, DC: World Bank.

World Bank. 2003. *Benin Poverty Assessment.* Washington, DC: World Bank.

7

Rural Development Is More Than Commodity Production

Cotton in the Farming System of Kita, Mali

Dolores Koenig

WEST AFRICAN FARMERS HAVE RECENTLY FACED stagnating cotton prices and reduced soil fertility. Like many others, Malian farmers are well aware of these challenges to earning a good living by growing cotton. Yet many farmers continue to grow this crop, and the expansion of the cotton organization into new areas was greeted with enthusiasm. Why do farmers embrace cotton cultivation when they are well aware of the difficulties that they may confront while doing so? We can understand this paradox by conceptualizing cotton growing as part of larger systems of which farmers are a part. In other words, farmers value cotton production for more than its potential or actual income alone.

In rural Mali the farm is part of three larger systems that affect farmers' evaluations of particular crops. First, farmers are part of households, and their role within the household influences their assessment of a crop. Household heads evaluate crops not only by their ability to provide food or income for household needs, but also by their capacity to retain household labor. Non–household heads, both men and women, evaluate crops by their capacity to generate individual resources, both cash and food, to meet their responsibilities;

since their access to land, labor, and extension services is often different from household heads, they may grow different crops.

Second, each farm community is part of the larger Malian political economy. Communities have differential access to government and private services that vary substantially from one region to another. To optimize crop production and income, farmers need access to credit, inputs, and markets; these depend, in turn, on the available infrastructure. Soon after independence, the Malian government began to structure access to rural resources through regional rural development organizations (RDOs, opérations de développement rural); other rural government services tended to be less well funded. Thus, the third system is the local RDO itself. For much of its life, through early 2000, Mali's RDO for cotton, the Compagnie Malienne de Développement des Fibres Textiles (CMDT) intervened in multiple spheres of the Kita zone economy to enhance local production potential.

The CMDT's activities allowed many farmers to meet their family responsibilities and sustain their livelihoods, increased options available to both households and families, and enhanced access to resources within the larger political economy. Thus, despite its problematic aspects, many farmers made its cultivation a part of their livelihood strategies.

Regional and Household Economy in the Kita Zone

The Kita zone, in western Mali's First Region, has long been characterized by its relative isolation (see fig. 7.1). The railroad from Dakar (in Senegal) to Bamako arrived in Kita in 1881; for a long time it served as Kita's main link east to Bamako and west, through Mali and Senegal, to the coast. Although this was Mali's first major modern transport infrastructure, transport by road became more important over time. However, national road construction was concentrated south and east of Bamako, leaving Mali's entire First Region dependent on train transport. For many years, Malian officials appeared to believe that a good road along the rail line would siphon off railroad clientele, since trains were very slow and often late. Sometimes washouts during the

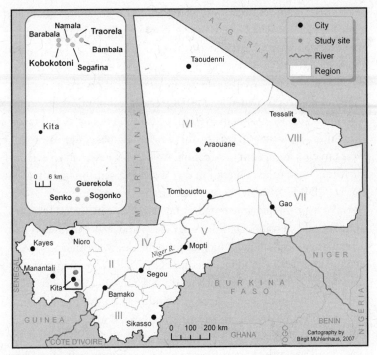

Fig. 7.1. Map of study sites.

rainy season stopped train travel altogether. Bus and truck transport offered greater flexibility.

Kita's dependence on the railroad was one of its defining features and affected the availability of resources to farmers. In particular, fewer private merchants and transporters appear to have been active there compared to areas in Mali's southeast, and cash-crop production focused on products that could withstand long storage. In other words, the regional political economy provided less opportunity to access resources privately, and Kita farmers were more directly dependent on government services, including markets, than were farmers in some other regions.

Mali became independent in 1960 with a socialist government that emphasized centralized control of the economy, but the country was simply too poor to provide the array of government services that it would have liked. By the late 1960s and early 1970s, government services in many regions were provided through donor-financed, parastatal RDOs, which came to accentuate integrated rural development, particularly after the Sahel drought of the 1970s.[1] Thus, to say that Kita farmers were dependent on government rather than private services was also to say that they were dependent on the infrastructure and services provided by an RDO. The larger political-economic system and the RDO system overlapped through the 1970s and 1980s.

Within this system, areas to the west of Bamako, Mali's capital, were targeted for peanut production. An organization, which eventually came to be called Opération de Développement Intégré du Mali Ouest (ODIMO), began to encourage farmers to grow peanuts in 1967. By 1981 it promoted integrated rural development. In addition to agricultural extension, ODIMO upgraded rural feeder roads and had an extensive local-language literacy program. Many farmers who grew peanuts could earn good incomes for rural Mali in the late 1970s, and the level of equipment use increased markedly (Koenig 1986). With German collaboration, a factory was built in Kita to process peanut oil for export. Yet, by the mid-1970s, the international peanut market was growing uncertain (Steedman et al. 1976). By the mid-1980s not only had the world price of peanuts fallen, but peanut oil had to compete with cheaper cottonseed oil within Mali. By the late 1980s ODIMO was stagnating and on its way to disappearing.

Economic liberalization in the 1980s led to a decline in government-sponsored activities. Macroeconomic policy changes required RDOs to become economically self-sufficient, but most, including ODIMO, required net infusions of cash from donors to survive. It could no longer earn sufficient income from international peanut sales, and it had gained a reputation for inefficient management. Despite several attempts to revive ODIMO, it was abolished in 1996. Because of policy changes, private-sector goods and services could in theory move into areas where government or parastatal organizations had moved out. But private-sector operators often lacked the resources to address the poor infrastructure of the First Region, and they did not create substantial new economic opportunities in the zone.

Nevertheless, southwest Mali saw striking new developments during this period. At Manantali, approximately one hundred kilometers west of Kita, the Senegal River Basin Authority (Organisation de Mise en Valeur du Fleuve Sénégal) built a high dam for electricity and irrigation. Soon after, exploitable gold was discovered at Sadiola (northwest of Manantali, south of Kayes) and a mine created there. People living and working in these areas needed goods and food, stimulating market links between them and production areas. Some roads were improved, including the link from Kita west to Manantali. However, through 1999 the two-hundred-kilometer national road east from Kita to Bamako was little more than a track and was negotiable only during the dry season. While new development activities stimulated some private-sector growth, poor transport infrastructure still constrained development.

Nevertheless, Kita town and its market did grow slowly and steadily, offering more commercial possibilities to its rural hinterland. By 1999 the items for sale in Kita's market increased substantially to include perishable foods such as lettuce, tomatoes, and cucumbers in quantity in all seasons. When ODIMO stopped buying peanuts, private merchants bought them from farmers in Kita's hinterland and sent them to other cities, especially Bamako, on the train or on trucks when the road was practicable. However, farmers complained of low peanut prices, dependence on relatively few traders, and lack of alternative opportunities.

Although increasingly active rural weekly markets and private-sector merchants could increase commercial outlets, farmers still looked to RDOs for access to other resources. Nor was the Malian government content to let all major parastatals become privatized. Despite ongoing encouragement from both multilateral and bilateral donors to sell its stake, the Malian government retained ownership in the CMDT, which, since its creation in 1974, has been owned by the Malian government (60 percent) and Dagris (40 percent), formerly the Compagnie Française pour le Développement des Fibres Textiles. Moreover, the macroeconomic policies that led to the termination of ODIMO also allowed the expansion of "successful" RDOs; in practice, that was the CMDT. By the 1980s the CMDT had increased activities in southeastern Mali, particularly in underserved areas of the original CMDT. Farmers in western Mali also believed that the CMDT was a rural development organization that could assist them.

In 1989 a Kita-based nongovernmental organization began to lobby the CMDT to begin cotton extension there, in the belief that that would help Kita farmers. Their efforts were successful and the CMDT began its first full year of work in 1995/96. By 1998 personnel had been in Kita for several years, infrastructure was in place, and farmers had begun to plant cotton. Kita farmers mostly greeted CMDT interventions with interest. Although they continued to cultivate and sell peanuts, they had lost guaranteed markets and prices. In contrast, cotton was a crop that could be sold to a known seller at fixed prices. Many wanted to give it a try.

Cotton also appeared to fit well into the household farming system. Mali's RDOs were committed to working with small-scale household farms, whose major labor force was unwaged household members. Family farms in contemporary Kita were organized as patriarchal and patrilocal extended households; a male head of household and his younger brothers and sons, their wives, and children lived together, ate from a common cooking pot, and cultivated household fields. On collective fields managed by the household head or a married male appointed by him, food, usually sorghum, was cultivated to feed the family. Other crops, such as peanuts or cotton, were grown to earn cash. To produce enough food and cash, household heads needed to retain young men's labor, and they assessed CMDT activities in this light. The complementary resources offered by an RDO were important in making rural life attractive to youth.

Alongside the household fields, both men and women could cultivate individual fields. In fact, women were expected to do so to provide sauce ingredients or money with which to buy them. They usually grew peanuts as their primary crop; it was a major ingredient for sauces but could be sold as well. They rarely grew cotton, in part because they had less direct contact with CMDT personnel, in part because it did not meet their need for food. In contrast, younger men were more interested in earning cash and often began to grow cotton in their individual fields; they were also interested in the complementary resources brought by cotton.

The data used in this analysis come from a 1999 study of sixty rural households, organized according to the cultural principles described above, in two village clusters in the Kita hinterland. These clusters were centered in the communes of Namala, approximately forty kilometers to the north of Kita town, and Senko, approximately thirty kilometers to the south. Namala residents were primarily Malinke, while Senko residents mostly identified themselves as Birgo Fulbe. However, both groups considered themselves to be primarily sedentary farmers, spoke Malinke, and had similar lifestyles, asset accumulation, and income-earning patterns. The study as a whole collected a variety of information on multiple aspects of rural life.[2] This chapter draws on both quantitative data and extended interviews.

The Drawbacks to Cotton Cultivation

Even though people looked forward to what they saw as the advantages of cotton cultivation, they faced many difficulties, including obtaining sufficient labor as well as unpredictable prices, payments, and rainfall.

First, Kita farmers so needed money that when the CMDT arrived, some put too much land and labor into cotton; they found themselves with insufficient food. CMDT personnel at all levels consistently recommended that farmers use a three-year rotation of cotton, food grain, and maize, but many did not follow that counsel. CMDT staff also said that farmers often sold cereals as well as cotton, leaving them with neither enough seed nor enough to eat.

Some farmers recognized the problem and even criticized themselves. As one said, "Before the arrival of cotton cultivation, my harvest was sufficient to nourish my family; but with cotton, I don't have time. I want to earn everywhere, and I no longer produce the quantity of cereals I need." Even some critics of the CMDT put part of the blame on farmers. A former ODIMO employee noted that Kita no longer produced surplus food but had become a net food exporter as people moved fields from sorghum into cotton. This led to rising grain prices; he noted (in March 1999) that a hundred-kilogram sack of sorghum was selling for 10,000 CFA francs (FCFA) (US$15) in Kita but only FCFA 8,000 ($12) in Bamako.[3] He expected that grain prices might rise to FCFA 12,500 to 13,500 ($19–21) before the next harvest. One farmer, however, believed that people were learning the new system. After having decreased the size of grain fields, many realized that they should cultivate cotton in addition to cereals and peanuts rather than substituting it entirely for an existing crop.

However, some farmers believed that they did not have enough labor to implement a strategy that produced cotton, sufficient grain, and peanuts as well. People in Kita often believed that cotton required more work than their traditional crops. Some specifically said that it was too demanding. One person noted that cotton required three and sometimes four weedings but that most of their other crops needed only two; many did not think cotton worth the extra work. Others said that people might sow enough cereals, but later in the crop cycle, when cotton demanded more work, they worked on that and did not spend enough time on grains. They were more concerned with paying debts than with having enough to eat.

Some farmers did not grow cotton because they did not have enough labor; one even said that too many of his children were at school for him to have a cotton field. Although young men were supposed to work on household grain fields, at least one household head said that he did not have the labor he needed on those fields because young men had individual cotton fields, which demanded a lot of upkeep. At the same time, two women complained that they did not have enough time for their individual peanut fields, because the whole family was needed to help with the cotton harvest. While farmers knew they had to keep growing sorghum for food, many thought that they had to choose between cotton and peanuts.

Second, people were concerned about the falling price of cotton. Although Malian farmers had benefited from rising cotton prices for many years, soon after Kitans started cultivating it, the price went down. The floor price did not necessarily decrease, but the negotiated price of cotton had two parts: a floor price and a rebate (the *ristourne*). In 1998/99, according to the CMDT personnel, the floor price was FCFA 145 (22 cents) per kilogram for first quality, with FCFA 40 (6 cents) per kilogram rebate. But lower international prices led the CMDT to lower the rebate significantly. In 1999/2000, it was only

FCFA 5 (less than one cent) per kilogram, for a total maximum price of FCFA 150 (23 cents) per kilogram. Farmers interpreted this as a price reduction, and many refused to grow cotton in 2000/2001 (Ministère de l'Agriculture 2004).

Farmers were also concerned about late payments of the money they did earn; they said they could wait months between the cotton harvest and when their cotton was picked up and then again between cotton collection and when they received payment. CMDT personnel themselves admitted that late payments were a problem. To encourage farmers, the government and the CMDT had decided that all payments would be made before April 30, even if the cotton had not yet been picked up, but CMDT staff believed that that was an unrealistic promise for Kita, a large zone with more than three hundred villages and eighteen thousand cotton farmers. Staff claimed that they had encouraged farmers to harvest and sell early but that farmers often waited until the bolls of all their cotton opened to begin harvesting. Then, everyone was looking for trucks at the same time. CMDT staff said that the lack of organization at all levels impeded expeditious marketing, but they also admitted that the CMDT often did not have cash on hand to pay farmers earlier.[4]

Third, in the 1999/2000 season, Kita farmers also faced the problem of too much rain. From one point of view, more rain in the savanna is a good thing, but farmers had become used to adapting to rain shortages, not surpluses. Many had planted cotton in lower-lying wet areas, and these fields were flooded. In contrast, sorghum and peanuts were less affected by the heavy rain. Farmers often had planted them in higher and drier areas, but it also appears that the local seeds used for these crops were better able to withstand variable climatic conditions. As farmers learned about the lower cotton prices, some of them neglected or abandoned the crop. Most farmers got lower cotton yields than they had the preceding year, and many faced losses. The farmers who did have substantial cotton harvests often forfeited their returns to pay off the debts of others, because credit came through village associations that used a solidarity guarantee (see below).

By June 2000 many farmers were skeptical of cotton and considered whether or not to grow it in 2000/2001. A few farmers came out clearly against the crop. One older man said, "If you ask me about cotton, I'll react strongly. I consider cotton to be a bad weed. A single cotton plant in my field will make me angrier than almost anything. Listen, you can't eat cotton; it brings famine." Many farmers, however, were ready to try again, and production figures from the Kita office of the CMDT in 2004 suggest increased production in the zone as a whole between 1999 and 2003.

The Benefits of Cotton Cultivation

Farmers are, overall, rational producers; they continue to cultivate cotton because they see benefits, despite the problems. On the one hand, the contemporary political economy demands that rural households have cash, and crops that offer assured incomes through participation in commodity-production services are one of the few reliable ways to earn it. In this sense, Kita farmers may have few alternatives to cotton if they wish to earn substantial farm incomes. However, data from Kita suggest that this analysis is insufficient on its own. Given the household and regional political-economic systems of Kita farmers, the CMDT has offered them multiple benefits that sustain their livelihood goals. Some benefits were limited to cotton producers and induced some to grow cotton when they might otherwise not do so. Other benefits were linked to cotton production but flowed to those with subsidiary relationships to it, for example, smiths who produced agricultural equipment or those who raised livestock. A few benefits, however, were available to all residents of the zone; they existed because the CMDT continued to act as an RDO and not simply as a commodity-production organization.

BENEFITS FOR COTTON CULTIVATORS

When Kita farmers decided whether or not to grow cotton, they looked not only at the money they hoped to earn from cotton sales but also at the other resources they could get. These included agricultural equipment, inputs, and credit; access to credit was primary because it gave farmers access to equipment and inputs. Agricultural equipment (plows, seeders, and multipurpose tool frames) as well as draft oxen to pull them were available through private sellers in this part of Mali, and local residents did buy through private-sector networks when they had sufficient cash, but few private sellers were willing to give multiyear credit. Village banks had recently been created in this zone, but they too were often hesitant to accord large, multiyear loans that people needed to buy equipment.[5]

Inputs were even harder to get because they were rarely sold privately in this part of Mali. Evidently distributors found it easier to sell large quantities to agricultural extension organizations rather than to encourage the development of small-scale private distribution networks (Koenig, Diarra, and Sow 1998). Thus, access to fertilizers, herbicides, and insecticides came primarily through RDOs or similar organizations.

Since equipment and inputs were sold on credit through the CMDT, only cotton farmers could easily get them. Cotton farmers in a single village joined together to create an *association villageoise* (AV), which when certified by the CMDT could take a loan from the Banque Nationale de Développement Agricole. Repayment of loans was guaranteed by the solidarity of the AV. A village could not get a new loan for the following year unless the previous year's loan had been repaid. Kita farmers compared this system negatively to the individual loans that had been granted during the ODIMO years, when there were, however, relatively high default levels among farmers.

Many farmers said they began to cultivate cotton so that they could purchase agricultural equipment. Kita farmers were almost unanimous that the major resource needed to increase agricultural production in this zone with relatively good land resources and rainfall was increased equipment. Said one, "Equipped farmers produce much more." Said another, "Equipment is the only thing that can better the lives of farmers." A third said, "Before, people only needed *dabas* (hoes) to produce, but it's different today. We are more and more aware of innovations." Less-wealthy farmers noted that lack of equipment was an obstacle to greater production.

Access to equipment also helped household heads keep the other major resource needed for agriculture, human labor, particularly the labor of sons who might otherwise leave on wage-labor migration. One poorer farmer suggested that the only strategy that would keep young men at home and working on the collective fields was "to be rich"; otherwise they might simply leave. Another farmer noted that he did not grow cotton because his grown children were not in the village with him. In this zone, cotton needs both equipment and a relatively large labor force. To be sure, equipment could replace people by rendering more efficient the human labor available; as one farmer noted, "It's important to have equipment because it can do the work of five or six persons in no time." Yet many Malian farmers used equipment to increase the land area they cultivated; they needed more labor for the tasks, particularly harvesting, still done by hand. As one wealthier farmer noted, equipment allowed a household to add cotton to its portfolio without reducing the area in peanuts and cereals. Access to equipment and labor were linked, and the local meaning of being rich included having a large family as well as owning multiple pieces of agricultural equipment. Although farmers were most interested in equipment to increase the productivity of annual crop agriculture (cotton, sorghum, and peanuts), they also saw other uses. A young gardener noted the importance of equipment for improving his production and sales; farmers wanted carts to decrease transport costs.

Thus, a major reason to pursue cotton cultivation was to get access to agricultural equipment. In the sample households, a majority owned at least some equipment, but ownership was quite stratified. The wealthiest households had the most equipment, and the poorest households had very little (Koenig 2005), a pattern also found in Lacy's chapter in this volume. However, in this sample, the greatest number of CMDT equipment loans was reported by those in the middle socioeconomic stratum, who used them to buy plows, seeders, and oxen. For those who already had a plow and seeder, the CMDT offered a chance to get a cart. Some farmers said they would stop growing or reduce their field area in cotton as soon as they paid off their CMDT loans, which stretched over five years. However, the possibility of getting more equipment was enticing. A farmer who considered reducing the size of his cotton field once his debt for a plow was paid said that he still wanted a cart. Even some who had problems producing enough to pay their debt were enthusiastic about getting equipment. One pair of brothers said that they had sold a bicycle and some agricultural equipment to pay, but they had kept other equipment and an ox they had received through the CMDT; they planned to borrow more the following season.

In contrast, neither the poorest nor the wealthiest farmers made great use of equipment loans. The poorest farmers were not approved by the CMDT or their local AV, because they did not have potential production large enough to merit an equipment loan. At the same time, few of the wealthiest farmers took equipment loans, because most already had equipment bought privately or from ODIMO. This equipment could be twenty to thirty years old, but farmers had carefully repaired it; moreover, unlike the less wealthy, they had never needed to sell it to make ends meet. A few younger farmers in wealthy families were using equipment inherited from their fathers. One richer farmer claimed that the older equipment he was using was better quality than the CMDT equipment, even after repairs; he said that CMDT equipment had begun to break already. Yet even wealthy farmers were not completely detached from the equipment circuits of the CMDT. One AV president noted that he had received a pair of oxen, two carts, and two seeders on credit; he had in turn given them to other farmers on credit to himself, presumably reinforcing his role as a village patron. The AV president in another village, who had plenty of equipment, was trying to figure out how to get a tractor from the CMDT.[6]

However, because wealthier farmers were the biggest cotton producers, they did take loans for inputs (Koenig 2003). The fact that these farmers took credit primarily for inputs and only rarely for equipment should have meant a greater return on their crop than among middle-stratum farmers, many of whom were required to pay off proportionately larger equipment debts. However, the use of the AV meant that debt repayment fell disproportionately, at least over the short term, on the backs of the biggest producers.[7] One large household that had produced seven metric tons of cotton received very little because its income covered other people's debts. One married man in this household had produced 1,587 kilograms, and he calculated that should have netted FCFA 140,000 ($215), but he ended up with nothing. In the same village, one less-wealthy farmer with an equipment loan had produced 1,425 kilograms; he ought to have netted FCFA 45,000 ($69), but he received only FCFA 10,000 ($15). Another middle-stratum farmer was relatively nonplused about his debt, arguing that because of the 1999 rain, nobody had a very good harvest and everyone was in debt because of cotton. As one farmer said, "In the past, authorities came with their scale and paid each person. Now we weigh among ourselves . . . after the debts are paid, they [the CMDT] send us the rest and we arrange things among ourselves. There are some who have too many debts in comparison to their income; we have this problem here."

AV presidents, usually among the bigger growers, had varying responses to this situation. A few noted the responsibility of village leaders to solve village problems. One said, "You can say that the AV is on my back; as head of the AV, I'm the first to suffer. I am angry . . . but those who have lost, they have nothing and you can't make them pay; they have nothing." However, in two villages, the AV was able to put some pressure on members to repay. Some people sold goods to pay cotton debt, either because they felt coerced or because they too did not want neighbors to suffer. Some AVs also planned to be more exigent the following year. Said one AV leader, "We've decided to drop those who had debts with the CMDT this year, because some of them don't work, even though the CMDT has given them equipment. We won't give equipment or inputs to those who don't work hard." At the same time, some wealthier farmers were looking for ways to divide AVs into smaller groups or be treated as individual growers. The CMDT did not accept the latter option because, as one farmer noted, "an individual could take the money and disappear."

Many farmers preferred the ODIMO system, where responsibility rested with the extension organization, to the CMDT, where the village was responsible for its debts. One wealthy farmer said, "I worked with the people of ODIMO; they were more interesting to me than the CMDT. At least they didn't talk about AVs; I am discouraged by the AV system." It seems unlikely that wealthier farmers will subsidize their less-wealthy neighbors over the long term.[8]

All cotton growers had access to inputs, primarily fertilizers, and insecticides. The CMDT attempted to ration these according to the amount of field area devoted to cotton. Fields were measured ahead of time, and farmers were able to buy on credit only the amount needed for the size of their fields. Nevertheless, there was some diversion, as farmers used some of the fertilizer on other crops or sold it. At least one farmer told us that he grew cotton primarily to get the fertilizer, which he then used on his peanut field.

In addition to the tangible benefits of equipment and inputs, many farmers appreciated that they could learn about new technologies and gain new information from extension agents. In general, people commented positively on what they had learned from CMDT agents, who usually lived in rural villages. Many believed that production possibilities had increased and that CMDT counsels were sound. As one said, "I am now convinced that those who respect [CMDT] advice will have fewer production problems." Many mentioned ideas that might have been offered by any extension agency, for example, strategies to prepare and clear fields more effectively, techniques to measure fields, recommendations on the use of fertilizers and insecticides, and strategies to limit field areas seeded to those that a farmer could easily maintain. However, since the stagnation of ODIMO, they had few learning opportunities. Moreover, the CMDT attracted complementary projects. In Kita, for example, a German-funded project worked on environmental issues. Farmers mentioned that they had learned how to make better use of organic manure on their different crops, to use rock lines,[9] and to grow *pourghère* (*Jatropha curcas,* a shrub grown as a hedge) to control erosion. However, since only cotton farmers had direct access to CMDT agents, they had disproportionate access to new knowledge. One said he was interested in all that he could learn to aid him, but that he had not worked with an agricultural agent because he did not grow cotton. One woman noted that since only a few women grew cotton, they had much less access to CMDT agents.

Clearly, farmers grew cotton not only because of the income they expected to earn from its sale, but also because of the other resources they could gain: credit, inputs, equipment, new knowledge. At the same time, because these benefits came through the CMDT, they were directly available only to those who grew cotton. The dependence of benefits on cotton cultivation pushed some individuals, who might have preferred to grow other crops, into cotton as a means to get them. In many contexts, wealthy farmers benefit disproportionately from extension activities, but in 1999, the largest benefits appear to have accrued to middle-level farmers who received credit for equipment purchases. Because middle-level households formed more than half the sample (thirty-three of sixty households), access to the complementary benefits of cotton cultivation was quite high.

SPECIALIZED BENEFITS LINKED TO COTTON PRODUCTION

The CMDT offered some benefits to those who offered support activities to cotton, including blacksmiths who fabricated agricultural equipment and livestock producers who raised oxen. It also offered some specialized training, for example, in gardening. The sixty-household sample had individuals in all these categories.

To furnish agricultural equipment, the CMDT had turned to a strategy that used local blacksmiths.[10] At first, most equipment was produced in southeastern Mali, in the CMDT heartland, but the CMDT later decentralized production. One of the smiths in our sample was a member of a cooperative of Kita smiths that made equipment for the CMDT. He was originally trained by ODIMO, whose instruction reinforced and "modernized" skills he already had. ODIMO also furnished credit for additional tools. Upon its arrival, the CMDT hired the association to produce equipment; it also provided raw materials. The CMDT was the association's only client, but each smith continued to work individually for his own customers. This smith was one of the most affluent artisans in our sample; clearly his work for the CMDT had benefited him.

Not all smiths gained from this extra work. A younger smith, who was not an association member, had to rely on individual clients and was not as obviously successful. He noted that in order to participate in the association or get further training from the CMDT, a smith had to apprentice with someone who would give him a written certificate. A smith could not get the training unless he had an appropriate recommendation. At the same time, he said, the presence of the CMDT made the price of scrap iron go up because it created competition for existing stocks.

The CMDT also bought its oxen locally, even frequenting the local market to buy it. Staff noted that oxen were so easy to get that farmers sometimes received oxen before their plows or other equipment. One of the sample farmers who had sold some of his stock to the CMDT said that he usually sold his livestock in the local weekly market. He noted that although itinerant sellers might propose higher prices, they tended to pay only half the agreed price up front, and it was often difficult to get the remaining sum. In contrast, those buying traction animals for the CMDT would pay the entire amount in cash.

Blacksmiths and livestock sellers could benefit because they were involved in activities directly linked to cotton production. Sometimes, in its role as an RDO, the CMDT supported other activities as well. One young man, interested in gardening, had sought to increase his skills by working for experienced gardeners in urban peripheries. Upon his return home, he had taken over management of a large garden begun by his father. Well known in his village for his passion for gardening, he was chosen by the CMDT for further training; CMDT programs sent him to other Malian towns to learn improved grafting techniques for old and new species. He also learned procedures to make wild trees like shea (*Butyrospermum parkii*) more productive. This involvement with the CMDT upgraded his skills, but did not directly provide added income. Nevertheless, he was expanding his garden during the study period.

In another village, a twenty-eight-member women's association created a community garden. They enclosed their large garden with wire fencing, paid for by a loan from the CMDT. They had reimbursed part of the loan with money they earned from growing tomatoes, lettuce, and other garden crops but planned to grow a cotton field in the following year to finish paying off their debt. After that the women could use their earnings for further investments or to divide among group members. The women in the group included several from the family of the dynamic and politically active AV president; this man gave us a tour of the garden in the hope of finding a donor to improve its wells. This relatively rare experiment built on infrastructure brought by the cotton organization.

Other resources provided by the CMDT were potentially more widespread. For a long time, the CMDT has had a policy of transferring control of certain activities to local farmer organizations. Although the policy was due in part to a desire to devolve financial responsibility away from the CMDT, it created a group of people with useful skills. For example, the CMDT began local-language literacy and numeracy programs in the 1970s so that villagers could weigh crops and measure fields. However, not all literate members had to be active farmers, and the benefits of these programs could spread beyond AV participants. In the Kita sample, one of the store owners said that he had no formal schooling, but he had received literacy training, which he used to keep business accounts, recording loans, purchases, and income.

The CMDT also made cottonseed residue, a popular cattle feed, available to anyone with money to purchase it. One woman in the sample, who owned cows and goats, said that she fed her animals cottonseed that she bought from the CMDT, because it was good feed if you wanted to make your cows fat.

Although these benefits were varied, their impact was limited; five different households in the sample of sixty mentioned one of them. Because they built on existing skills or connections, the benefits tended to favor those who already had more resources; most that benefited were from more affluent households. Benefits could spread; for example, although the women in the gardening association had access to this loan because of links to the family of the AV president, the membership included other women as well. Nevertheless, in contrast to the benefits from cotton cultivation itself, which enabled the vast middle part of the population to get additional resources, these were biased toward those who had resources or skills on which to build. In turn, access to these benefits enabled these individuals and households to improve their relative position even more.

As noted, the defining feature of the Kita zone through the 1990s was its dependence on the railroad and its consequent isolation. Within the zone, some good roads did link major production centers to Kita town and the railroad. In its heyday ODIMO had built and maintained feeder roads that linked peanut-producing villages to Kita, but as it stagnated, so too did the state of the roads. When the CMDT moved in, one of its first activities was to improve the road network. By the time we began our fieldwork in Kita in 1999, the CMDT had built a major road parallel to the old Bamako road, from Kita east to another major production and rail center, about one-third of the way to Bamako. It had also improved interior roads and built bridges and improved river and stream crossings to render all-season travel easier. In 1999 the CMDT roads were complemented by a national improved, but unpaved, road between Kita and Bamako; a bus route arose almost immediately.[11]

Although built to facilitate the work of the CMDT, the roads became part of a public network, and the benefits were not restricted to the CMDT. They enabled the growth of public and private transport, greater activity of private traders, and easier sales of peanuts and other crops.[12] In response to these changes, Kita town and its market continued to grow. Kita farmers were most aware of the subsequent increase in peanut prices.

As discussed above, farmers in Kita complained of falling peanut prices from the late 1980s through the mid-1990s, as ODIMO stopped buying and private merchants moved in. Yet by 1999 the price of peanuts had increased substantially, which people generally attributed to the presence of the CMDT. As one said, "It's easier to have money now than twenty years ago. Peanuts didn't used to work, but with the arrival of the CMDT, peanuts have known a price that encourages people to trade them." Although a few people claimed that the price of peanuts had gone down, most said that it had increased. Some suggested that people should cultivate more peanuts. Another farmer said, "Here in the zone, there is money now. Even peanuts are sold more easily. Before the arrival of the CMDT, it was often difficult to sell peanuts, because ODIMO had failed. If you have cotton money, you can sell your peanuts when you want. The price of peanuts has increased considerably since the arrival of the CMDT." Another noted that with the arrival of the CMDT, everything produced on the farm could be sold.

Some attributed this change directly to supply and demand; when cotton arrived, fewer peanuts were cultivated. As one farmer said, "The price of peanuts is good now. This is due to cotton. Before we only grew sorghum and peanuts, but now there is also cotton. This means we cultivate fewer peanuts, which has raised the price, because what is rare is dear." One farmer attributed this to the fact that young men were more likely to put their individual fields into cotton rather than peanuts. However, another noted that there was also a lack of peanut seed.

The route infrastructure improved the efficiency of markets in general, lowering transport costs and facilitating commercialization. In contrast to cotton, bought only once a year by the CMDT, peanuts could be sold virtually anytime and anywhere. Peanuts were bought in every village by individuals as well as at regular day and night markets; farmers could bring their peanuts to Kita or even sell in Bamako or Kayes. Some farmers believed that peanuts therefore provided a surer source of income than cotton. Prices did vary seasonally; one grower noted that if you stocked your peanuts and then sold them at the beginning of the rainy season, prices were better. Quantitative data showed that all households sold some peanuts soon after the harvest, but wealthier households often held some stock to sell when prices were higher. These sales, by women as well as men, sometimes involved several hundred kilograms of peanuts.

Farmers were not especially happy about the price variability of peanuts, but they understood it to be a function of the private market. At the same time, the fact that they could earn a fixed price for cotton, in a large sum at a single time, to complement the more variable and spread-out peanut earnings was an incentive to grow cotton. The ideal strategy was to combine cotton and peanut earnings. As one farmer said, "peanut sales can meet small expenses of the family, but cotton brings more, although the money doesn't come fast. I'm also concerned that the problem of low prices may reappear; it's thanks to the CMDT that peanuts have reached a better price. If not for them, peanuts wouldn't even sell." Although virtually every sample household grew some peanuts, if only for consumption, wealthier households were most able to realize the goal of simultaneous cotton and peanut cultivation, because they had both the labor and the equipment to put significant areas in both crops. On average, wealthier households reported higher production levels and more than twice the income from peanut sales than did poorer or middle-income households (Koenig 2003).[13] One of the largest farm households, which had produced seven metric tons of cotton, also harvested three hundred sacks of peanuts, an estimated fifteen to thirty metric tons. They planned to keep a hundred sacks for family consumption and seed and sell the rest. The head of this household nevertheless believed that he could earn more from cotton under the right conditions.

People made sophisticated calculations of the benefits they could expect from sales of peanuts at different times and in different places, taking transaction costs into account. In the past, there had been a trade-off between lower local prices with no transport costs and potential higher prices at more distant markets, but with transport costs to get there. The improved transport brought by better roads changed the local terms of trade. Buyers came to local markets and even to the farms of big growers. One farmer claimed that prices were often the same in his village and in the local weekly market. Another said, "Traders from Kita who know me come here to buy in the family. I sell at the same price as when I go to Kita and this avoids the need to pay for transport." Smaller growers could sell as well when merchants came to buy stocks of larger producers. People also tried to increase what they earned from peanut sales by adding value; many sold shelled peanuts, which brought more money than unshelled ones, at little opportunity cost, since people sat around the fire in the evening hand-shelling peanuts as they visited. In contrast to cotton income, limited to men, virtually all women had peanut fields and many sold peanuts. Therefore they benefited directly from the increased route infrastructure, even though they usually did not cultivate cotton. Like men, they understood that the arrival of the CMDT had increased the prices they could get for their peanuts.

CMDT personnel often expressed ambivalent attitudes about peanut cultivation. Insofar as the CMDT was conceptualized as a commodity-production organization that earned its income from a single crop, personnel accented cotton. Peanuts, sold entirely within the private sector, brought no earnings to the CMDT. Moreover, the expertise of CMDT personnel was in cotton; a veterinarian in Kita noted that the CMDT might encourage farmers to grow other crops, but the staff did not really have expertise in anything except cotton. In some zones, the CMDT encouraged the cultivation of complementary crops such as cowpeas and soybeans, sweet potatoes, and yams, but in Kita, discussion usually revolved around the standard CMDT rotation of cotton, sorghum, and maize. Nevertheless, some CMDT staff believed that farmers could cultivate peanuts at the same time that they grew cotton. They noted that the quality of peanut seed had declined since ODIMO's fall, and they wanted to improve the quality of peanut seed available to farmers. Because the end of the peanut harvest overlapped the beginning of the cotton harvest, another possibility was to facilitate creation of peanut varieties with a shorter growing season, which would allow farmers to combine the two crops more easily. However, in 1999/2000, CMDT personnel did very little to improve peanut production.

Many, both within the CMDT and outside it, believed that the organization should not be just a commodity-production organization but also an RDO concerned about rural development in general. From this perspective, CMDT personnel recognized that peanuts played an important role in a diverse production system. Moreover, peanut production had become an essential element in the culture and identity of the Kita Malinke.[14] One CMDT staff member in Kita, himself Malinke, remarked that Malinke could not stop growing peanuts. Like farmers, personnel realized that the arrival of the CMDT had facilitated rising peanut prices, encouraging production and sales. Village-based extension agents were often even more aware of the challenges faced by farmers and the importance of peanuts, both economic and cultural, in addressing them. As one farmer noted, "The

CMDT technician told us not to do only cotton but to do something else like peanuts, which would help us have money."

The increasing efficiency of markets facilitated by the CMDT infrastructure was not only confined to peanuts but also affected other activities and crops. A few people mentioned that they earned more from selling maize than from selling cotton. Even more popular was the strategy of selling fruit, which made its way to Kita and sometimes to other cities. Some sold oranges, bananas, and mangoes. Many in Senko, the commune south of Kita, grew and sold watermelons. Livestock sales and purchases also increased; women as well as men could buy livestock with income from crop sales. One woman said that she bought two of her three cows with money earned from selling peanuts. Like peanuts, livestock could now be bought and sold within villages without going to Kita or a livestock trading center. Said one larger farmer, "I sell my animals here. In Kita, the butchers often ask you to sell your animal on credit, which can pose problems. You do a lot of going and coming to get your money. I think that even if you don't get as much, it's better to get all your money here."

Clearly, better commercial infrastructure and increased market efficiency facilitated trade at multiple levels. Almost anyone could enter the peanut trade, at least on a small scale, and a number of men and some women in the sample were or had been peanut traders, buying from their neighbors and reselling in other markets. In several households, individuals earned relatively large amounts from trade; these included one young household head who was a peanut, sorghum, and livestock intermediary. He earned relatively small amounts on each transaction, but brought in a substantial sum overall. Another young man owned a large store in a weekly market town. He noted that some twenty years ago, the Malinke thought that trade was an affair for cheaters; at that time they only farmed and people came from elsewhere to buy and sell. Now, Malinke themselves had entered the market. However, his business depended on good harvests; "if farmers don't produce a lot, they don't buy," he said. One small trader said that he used income from peanut sales to build and stock his small store; in turn he used some of the benefits he earned from the store to buy inputs for peanuts. Women as well sold peanuts to earn a fund to invest in livestock or begin trading enterprises.

The greater ease of selling commodities allowed people to improve consumption and stimulated new activities by village residents for their own neighbors. One man, for example, learned to fish and earned by selling fish to village residents. There were also bakers and radio repairers. Another man bought a donkey with money from peanuts and then a cart; he transported grain from outlying farms to the village. One older man said that even if you did not grow cotton yourself, you could go to those who did earn money from it and ask them to lend you money or provide you another service.

Although structural adjustment and its associated price liberalization have had many negative consequences, they positively stimulated activity among local traders and transporters in rural Mali, because they no longer had to confront price controls. However, until the CMDT improved roads and bridges to facilitate its own commodity work, activities in Kita still were constrained by poor infrastructure. Since the roads were public rights of way, all could benefit and there were many positive spread effects. Greater commercialization was not a benefit to everyone, as those who fell into debt might testify. However, the great majority of rural residents appreciated the commercialization possibilities brought by improved infrastructure, and positive effects were widespread at the individual, household, and community levels. In particular, household heads noted that new local earning opportunities decreased the pressure on young people to migrate for purely economic reasons. Not only could they grow cotton to earn money, they could also enter remunerative complementary activities, including crops, crafts, and trade. At the same time, increased access to consumer goods improved the quality of life for rural residents. Thus, the impact of the CMDT went well beyond its impact in cotton cultivation.

Insofar as the CMDT existed as an RDO, it offered multiple resources to rural residents. The value that Kita inhabitants placed on these resources explains why they appreciated the arrival of the CMDT, even though they were not happy with cotton incomes. As an effective RDO, the CMDT enhanced the regional political economy, thereby allowing many farmers to preserve the family farm system. The greater availability of transport, markets, and consumer goods made rural life more attractive to young people; the equipment and inputs available through cotton cultivation modernized farming and also encouraged younger people to stay. Although the very poorest rural residents (in our sample, about 15 percent of households) were not always able to access these benefits, they were widely distributed among the other 85 percent of the population. Therefore, Kita residents on the whole wanted CMDT programs.

However, the CMDT has been encouraged to privatize since the early days of structural adjustment; a part of this strategy includes making the organization more focused on commodity production. In 2002, in a move to increase efficiency, the CMDT laid off some five to six hundred workers and reduced its auxiliary programs in rural roads, village water supply, and literacy (Traoré 2002). By 2004 the CMDT had substantially scaled back activities in the Kita zone, even as its own figures showed increased cotton production. In Manantali, just to the west of Kita, each commune had a single agent, in comparison with the several it had had earlier. German technical assistance had scaled back its erosion-control project; it had pulled out of Manantali entirely and was concentrating only on selected areas of Kita. The personnel at the regional office in Kita had been drastically reduced, with remaining personnel reassigned to cover field positions.

Nevertheless, complete privatization was consistently delayed. Believing that the Malian government was not moving expeditiously toward this goal, the World Bank decided at the end of September 2004 to freeze an anticipated structural adjustment credit. However, further negotiations to free up this loan led to an agreement to delay full privatization until 2008, although several steps were to be undertaken earlier (Touré 2005). The ability of the Malian government to delay privatization was greeted with a certain amount of pride by the Malian press (Touré 2005).

That delay has not, however, increased in any obvious way the ability of the CMDT itself to act as a rural development organization.

However, other actors have stepped in. In 2003 four cooperatives in the Kita zone began to produce fair trade cotton under a project run by Max Havelaar France in association with Dagris (one of the CMDT's shareholders). This cotton earned a bonus, meant to be used for local investments such as school and health center construction, literacy programs, and the purchase of agricultural equipment, precisely the activities that would have been done by a rural development–oriented CMDT (Max Havelaar France 2005). This rural development approach has evidently proved attractive to farmers, because the number of cooperatives increased to sixteen in 2004 and ninety-two in 2005; 57 metric tons of fair trade cotton were produced in 2003, 300 metric tons in 2004 (Dembélé 2005).

Clearly, farmers have continued to appreciate the importance of complementary activities in enhancing their regional political economy. The requests to Mali's prime minister when he visited Kita in 2004 show what farmers think is important. Above all they stressed their need for better access to resources to increase production: more equipment, more agricultural credit, and lower costs for inputs, including fertilizer. However, they also wanted better infrastructure so that they could market more goods: increased road construction between producing areas and Kita town, revitalizing the railroad, paving the Kita-Bamako road, and more telephone lines. They also wanted better infrastructure for villages: more schools and health centers, more sanitary water points, and telephone access (Coulibaly and Kouyaté 2004).

Insofar as the CMDT acted as an RDO, it increased its attractiveness to rural populations by the many services it provided. This was especially so in the years that the Malian government used RDOS to provide rural services and left other agencies underfunded. As the CMDT becomes more focused on commodity production, other organizations will need to provide these services. Indeed, as RDOs began to disappear, the state did create or enhance local agencies, but interviewees at both Kita and Manantali suggested that the resources available to them were far less than those earlier available to RDOs. Sometimes nongovernmental organizations stepped in to offer supplementary services, for example, village-level banks, which offered credit to those who did not cultivate cotton. However, the amounts of credit that these banks were able and willing to give were both smaller and shorter term than that available through the CMDT. When the prime minister visited Kita in 2004, one specific request he heard was for better bank credit for craft and commercial activities (Coulibaly and Kouyaté 2004).

The fact that CMDT activities improved access to multiple resources, sometimes even those competitive with cotton, is a major reason that farmers have participated in its activities and valued its presence. The RDO-type CMDT contributed to development in the zone in many ways besides providing cotton income. If the CMDT were to offer higher cotton prices, but at the cost of dropping its so-called complementary activities, it would likely meet much greater criticism from Kita farmers. In an ideal world the Malian government and the private sector would adequately fund institutions to provide the array of rural services previously furnished by the CMDT. It remains to be seen if Mali, still poor, can find alternative strategies to enhance regional political economies.

Notes

This chapter is based on research funded by Fulbright Hays PO19A80001, NSF SBR-9870628, and USAID LAG-A-00–96–90016–00 (BASIS CRSP). Many Malian and U.S. agencies in Bamako facilitated the research; most important was the collaboration of Malian colleagues from the Institut des Sciences Humaines, especially Tiéman Diarra, Mama Kamaté, and Seydou Camara. I also thank Tiéman Diarra for comments. I bear sole responsibility for the views presented here.

1. For more information on this period, see Koenig, Diarra, and Sow (1998). A parastatal is a specialized agency owned or controlled wholly or partly by a government.

2. Basic census information was collected on entire households. Other data, on topics such as activities, incomes, expenditures, and agricultural work, were gathered from individuals, because the members of West African households keep individual budgets and rarely pool incomes. Within each sample household, up to five people were systematically interviewed, one from each of five categories that reflected major social

roles: the head, one married man, one unmarried man, one older married woman, and one younger married woman. The entire sample included 229 individuals. Household information was created by aggregating individual data.

To capture seasonal variation, data on work, income, and expenditures were gathered at periodic intervals by Malian research assistants who lived in study villages throughout the 1999/2000 agricultural season. Quantitative data were supplemented by the knowledge gained by them as well as from eighty-two additional interviews and oral histories in the nine study villages. Further information on the study as well as preliminary results on other topics can be found in Camara et al. (2000) and Diarra et al. (2000).

3. At the time of the study, FCFA 650 was equal to one U.S. dollar.

4. These problems did not disappear; in late May 2004, when I traveled through Kita to Manantali, cotton was sitting in village collection sites waiting for pickup, even as the rainy season was beginning. Farmers growing cotton in Manantali continued to complain about late payments.

5. The length of the payback period in Kita is not known, but Manantali's active village banks required that all loans be paid within one year, a period too short for substantial loans.

6. In some zones, the CMDT approved minitractor loans for the biggest producers. In the study communes, all equipped farmers used ox-drawn equipment at the time of the study.

7. In chapter 8 of this volume, Lacy notes that AVs absorbed debts when producers defaulted on individual loans. However, since AVs have few resources of their own, separate from those of individual farmers, the wealthier members absorbed the debt, as Kita farmers discuss here.

8. The CMDT continued the strategy of using the entire village as the only option for an AV through 1999, although it has been questioned for a long time (McCorkle 1986). Nevertheless, there was much discussion of the option to form smaller groups. For example, in the 2000/2001 season, the CMDT in Kita planned to allow a ten-person group, if it had at least five literate members. That would be difficult to achieve, however, since CMDT personnel said that only 30 percent of households had at least one literate member. I have no information on whether it was implemented or not. Lacy's contribution to this volume (chapter 8) documents the institution of smaller groups and its impact in another CMDT zone.

9. Rocks are placed in a line following the contour of the land to conserve water and sediment and control soil erosion.

10. In the 1970s farm implements were produced by a national factory for distribution throughout the country (Steedman et al. 1976). Later,

supplemental production was carried out by village-based blacksmiths through RDO training programs, which adapted plow designs from elsewhere (Toulmin 1992). The CMDT began smith-training programs in 1970.

11. This road linked to other roads built in conjunction with Manantali and Sadiola. By 2004 it was possible to travel west from Bamako, through Kita and Manantali, to southwest Mali, over relatively decent roads. When the railroad was privatized, it substantially decreased passenger activity, and trucks quickly moved into long-distance transport. Because these roads were not yet paved, however, significant truck traffic had a negative impact on them, especially during the rainy season.

12. The term *public transport* is ambiguous in the Malian context, since most buses, passenger trucks, and taxis are privately owned. Individuals buy these vehicles and then procure appropriate licenses for passenger transport; they usually put them on routes where they think they can earn money. Attempts at national publicly owned bus companies have not been very successful.

13. Lacy, (chapter 8 of this volume), showed a similar trend in regard to the links between sorghum and cotton production in Dissan.

14. This role was nationally recognized; Malian media consistently referred to Kita as Mali's peanut capital.

References

Camara, Seydou, Tiéman Diarra, Mama Kamaté, Dolores Koenig, Fatimata Maiga, Amadou Tembely, and Sira Traoré. 2000. *L'économie rurale à Kita: Étude dans une perspective d'anthropologie appliquée (rapport intérimaire).* Report to USAID and Malian agencies. Bamako: Institut des Sciences Humaines. July.

Coulibaly, M. and H. Kouyaté. 2004. "Visite du premier ministre à Kita: À coeur ouvert avec les producteurs de coton." *L'essor,* November 29. http://www.africatime.com/mali/popup.asp?no_nouvelle=158793.

Dembélé, Sidiki. 2005. "Coton: Les producteurs africains en quête d'équité." *Les Échos,* November 11. http://www.maliweb.net/news.php ?pageid=4&news_no=7890&cat=72.

Diarra, Tiéman, Ladji Siaka Doumbia, Mama Kamaté, Dolores Koenig, and Amadou Tembely. 2000. *L'économie rurale à Kita: Resultats de la première étape.* Report to USAID and Malian agencies. Bamako: Institut des Sciences Humaines. March.

Koenig, Dolores. 1986. "Research for Rural Development: Experiences of an Anthropologist in Rural Mali." In *Anthropology and Rural Development in West Africa*, ed. M. M. Horowitz and T. Painter, 29–60. Boulder: Westview.

———. 2003. "The Politics of Production on the Cotton Frontier of Kita, Mali." Paper presented at the Colloquium Series, Program in Agrarian Studies, Yale University, October 10.

———. 2005. "Social Stratification and Access to Wealth in the Rural Hinterland of Kita, Mali." In *Wari Matters: Ethnographic Explorations of Money in the Mande World*, ed. S. Wooten, 31–56. Münster: Lit Verlag.

Koenig, Dolores, Tiéman Diarra, and Moussa Sow. 1998. *Innovation and Individuality in African Development: Changing Production Strategies in Rural Mali*. Ann Arbor: University of Michigan Press.

Max Havelaar France. 2005. "Coopérative des producteurs de coton de Dougourakoroni, Mali." http://www.maxhavelaarfrance.org/produits/coton.htm.

McCorkle, Constance. 1986. *Farmers' Associations Study: Opération Haute Vallée II, Mali*. Washington, DC: Checchi and Company.

Ministère de l'Agriculture. 2004. "Filières agricoles." http://www.maliagriculture.org/filier_a/coton/index.htm.

Steedman, Charles, Thomas Daves, Marlin Johnson, and John Sutter. 1976. *Mali: Agricultural Sector Assessment*. Ann Arbor: University of Michigan Center for Research on Economic Development.

Toulmin, Camilla. 1992. *Cattle, Women, and Wells: Managing Household Survival in the Sahel*. Oxford: Clarendon Press.

Touré, Bréhima. 2005. "Coton malien: La privatisation attendra." *Maliba*, March 21. http://www.malipages.com/presse/news_03_05/news_0089.asp.

Traoré, Fousséni. 2002. "CMDT: Un nouveau schéma pour la privatisation." Communiqué de Conseil des Ministres. *Le républicain*, September 10. http://www.cefib.com/presse/actu2.php?page+40.

8

Cotton Casualties and Cooperatives

Reinventing Farmer Collectives at the Expense of Rural Malian Communities?

Scott M. Lacy

BEFORE THE FRENCH-LED INTENSIFICATION of cotton production in colonial West Africa, family farmers in southern Mali grew regional varieties of cotton for a strong domestic market and for self-sufficient household consumption (clothing, blankets, fishing nets, string, etc.). Starting in the 1890s, commercial and colonial interests worked for decades shaping Malian cotton production in an attempt to capture cotton harvests for French textile mills. By 1950 the colonial state was spending approximately 70 percent of its resources on the intensification of cotton production, targeting southern Mali through the introduction of new varieties, agricultural extension, price subventions, and support for rural investment in machinery and fertilizer (Roberts 1996, 280). Before the introduction of incentives like agricultural extension and credit for purchasing plows and agrochemicals, family farmers in Mali resisted expanding household production beyond local needs.

In Dissan, a village in the Bougouni region of southern Mali (fig. 8.1), elders explained that cotton came with plows; widespread extra-household cotton production and farmer credits followed the installation of a regional cotton processing facility in the 1960s. Dissan

Fig. 8.1. Location of Dissan study site.

farmers acquired plows in the 1960s from the Compagnie Malienne pour le Développement des Fibres Textiles (CMDT), a state agency created by the government of Mali's first president, Modibo Keïta. In the 1970s the CMDT worked with villages to organize cotton producer collectives and began transferring to these village associations production responsibilities such as ordering and distributing inputs, and managing credits and payments (Bingen, Serrano, and Howard 2003, 410–11). The efficacy of the village association strategy developed by the CMDT in the 1970s eventually transformed this once regional program into a national one. Today the CMDT remains the primary agency for agricultural extension services in many southern Malian communities.

Before 2003 communities throughout Mali organized cotton production through village associations (AV) based on the CMDT model, one association per village. For decades this AV system endured few substantial changes, but starting in late 2002 CMDT extension agents across southern Mali visited villages to explain that farmers would soon be given the freedom to determine the membership and size of their cotton collectives, including the option of forming multiple subvillage collectives. The freedom to choose the membership and size of one's local cotton grower association may help some producers prevent monetary losses stemming from the crop failures of other village producers, but this freedom may further complicate the economic and social viability of producers and communities in crisis.

Farmers in Dissan first learned in November 2002 of the new CMDT system for cotton collectives, and within two years the former AV splintered into two independent collectives. Together, the new collectives reaped a 2004 harvest nearly equal to Dissan's combined 2002 and 2003 harvests (see table 8.1). Following a description of both the old and new systems for organizing community cotton production through the CMDT, I describe farmer perspectives of their transitions into the new system, including the immediate and potential long-term impacts of these changes in rural Malian communities.

Table 8.1. Aggregate Dissan cotton harvests recorded at CMDT facility, Bougouni, 2002–4

	Cotton collective system in use	Total number of cotton grower households	Aggregate harvest (kg)
2002	1 AV	50	70,740
2003	1 AV	52	70,700
2004	2 CPCs	49	113,960

Methods

This chapter is based on two field studies in southern Mali: a fifteen-month study in 2001/2 and a two-month follow-up study in 2004. While living and working with family farmers in the village of Dissan, I conducted two extensive surveys to learn about household agricultural production, including farmer practices and knowledge of local crops and growing environments. In the first two months of the study, I surveyed all sixty-six Dissan households and conducted a comprehensive census of the community to acquire baseline data on household farm production and resources. Before the planting season, in March and April 2002, I interviewed a stratified sample of Dissan households ($n = 20$) to further investigate farmer knowledge and production practices. After completing the two major surveys, I spent the growing season apprenticing with four households to actively learn about the resources and annual production cycle of Dissan farmers. In 2004 I returned to Dissan to conduct a brief follow-up study. Qualitative data used in this chapter come from ethnographic field notes, individual interviews, and a series of informal group interviews recorded during the 2001/2 and 2004 field studies.

Study Community

I was introduced to Dissan in 1994 when I lived there as Peace Corps volunteer. Dissan is a farming community of less than a thousand people who trace the origins of their village as far back as the seventeenth century (Lacy 2004, 83–85). Bamanakan is the primary language spoken in Dissan, however, some community members also speak other languages including Arabic, French, Fulani, and Wolof. Every family in Dissan depends on rain-fed agriculture for subsistence, including the three teachers of the village primary school who farm when school is out to supplement their salaries.

Dissan is located twenty-eight kilometers from Bougouni—an industrial town with an urban/periurban population of approximately 273,000 (Ministère de l'Administration Territoriale et de Collectivités Locals de la République du Mali 1998). Bougouni and Sido, two market towns frequented by Dissan villagers, sit on the paved road that extends south from Mali's capital city Bamako onward to Ferkessédougou, Côte d'Ivoire.

In December 2001 there were 881 people living in sixty-six households in Dissan. The household is an extended family that lives, eats, and works together using common resources. Depending on its size, a household (*du*, in Bamanakan) shares either a single compound or a conglomeration of adjacent compounds composed of shaded sitting areas, sleeping quarters, cooking huts, and various storage constructions. The mean number of people per household was thirteen (SD = 8.9). Annual rainfall in the region is low and extremely variable, making rain-fed agricultural production a complex and risky enterprise (Touré 2003). Though Dissan is in a relatively wet region of Mali sometimes referred to as the cotton zone, even in good years when many households harvest enough grain to last the year, other households will suffer food shortages.

In 2001, Dissan households used hand-held hoes, collective labor, and animal-traction plows to cultivate a combined total of nearly 350 hectares of field crops. In this village, area devoted to cotton production is second only to sorghum, the most widely grown cereal in the community. Among the households that grew cotton, the mean was 1.59 hectares per household ($n = 37$), compared with 2.35 hectares of sorghum per household ($n = 58$). Farmers typically produce sorghum for household consumption and grow cotton as a cash crop or as a means for procuring agricultural inputs and short-term credit (or both). Data from the 2001 survey show that households who acquire credit and inputs through the CMDT are the households that plant the most sorghum; they also are more likely to have expensive farm equipment like cultivators, seeders, plows, donkey carts, and sprayers for applying chemical inputs such as pesticides (table 8.2).

Table 8.2. Sorghum cultivation and ownership of farm equipment by household, Dissan, 2001

| | Mean sorghum ha/HH | Percentage of HHs owning: | | | | |
		Plow	Cultivator	Seeder	Donkey cart	Spray pump
CMDT households, $n = 41$	2.8	88	71	46	61	49
Non-CMDT households, $n = 25$	1.7	36	12	4	8	0

CMDT and Collective Cotton Production
in Dissan, 1974–2002

In 1974 the CMDT started the process of transferring to villages responsibility for cotton grading, weighing, orders for equipment and inputs, and credit management (Bingen 2000, 357). At first, the CMDT appointed existing village social organizations as the body responsible for such tasks, but by the late 1970s it had established an AV system for southern Mali managed by community officers, including president, treasurer, and secretary. With World Bank financing, the CMDT organized literacy and numeracy programs in Bamanakan to teach farmers skills for effectively managing village cotton production. The AV program proved to be so efficient by CMDT standards that it eventually became national policy.

As the AV system took hold in southern Mali, many Dissan farmers began acquiring more household money through cotton production. The AV system consolidated all Dissan farmers into a single cooperative for organizing local production (see table 8.3). This system and responsibility spread individual risk among all village cotton farmers and consolidated fiscal accounting into manageable units for the CMDT. Every year, after receiving one lump sum for the entire village's cotton harvest, the AV distributed crop payments to individual members. When poor harvests or household crop failures led any number of producers to default on their individual loans, the AV absorbed those debts. In 2001, for example, two Dissan households defaulted on their loans and although both households repaid over half their debts, an outstanding balance of roughly US$300 remained. A small number by some standards, $300 accounted for only 2.5 percent of all Dissan loans that year. From an individual perspective that total is much more daunting considering that the annual per capita income in Mali was $239 in 2001 (World Bank 2003). Furthermore, these economic indicators fail to capture any social discord or peripheral economic hardships endured by individuals and communities as a result of loan defaults.

Once established, the AV system provided farmer access to credit, it established de facto community security nets for cotton farmers and gave rural populations a formidable voice in regional and national agricultural policy. Siaka Sangare, long-standing secretary of Dissan's AV, explained that in 1989, when the CMDT attempted to restructure the AV credit system, producers across the country, including Dissan, used their AVs to organize a cotton strike. Through AV leaders, the CMDT brokered a deal that was acceptable to farmers, and the strike was averted (USAID-Mali 2003). However, in 2000 many Dissan farmers joined a national cotton strike in protest of unpaid harvests and low purchase prices. The CMDT typically set purchase prices after the planting season for cotton, forcing farmers to purchase inputs on credit and organize production without any certainty of how much they would earn for their investments. Largely due to a saturated global market, not to mention enormous U.S. subsidies for industrial U.S. cotton producers, international prices for cotton fell significantly in 1998 and 1999. Falling prices translated into significant operating deficits for the CMDT, which meant farmers in Dissan and elsewhere had to bear the brunt of these economic losses. In 1998 the CMDT purchase price for cotton was 185 CFA francs (FCFA) per kilogram, and the price dropped to FCFA 150 in 1999 (USAID-Mali 2003). Secretary Sangare noted that unexpected lower prices in 1999 put some Dissan farmers in debt, leading many to abandon the crop the following year. However, in 2001, when the CMDT guaranteed a good purchase price before planting (FCFA 200/kg), many farmers returned to cotton production. The national cotton strike certainly influenced the favorable price of cotton in 2001, but rippling effects of the strike extended further; in late 2002 the CMDT announced the AV system would undergo major organizational changes.

The Meeting

In November 2002, shortly after most households had harvested their cotton, the CMDT extension agent who works in Dissan, visited the AV to call an important meeting. The extension agent was an agricultural engineer trained in Katiabougou, Mali, and at the University of Dijon in France. The meeting was one of thousands throughout Mali, organized to familiarize farmers with fundamental changes to the organizational structure of cotton collectives in Mali (Diallo 2004). Though renamed, the AV could still serve as a villagewide collective, but under the new system, the AV could be composed of any number of independently organized, subvillage collectives. Using diagrams on the chalkboard of a dilapidated one-room schoolhouse, the extension agent explained in Bamanakan how the new system would empower farmers.

With children peeking in windows and with the sounds of chickens and donkeys in the background, the extension agent sat at a table in front of thirty-five farmers seated on weathered desktops. The CMDT representative began with an announcement: after the 2002 harvest, the CMDT would encourage Malian cotton farmers to establish new collectives that permit members to associate themselves at the subvillage level. According to the agent, villagewide associations reduce incentives for skilled, large-scale producers, because these producers would bear financial liability for the catastrophic crop losses and the irresponsible credit management of other farmers. The agent occasionally looked down at his notes as he discussed the regulations for forming the new cotton collectives. Farmers listened patiently, a few with modest disinterest, as the agent described eight new rules.

- Each group will be called a CPC (coopératif pour les producteurs cotonnière).

- Each CPC must have at least five producers And/or a minimum of ten separate cotton fields.

- Each CPC must produce an annual minimum of 30 metric tons of cotton (slightly less than half of Dissan's combined total of 70.7 tonnes produced in 2002).

- CPC members must be from the same village (associations with people from multiple villages are prohibited)

- Every CPC member must have a certificate of residency (obtainable for a small fee from a regional administrator)

- Each member must sign an official document containing CPC bylaws, organizational structure, and a description of responsibilities for each CPC officer. The document, written in Bamanakan, is made official with the approval and signature of all CPC members and a CMDT officer.

- Each CPC operates for three years, after which it must be renewed as is, modified and renewed, or disbanded.

- All Dissan CPCs collectively constitute the Union des Coopératif de Dissan.

The extension agent reinforced several CPC policies before taking questions from farmers. First, he explained some of the benefits of the new CPC system. For example, if someone in a CPC turns out to be a poor associate or a bad worker, at the end of the three-year term of the CPC, members can vote to expel the underperforming associate. Meanwhile, CPC members must pay the debts of fellow members in default, but as CPC members they would have recourse. If necessary a CPC can take legal action against members in default using a CMDT legal service available to all CPC members. Some farmers raised their eyebrows when the agent described how the CPC system deals with chronic debtors and rule breakers: in the worse cases, a judge will dispatch gendarmes to claim payment or in-kind restitution. The agent also said that the CPC system will equate to money for community improvements and projects. Under the former system the AV received from the CMDT a sum equal to 2 percent of the gross price of all Dissan cotton delivered to the CMDT scales. These funds were used according to AV by-laws for: operational costs (20 percent), officer stipends (30 percent), and community development projects (50 percent). The extension agent explained that under the CPC system, defaulted loans of farmers who lose money on cotton production would no longer drain funds earmarked for community service.

Throughout the meeting, the CMDT representative focused on a central theme, the power of a strong collective voice. Farmers in attendance nodded their heads as the agent recalled how AVs unified farmers during the cotton strike of 2000. Using an intricate diagram of circles within circles, the extension agent demonstrated that the work and efforts of each CPC will have a single, strong voice, while the village collective—the Union des Coopératif de Dissan—will have an even stronger voice that can represent all Dissan CPCs. Although this well-worn selling point may sound trite, there is no doubt that AVs helped farmers organize and amplify their voices en masse in 1989 and 2000, when they successfully convinced CMDT authorities to address farmer concerns regarding AV policy and cotton prices (Lacy 2004, 107–8).

From my perspective as an observer, perhaps the most salient yet understated point raised by the extension agent during the meeting was that farmers could use the management skills they develop as members of CPCs to form cooperatives for other crops or animal husbandry. As the meeting drew to a close, some of the biggest cotton producers in Dissan voiced skeptical interest and tacit approval for the new system, but a few producers—one of whom with considerable, old cotton debts—expressed concern about the potential difficulties they may face if they hope to join a CPC to obtain credit.

Farmer Perspectives of the CPC System

Following the meeting I talked with several farmers and asked them to describe their reactions to the CPC program. Although most farmers voiced cautious or little interest in the new CPCs, two of them held completely opposite opinions. The first farmer, an elder named Sidike Sangare said he was suspicious of the new system. During the meeting Sangare remarked that farmers who default on loans eventually pay their debts, and should not be expelled from a group, chased by gendarmes, nor excluded from cotton production, particularly when their households may be in crisis. Under the CPC system the de facto safety net provided by the AV would be transformed into several smaller nets, spreading larger risks among smaller groups of producers. After the meeting Sangare predicted he would not grow cotton the following year.

On the other side of the spectrum, AV officer Burama Tarawele expressed great optimism about the CPC system. Tarawele was visiting Dissan from Bougoumbala, a neighboring village, and was present at the Dissan meeting. Immediately following the meeting Tarawele said he was pleased the CMDT was finally addressing the problem he termed, "the politics of CMDT." Echoing the extension agent's words, from Tarawele's point of view, the former AV system was counter-productive for large-scale cotton producers like him. Before the formal initiation of the CPC program in the region, Tarawele had already created a CPC in his village; he and two other farmers decided to create a subvillage collective to independently procure credit and inputs through the CMDT. Though leaving their village-wide cotton association created some quarreling in the village, Tarawele believes people now understand why he and his two partners left the Bougoumbala AV (*decentralization* was the term Tarawele used). He said that the CMDT cooperated with this decentralization because he and his co-horts—all large-scale producers—threatened to refuse to grow cotton. Tarawele said the CPC program will be good for Mali cotton farmers, but warned that many farmers do not really have the skills to apply for, acquire and properly manage independent loans. He acquired his banking and management skills in CMDT workshops and as the former secretary of his village AV. Tarawele plans on intensifying cotton production in order to invest in cattle and animal husbandry.

Dissan Creates Two CPCs

In 2003 Dissan farmers were able to create the first CPCs but instead they chose to remain as a single AV. Later that year, however, after several quarrels related to a confidential financial dispute, farmers made a decision that would not have been an option just two years earlier. Because the new CPC system encouraged subvillage collectives, farmers resolved their dispute with the dissolution of the villagewide AV. Then the former AV leader formed a CPC with seven other households, while the remaining forty-one cotton-producing households banded together to form a second, much larger CPC. The larger of the two groups built a separate storage shed, and by the start of the 2004 growing season both CPCs were operational. Though factors like rainfall and pest control have plenty to do with successful cotton

Table 8.3. Annual cycle of cotton production under AV system, 1974–2002

March–June	**AV officers organize input orders and credit** Officers solicit initial orders from members (for seeds, input, and credit) Officers request materials and credit based on preliminary orders Officers receive CMDT form and deliver it to BNDA to activate credit
	Inputs purchased and delivered on credit via CMDT BNDA transfers AV loan money to CMDT CMDT delivers seed and inputs via contractor AV receives and distributes seed and inputs to members
June–December	Individual households farm their cotton fields
December–January	**AV coordinates "cotton market" after harvest** Households deliver their cotton to central location in village CMDT sends scale to village, followed by one of many trucks AV hires farmers to weigh each household's harvest before loading trucks AV workers fill truck; truck hauls cotton for processing Truck returns for next load until all cotton is weighed and transported
February–March	**AV manages payments to members** CMDT delivers lump-sum payment for cotton crop (minus credits) AV officers account for credits, debts, and salaries for officers and workers AV officers distribute remaining money as payments to farmers for their crops

farming, they alone do not explain why aggregate Dissan cotton harvests nearly doubled in one year under the stewardship of two independent subvillage collectives (see table 8.1). Following wildly successful harvests, Dissan farmers report positive initial experiences with both CPCs, but their long-term experiences may not be so optimistic.

Membership in the smaller CPC was not directly based on production levels, but on family alliances and relationships. That said, a cursory look at some of the characteristics of "small-CPC households" indicates that the bifurcation of Dissan's AV consolidated some of the village's more wealthy households apart from the larger community (see table 8.4). In other villages across southern Mali, cotton cultivation has been shown to contribute to the exacerbated economic disparity among households (Moseley 2005, 46–49). In 2007 both Dissan CPCs will have the choice to renew or modify their membership rosters (or both), and by then farmers' evaluations of the CPC system will begin to demonstrate the positive and negative effects of the decentralization of villagewide collectives.

Table 8.4. Smaller CPC households versus all other households, Dissan, 2001

	small CPC HHs	other HHs
Number of		
households	8	58
people per HH	23	12
field hectares cultivated, 2001	10.3	5
% households owning		
plow	100	65
cattle	100	58
cultivator	100	46
donkey cart	100	42
seeder	83	25

Note: Based on data from household survey, November 2001.

Will Subvillage Collectives Increase Poverty, Wealth, or Both?

Every year after the CMDT has collected cotton harvests from villages all across the region, local farmers listen intently as Bougouni radio stations announce final production totals for their villages. Cotton is undeniably a major focus of household agricultural production in southern Mali, and transforming the AV system with subvillage-level cooperatives (CPCs) will affect different farmers in different ways. Depending on the resources, skills, and experience of individual producers, the CPC system could equate to new opportunities and exclusion from cotton production and farmer credit.

In the short term, successful cotton farmers capable of acquiring and managing credit stand to gain more autonomy over production choices. Furthermore, provided they associate with other stable producers, these farmers may reduce the risk of losses from cotton profits due to crop failures or mismanagement by others. Farmers known to have defaulted on previous loans, whose households may be in crisis (labor shortage, debt, chronic crop loss), face potential difficulties if they ask to join or create a CPC. Just as elder Sidike Sangare predicted he would stop farming cotton because his old cotton debts make him an undesirable associate, Burama Tarawele formed his own CPC to avoid associating with unreliable or crisis-prone farmers. Cotton may not be an equally appealing nor accessible crop choice for farmers of different means.

Elder Sangare was not the only farmer to question whether cotton farming was a worthwhile endeavor. Even before the CMDT announced the changes for cotton collectives, Dissan farmers debated whether or not cotton was "worth it." The Dissan *ton* (a villagewide collective labor organization) decided that in 2002 they would grow peanuts instead of cotton to raise group funds. This decision was based on the idea that peanuts were a less risky crop and would not require nearly as much labor, in contrast with cotton. Equally important, peanut crops do not require major investment costs for fertilizer, herbicide, and insecticide.

In June 2002, when the Dissan AV met to distribute cotton inputs to village producers, the AV officers arrived at the meeting to find farmers arguing over the risks associated with cotton production. AV secretary Sangare temporarily subdued the heated discussion by delivering a message from the CMDT; the regional extension agent asked Sangare to remind farmers that cotton would remain a good way to earn money. Sangare explained that the agent recently visited several local communities only to learn that many farmers in the region had decided to forgo cotton production. After Sangare's announcement, farmers discussed the relative merits and risks of cotton farming, but the discussion was a brief and relatively futile exercise because by their very presence at this particular meeting, those farmers had already decided to grow cotton in 2002.

Ultimately, cotton production and cotton collectives are long established in the Dissan community and in villages throughout southern Mali. The CPC system is likely to generate new debates and questions about the social, ecological, and financial ramifications of household cotton production in southern Mali, but exactly how these subvillage collectives may or may not transform local production and socioeconomic dynamics has yet to be determined. In the long term, three critical issues will determine the success or failure of the CPC system: the exclusion principle, the efficacy of CPCs in expanding the idea and benefits of cooperatives beyond cotton fields, and strengthening the individual and collective voices of cotton farmers. In southern Mali, household cotton production typically excludes women and poorer households, who, as a result, have limited access to extension services and inputs (Moseley 2001, 187).

On the one hand, CPCs may lead farmers to exclude crisis-prone producers like elder Sidike Sangare, but CPCs also have the potential to open new opportunities for formerly excluded farmers. Investing in human capacity in terms of ensuring farmers who want to create a cooperative have the financial and literacy skills necessary to protect their own interests could also, with no small effort, bring women and poorer farmers into their own credit-worthy collectives, particularly if the CPC cotton model is successful in encouraging the formation of new cooperatives for other crops and animal husbandry. After all, if literate farmers with proven track records and strong financial management skills (acquiring and managing credit) break off into subvillage collectives, as they have done in Dissan, they might be less able or less willing to assist those farmers with different skill sets and resources. This new, localized manifestation of brain drain and wealth consolidation has the potential to exacerbate social and financial inequality, rendering cotton as a crop for relatively wealthier households. In the recent past, producer organizations like cotton collectives have been shown to amplify the voices of farmers in southern Mali (Bingen, Serrano, and Howard 2003, 407). In the end, what may determine the success or failure of the CPC program is whether or not it bolsters or diminishes the voices and opportunities of all farmers.

Note

I thank the village of Dissan and the four households that apprenticed me in their fields (Sumayila Sangare ka so, Sedu Mama Sangare ka so, Samba Sangare ka so, and Bakari Jakite ka so). I also thank Siaka Sangare, who collaborated in the 2001 and 2002 Dissan surveys, and Eva Weltzein and Fred Rattunde of ICRISAT-Mali for generously sharing their knowledge, time, and resources. I received support for the 2001/2 field study from Fulbright IIE, and the Department of Anthropology at UCSB. Additional support for project analysis was provided by the Fletcher Jones Foundation of Los Angeles and the University of California.

References

Bingen, James R. 2000. "Prospects for Development and Democracy in West Africa: Agrarian Politics in Mali." In *Democracy and Development in Mali*, ed. James R. Bingen, David Robinson, and John M. Staatz, 349–68. East Lansing: Michigan State University Press.

Bingen, Jim, Alex Serrano, and Julie Howard. 2003. "Linking Farmers to Markets: Different Approaches to Human Capital Development." *Food Policy* 28:405–19.

Diallo, Madou. 2004. "Situation scolaire: L'heure de vérité à Koulouba." *Le républicain*, December 8. http://www.planeteafrique.com/Web/

LeDiplomate/Index.asp? affiche=newsdatabase_show.asp&cmd
=articledetail&articleid=252.

Lacy, Scott M. 2004. "One Finger Cannot Lift a Stone: Family Farmers and Sorghum Production in Southern Mali." PhD dissertation, University of California, Santa Barbara.

Ministère de l'Administration Territoriale et de Collectivités Locals de la République du Mali 1998. Census data posted on the ministry's Web site, www.matcl.gov.ml, not accessible at the time this went to press.

Moseley, William G. 2001. "Sahelian 'White Gold' and Rural Poverty-Environment Interactions: The Political Ecology of Cotton Production, Environmental Change, and Household Food Economy in Mali." PhD dissertation, University of Georgia.

———. 2005. "Global Cotton and Local Environment Management: The Political Ecology of Rich and Poor Small-Hold Farmers in Southern Mali." *Geographic Journal* 171 (1): 36–55.

Republique du Mali. 1998. *Recensement général de la population et de l'habitat 1998: Résultats provisoires.* Ministère de l'économie, du plan et de l'intégration, Direction nationale de la statistique et de l'informatique, Bamako.

Roberts, Richard. 1996. *Two Worlds of Cotton: Colonialism and the Regional Economy in the French Soudan, 1800–1946.* Stanford, CA: Stanford University Press.

Touré, Aboucar. 2004. *Édition mensuelle—pluviométrie—Bougouni, 1980–2003.* Bamako: Institut d'Économie Rural.

USAID-Mali. 2003. "Production and Export Opportunities and Constraints for Coarse Grains." www.usaid.org.ml/mes_photos/production_and_e.

World Bank. 2003. *World Development Indicators 2003.* Washington, DC: World Bank. CD-ROM.

Part III

Alternate Futures

Genetically Engineered and Organic Cotton

9

Genetically Engineered Cotton

Politics, Science, and Power in West Africa

Jim Bingen

Problem Setting

IN OCTOBER 2005 the director of the National Agricultural and Environmental Research Institute (INERA) in Burkina Faso held an open house for 150 international researchers and journalists in Bobo-Dioulasso to publicize the "good results" of the institute's Bt cotton research trials. According to the director, these trials showed that pesticide use could be reduced by 80 percent, yet increase yields by 30 to 40 percent. The secretary general of the National Union of Burkinabé Producers, as well, welcomed the trial results and emphasized their promise of both production gains and the reduced need for highly toxic and risky pesticides.[1]

This enthusiasm for genetically engineered (GE) cotton[2] is not isolated to a research station in Burkina Faso. In fact, some argue that Africa is watching "the gene revolution pass it by." Recent production figures on biotech cotton would seem to confirm that observation. According to the International Cotton Advisory Committee (ICAC),[3] in 2003 biotech varieties of cotton were planted over 21 percent of the world's cotton area in nine countries, but on the African continent this included only South Africa.

Just across the border from the INERA research station, however, many Malian producers are much less enthusiastic about the promises of Bt cotton and they have joined a coalition of seventeen farmers' groups and regional associations to express their concerns about protecting the region's biodiversity (*patrimoine génétique africain*). Moreover, a recent report notes that smallholder Bt cotton production in South Africa has fallen by 80 percent since 2000.[4] After Indonesians burned their Bt cotton in 2002, and Indian farmers protested its introduction in Andhra Pradesh in 2004, perhaps the separate concerns from farmers in Mali and South Africa, as well as others, justify a critical look at the "bollgardization" of cotton production in sub-Saharan Africa.[5]

Within the last five years, West African cotton farmers have become politically prominent in the global trade debates surrounding cotton subsidies. This new international role and recognition reflects the results of several years of partnering and organizational investment among nongovernmental organizations to establish both local and regional networks representing the interests of cotton farmers. Confronted with the apparent benefits of Bt cotton, will they be able to take a similarly progressive global profile with respect to genetically engineered cotton? What are the opportunities and challenges confronting West African cotton farmers to move in solidarity with cotton farmers elsewhere in the world?

This chapter takes the position that the current promotion of genetically engineered cotton in sub-Saharan Africa embodies a mutually supportive set of business, scientific, and governmental interests which disempower smallholder African cotton farmers. Without question, the promotion of GE cotton illustrates the long-standing silver bullet mentality, and an easily seductive technocentric paradigm of African agricultural development. But I argue that the technological promises of GE cotton conceal the presence of a scientific-economic structure that undermines democratic development and jeopardizes many of the recent gains achieved by the collective global action of African farmers. Instead of investing in biotechnology, I suggest that investments in the democratization of research offers more promise for African agricultural and rural development.

GE Cotton—"Starting with the ABC of It"[6]

The letters *Bt* stand for *Bacillus thuringiensis*, a common toxin-producing soil bacterium. Molecular biological techniques are used to insert one or more genes from this bacterium into cotton. These genetically modified, or engineered, cotton plants then produce or express the Bt toxin as they grow, and thereby help to control boll-worm (*Helicoverpa* spp.) damage. In 1996 Monsanto introduced its trademark Bollgard variety, followed in 2003 by Bollgard II the next generation of Bt cotton varieties that controls for a wider range of caterpillar pests than the original Bollgard technology.[7] Dow Agro-Sciences introduced its trademark WideStrike variety in 2004, and Syngenta joins these companies in research to develop varieties that are both insect and herbicide resistant.

Very simply, Bt cotton is designed to eliminate the need to spray pesticides to control bollworm infestations. The second generation of Bollgard technology is intended to suppress damage by other pests and reduce the need for supplemental spraying, which was commonly required for the first-generation varieties. Some studies question the effectiveness of the new-generation technology, but it would appear to address the critical need to reduce pesticide use and thereby contribute to improved cotton production throughout sub-Saharan Africa. In particular, the commonly cited benefits of Bt cotton include reduced pesticide use, runoff, and farming risks as well as support for beneficial insects and wildlife.

THE COTTON PEST PROBLEM

Insects—not diseases or fungi—are the main cause of crop damage and losses in cotton throughout sub-Saharan Africa.[8] These insects include aphids, sucking and pricking insects, and worms (bollworms), all of which attack the leaves and bolls and feed on the cotton plant at various stages in its life cycle. Insect damage varies widely by country, but in areas where damage is considered to be "relatively moderate," yield losses may average 30 percent per year. For years, cotton pests have been controlled through program spraying—that is, by a specific number and type of applications over specified intervals of time throughout the growing season. A common formula involves a fourteen-day program with a total of four to six applications. Program treatments do reduce losses, but they also account for 25 to 30 percent of a smallholder's total input costs.

The insecticides used are pyrethroid-organophosphate mixtures, which are moderately toxic to mammals and usually quite toxic to birds, fish, and beneficial insects, including bees.[9] Few, if any, studies of the environmental impacts have been undertaken, but farmers report the alarming disappearance of bees in the older cotton-growing zones. Some groundwater pollution studies have been carried out long after the growing season and the last pesticide application, thereby making it difficult to identify the degree of pesticide contamination in ground or surface water.

Efforts to manage pesticide resistance with synthetic chemicals have created tragic results. In 1995 cotton bollworm (*Helicoverpa armigera*) resistance to the relatively nontoxic pyrethroids became problematic and was compounded by additional damage from whiteflies (*Bemisia tabaci*). In response, the cotton companies in West and central Africa reintroduced endosulfan, a highly toxic chlorinated hydrocarbon, that quickly proved disastrous. During 2000 in Benin, thirty-seven people were killed and at least another thirty-six became seriously ill from eating maize that had been contaminated from spraying cotton, and from reusing pesticide containers for drinking water. In addition, as many observers have pointed out for several years, farmers do not wear protective clothing and practically nothing is known about the chronic poisoning that occurs from inhalation and dermal exposure, especially since low-protein diets engender a higher susceptibility to pesticide poisoning.

Alternative solutions are also problematic and illustrate the well-known "pesticide treadmill." In the absence of developing biologically based integrated pest management programs to manage pest resistance, researchers continue to develop increasingly more powerful synthetic chemical formulations in order to respond to the resistance developed by insects. Research has helped to reduce the volume of pesticides used, but only by increasing the toxicity by weight.

Recent figures from India would appear to confirm the interest of smallholder farmers in adopting Bt cotton as a means to overcome the problems related to the continuing reliance on synthetic pesticides. However, as Stephen Greenberg from the African Centre for Biosafety observes, "only 5% of GM cotton is grown by smallholders in South Africa . . . [and the] apparent successes of the technology amongst African smallholders in South Africa are premised on concentrated institutional, financial and technical support that is unlikely to be replicated in many places" (2004, 4).[10] Evidence from current production, farmers' practices, and the production conditions imposed on farmers offers an equally ambiguous response.

"Getting . . . to the XYZ of It"

YIELDS

The initial field trials in Burkina Faso may be promising, but the Bt cotton yields achieved by smallholders are at best mixed. The available evidence does not suggest significant yield improvement with GE cotton varieties. A study of Bt and conventional cotton in India during 2003 showed that conventional varieties outperformed Bt varieties. In another study farmers' yields fell by 35 percent when they grew Bt cotton. Some differences may arise from the specific Bt variety planted. Hillocks confirms that adapting Bt varieties to local conditions is critical to the long-term success of a GE cotton strategy: "If they are not, then they will not out-yield the locally adapted conventional varieties" (2005, 135).

Hermann Waibel and his colleagues (2005) caution against an overoptimistic interpretation of initial studies. First, there is "a considerable degree of uncertainty" in "the data collected or made available for the assessment of GMOs" (154). Second, based on their retrospective analysis of the economics of pesticide use, they remind us that a "careful economic analysis . . . [and] . . . critical benefit assessment is important because there is a tendency among scientists to be overoptimistic at the beginning. . . . As long as the risks of GMOs are poorly understood, an overestimation of their benefits can be highly misleading. . . . Simply looking at yield can lead to the wrong conclusions" (153).

PESTICIDE USE

Bt cotton promises to lower input costs through reduced pesticide use, and fewer pesticide applications means reduced health risk and exposure for all family members. Nevertheless, even with Bt cotton, pesticides are required for the management of nontarget species. Confirming the results of a 1999 USDA survey, Mensah (2002, 104) found that the new generation of Bt cotton (Ingard) "did not result in a consistent reduction of pesticide applications on transgenic versus conventional cotton crops." Thus, fulfilling the promise of Bt cotton goes significantly beyond the adoption of a new genetically engineered variety, or a reductionist "component-by-component" approach to production. It requires taking a more systemic perspective on integrated crop management. This means that a new technology, such as a Bt variety, must be introduced in the context of agricultural diversification and not as part of a strategy to simplify and homogenize crop production. The introduction of Bt cotton must not be seen as simply a matter of adopting another variety or using a new pest management tool, but as part of a peasant farmer's overall crop management strategy.

Adopting this perspective raises some serious concerns about the conditions for the successful introduction of Bt cotton—conditions that are not being addressed through controlled trials on research stations such as those in Burkina Faso. Hillocks notes, "because of generally poor levels of crop management among cotton smallholders in Africa, Bt cottons are unlikely to deliver yield gains without addressing the crop management issues. . . . [Evidence from] . . . India [shows that without attention to crop management] . . . Bt cotton varieties have failed to deliver yield benefits sufficient to cover the purchase price of the seed and savings on pesticide have been insufficient to deliver an overall cost benefit" (2005, 135).

To date, the research results on the relationship of Bt cotton and integrated crop management are mixed. Some research indicates that

Bt cotton has no chronic, long-term effects on nontarget species, many of which are bollworm enemies. Other research in the United States indicates that some pests become more problematic because of a reduction in the use of broad-spectrum insecticides for boll worm control. Finally, in the absence of a clearly defined resistance management strategy that involves planting a non-Bt cotton "refuge" area, some cotton pests will develop resistance to Bt cotton.[11]

Contrary to expectations that resistance management simply involved the "need to routinely re-engineer cotton with new genes that will produce toxins with different modes of action" (ICAC 2000, 6), ICAC now recognized that "the evolution of resistance in the target insect pest or weed complex is the major challenge to the sustainable use of biotech cottons" (ICAC 2004, 3). Meeting this challenge requires combined technical understanding and institutional capacity, neither of which are obvious in Burkina Faso or similar trials planned in other countries.

First, "pragmatic, yet scientifically valid" strategies must be fashioned around "a sound ecological understanding" of different and specific farming systems and "an ordered process that engages all stakeholders to identify a workable response." Second, the assumptions guiding Bt cotton research for large-scale, mechanized conditions may be inappropriate for the "diverse mosaic" of African smallholder production systems (ICAC 2004, 3). Specifically, the conditions of smallholder cotton production raise serious questions about the effectiveness of relying on refuges in order to manage resistance to Bt. Can West African governments or cotton companies incur the costs of refuge monitoring and enforcement that in other countries are now incurred by the seed companies? How could cotton production programs prevent peasant farmers from planting only their poor-quality land—assuming they had access to additional land—in a refuge crop, and thereby compromising the effectiveness of the refuge? Under smallholder conditions, what kind of incentives could be designed to encourage farmers to plant refuges? Of all of the strategies under consideration—such as resistance user fees or tradable refuge permits, only the "mixed seed strategy," which requires farmers to plant mixed conventional and Bt cotton, appears feasible in West Africa.

However, such a strategy does not inform the current Bt cotton research agenda in West Africa and it further complicates concerns about protecting the region's biodiversity.

ENVIRONMENTAL EFFECTS

A large group of West African nongovernmental and farmer groups call for public attention to the effects of Bt cotton (and other genetically engineered crops) on the region's biodiversity.[12] This cautionary approach is based on several straightforward reasons: Bt cotton is not visibly different from conventional cotton, and mixing is therefore inevitable—especially if a mixed seed strategy as noted above is adopted.

The environmental and economic consequences of such mixing are serious:

- Once a transgene is introduced into the environment, it is difficult if not impossible to remove it if harmful effects for human or environmental health are discovered;

- Gene flow could occur between Bt cotton and local varieties or wild species of cotton, thereby jeopardizing these reserves of biodiversity; and

- Contamination by Bt cotton could compromise the entire production of organic cotton in the region, since organic certification criteria prohibit GMOs.

The available biological evidence suggests that protecting biological diversity in West Africa is more a management than a technical issue—but again one that is not incorporated into current research protocols. As the Second Expert Panel on Biotechnology in Cotton cautions, a pre-adoption environmental risk assessment "needs to take account of the limited resources available in many developing countries and, hence, set a priority on defining a required minimum set of locally derived data" (ICAC 2004, 3).

PROPRIETARY INTERESTS

Several aspects of the specific genes to be transferred, as well as cotton transformation and regeneration, are protected by patents. These patents identify intellectual property rights (IPR) that can stimulate new research and innovation. But these same patents may also create serious constraints that jeopardize the livelihoods of smallholder cotton farmers.

In West Africa, farmers receive their cottonseed and production supplies and sell their cotton to government-sanctioned cotton companies with monopsony power over production and marketing. Currently, farmers are free to exchange and redistribute their seed to neighbors, friends, and family members. With the introduction of Bt cotton, not only would this practice be illegal, but it is unlikely that farmers will be very interested in accommodating to the more restrictive conditions of the new technology.

If Bt cotton is introduced in West Africa, as it has been in South Africa and elsewhere, as a proprietary product, then farmers will be required to pay an additional "technology fee." Based on studies among smallholders in South Africa, the seed costs and technology fees outweigh any savings from the reduced need for insecticide. Equally important, if farmers are prevented from redistributing the seed, it is hard to imagine that they would willingly sign, much less accept the conditions of, the typical "technology use agreement" required to grow Bt cotton. Under these agreements, farmers must agree not to save seed for replanting or give seed to anyone else (including a spouse), and to pay a fine and legal fees if they violate the contract.

How many West African smallholders would even understand these contracts? Who will ensure that farmers understand the implications of the agreements? With no visible difference between Bt and conventional cotton, plus the need to cultivate both types together—as part of the resistance management strategy—how feasible is it for smallholders to separate their seed supplies? Who will enforce these contracts and play the police role that Monsanto has played everywhere else in the world to control its proprietary interests? How feasible will it be to enforce the agreements, much less ensure that resistance management practices are followed, in areas that are remote and often difficult to access during the growing season? At a minimum, if countries go forward with Bt cotton, they will need to consider farmers' rights as well as the costs and benefits of their seed multiplication and distribution regulations.

COTTON QUALITY

During the cold war between the World Bank and the West African cotton companies, the companies argued that quality control was the key to a competitive world market position for West African cotton. For years, hand harvesting helped to create some competitive advantage for West African cotton by meeting the textile industry's demands for reliable spinning quality. A high ginning ratio that improves spinnability has become an expected quality standard of West African cotton, and meeting this standard involves a continuing accommodation of the divergent interests of the textile industry, the growers, and the national cotton companies.

Contamination by bits of polypropylene used for wrapping bales and increased fiber "stickiness" caused by aphids has eroded the West African quality standard in recent years. But biotechnology changes may further modify cotton fiber quality and compromise the West African standard. Consequently, the introduction of Bt cotton may jeopardize West Africa's world cotton market advantage. This aspect of Bt cotton is not widely discussed, but in 2003 the head of Dunavant Enterprises, one of the world's leading cotton-trading companies, stated that the fall in quality was making it difficult to sell the U.S.-grown, short-staple Bt cotton. According to Dunavant, Bt cotton is deficient in length and strength—both quality features of conventional West African cotton. Clearly, the future for West African cotton farmers depends on more than resolving their concerns over subsidy payments.

Understanding GE Cotton, Power, and Development

On its face, the adoption of crop biotechnology, and Bt cotton in particular, appears to represent a freely taken and independent public decision and governmental strategy to address a particular technical (agricultural) issue or respond to a perceived development opportunity. But this next-generation "green revolution," embodies much more. Public foreign assistance agencies now directly mediate the establishment of "partnerships" in which national public research agencies "become dependent on [the] private-sector . . . for access to privately owned materials and techniques. As a result, for-profit companies are gaining growing influence over the research agendas" (McAfee 2003, 175).[13] These relationships can be outlined as follows.

Agricultural research scientists throughout much of West Africa are not in a position to challenge the proffered foreign investment in new scientific technology and further training, as represented by the Burkina Faso trials and the protocols proposed in Mali. As they welcome these externally driven, and largely private capital–financed, opportunities, the rate and direction of research becomes an integral part of capital that is controlled elsewhere. This is not an altogether new situation for agricultural research in sub-Saharan Africa. Starting in the late 1980s many national governments began to cut funding for research institutions, and the public flow of resources to research also became increasingly unreliable. The international donor community filled some of the funding gap until changing priorities and reduced levels of assistance led to further cutbacks.

In contrast, this new generation of funding lays the foundation for (continued) scientific dependence in which national scientific development becomes more conditional upon external resources and priorities and less responsive to smallholders. This happens in the following ways. Research scientists, a new "scientific or research bourgeoisie," gladly welcome the funding, professional networking and training opportunities available through foreign private and public opportunities to undertake Bt cotton research. In turn, private foreign investors in agricultural research, unconcerned about the democratic accountability of research, focus on promoting a mutuality of scientific interests with researchers that strengthens and enhances the authority and growth of this new bourgeoisie. Researchers are drawn quickly and willingly into networks of science-based economic and political power that ultimately delegitimize national democratic discourse and subordinate this important discourse to scientific development. This is the foundation for the "scientization of politics" that reinforces a "narrow instrumental rationality" in addressing development issues.

In many ways the new and seductive funding for biotechnology research simply strengthens a scientific discourse that makes agricultural research value neutral and obscures consideration and discussion of smallholder interests and needs. For some researchers, smallholders lack the credentials and therefore are not legitimate participants in any aspect of Bt cotton research. Based on this rationale—and one strengthened by the "bench science" nature of biotechnology research—it is a short step to replacing democratic accountability in research with "expertocracy." From this perspective, technological "imperatives" easily trump the ideals of equality and democracy. More broadly, biotechnology research offers one more way in which moral and political questions give way to the logic of science and technology.

Global Corporate Science and Development

NEW U.S. FOREIGN AID AGENDA— COTTON AND BIOTECHNOLOGY

In November 2005 the U.S. secretary of agriculture and the U.S. trade representative announced the West Africa Cotton Improvement Program (WACIP) to improve cotton production, transformation, and marketing for Benin, Burkina Faso, Chad, Mali, and Senegal. In the absence of responding directly to the World Trade Organization's decision to remove subsidy payments to U.S. cotton farmers, this $US7 million program represents a U.S. effort to show "real steps that can help West Africa, including its cotton farmers."[14] While West African governments and others are quite unlikely to see this program as a substitute for removing subsidies, the WACIP represents a watershed initiative in U.S. foreign aid, and one that was undertaken in closest consultation with the U.S. cotton industry.[15]

For years, a provision of the U.S. Foreign Assistance Act has protected U.S. cotton growers by preventing USAID funding for projects that directly support West African cotton. But it one fell swoop the

U.S. government, in close collaboration with the U.S. National Cotton Council, announced a seven-point plan to address West African cotton research, production, processing, and policy issues, including "the enabling environment for agricultural biotechnology" (USAID 2005, 4).

The announcement of the WACIP culminates a deliberate, strategic effort by several U.S. government agencies and the National Cotton Council to turn international attention away from continuing and well-publicized demands for ending U.S. cotton subsidies that encourage exports. In the summer of 2004 the National Cotton Council hosted a tour of the U.S. cotton belt by a group of West African dignitaries. A few months later, USAID funded a "rapid assessment" of cotton in the four countries covered by the WACIP in order to identify "potential solutions and interventions to improve production, transformation and marketing of cotton and its byproducts." By January 2005 a deputy undersecretary in the USDA, Jim Butler, met with Malian cotton farmers to pledge U.S. support for helping farmers increase their productivity.[16] As Kilman and Thurow suggest, this represents a "if you can't beat 'em, join 'em" strategy in hopes that West Africans will drop their demands and accept a gradual—and more politically palatable—reduction in subsidies to U.S. cotton farmers. Promoting biotechnology is central to this strategy.[17]

REGULATIONS MASK POLITICS

Thinking about biotechnology research as a technical undertaking sets aside social and political questions and puts smallholder cotton farmers at considerable risk. Public foreign assistance agencies—and especially the U.S. Agency for International Development (USAID) and the World Bank—lead this initiative to depoliticize biotechnology and pave the way for corporate investment by framing biotechnology issues as neutral matters of simply setting up the regulations and regulatory structures.

USAID (2005) asserts that if genetically engineered crops are to be introduced in Africa, then countries will need a biosafety system to regulate these new crops. Similarly, the ICAC's Second Expert Panel on Biotechnology in Cotton advises that "defining an appropriate science-based, risk assessment framework that addresses realistic and assessable risks to human health and the environment and balancing these against potential benefits is a key requirement for the adoption of biotech cotton" (ICAC 2004, 2).

On its face, there is little dispute over this position. But the issue lies not with the rationale for rigorous and science-based biosafety protocols, but in disregarding the political implications of this approach, and specifically how it excludes smallholder needs and interests in agricultural research. Instead of building on the years of investment in farmer-driven research (through farming systems research programs during the 1980s), policy focuses on strengthening the scientific competency for risk assessment, for risk management, and for crop inspection and monitoring.[18]

The "public information campaign" becomes an especially critical component of the USAID strategy. As noted in one consultant report, there is "much confused and confusing information" that "creates unfounded concerns . . . about the nature and the mode of development" of GE cotton. In response, the consultant recommends that "a well conceived and appropriate communication project with all stakeholders will do much to increase the chances of success of both the technological and the regulatory projects" (De Greef 2003, 6). With this type of approach, it is easy to understand how USAID is seen by some to be "making the world hungry for GM crops (GRAIN 2005b)." By helping construct the regulatory and legal systems, agencies like USAID are creating the basis for protecting corporate property rights and laying the foundation for corporations "to introduce their products (including seed) and to access commercially untapped genetic resources for future product development" (Greenberg 2005, 6).[19]

INTERNATIONAL RESEARCH NETWORKS

In support of these public policies, industry, research, and education partners have woven a new worldwide web of relationships to promote biotechnology research. In some cases, corporate biotechnology interests may have sought to promote an image of social responsibility by contributing to efforts such as the International Ecoagriculture Conference and Practitioners Fair hosted in 2004 by Ecoagriculture Partners in Nairobi.[20] When this occurs, some may understandably infer that such financial support represents a means to mask biotechnology interests behind the challenging ecoagriculture strategy that seeks to enhance farmer and community stewardship of ecosystems and biodiversity. That appears to be the conclusion drawn by the Institute of Science in Society in response to funding for the Nairobi event from the Syngenta Foundation for Sustainable Agriculture, Bayer CropScience, CropLife International, and the Sustainable Agriculture Initiative.[21]

The International Service for the Acquisition of Agri-biotech Applications (ISAAA) is perhaps the lead player weaving together the global scientific web in support of crop biotechnology. The ISAAA was incorporated almost fifteen years ago specifically to facilitate "the transfer and delivery of appropriate biotechnology applications to developing countries and the building of partnerships between institutions in the South and the private sector in the North." This group focuses on crops that are not covered by the international agricultural research centers (CGIAR/IARCs) and more specifically concentrates on "near-term bio-tech applications that have already been tested in industrial countries" (ISAAA 2007).

The ISSAA strategy for Africa is clear and sobering. According to the executive director, "The need for biotechnology applications is nowhere greater [than in sub-Saharan Africa], yet the region's national agricultural research systems remain, with some exceptions, relatively weak. Its extension services, too, have long been underfunded. . . . These circumstances explain why many fear that African countries will face great difficulty in absorbing and deploying biotechnology applications, with the result that investments in such applications will be poor investments" (ISAAA 1996).

In response, ISAAA's Africa strategy includes "strengthening the capacity for crop biotechnology." This involves an investment in establishing the Global Network of the Crop Biotechnology Knowledge Center, in association with the African Biotechnology Stakeholders Forum and other organizations in South Africa, Egypt, and pivotal countries in Francophone Africa. Established in 1994, the ISAAA AfriCenter focuses on "building strategic alliances that help to deliver more benefits to small-scale farming communities in Africa . . . [and] to keep Africa on the fast lane on biotechnology issues" (ISAAA AfriCenter 2007).

The monthly electronic newsletter, *Institut d'économie rurale et biotechnologie*, from Mali's National Agricultural Research Institute, the Institute for Rural Economy, illustrates one other way in which the ISAAA seeks to "keep Africa on the fast lane." Specifically, the creation of this newsletter—at the heart of a national research institute in which researchers continue to find it difficult to communicate with each other—responds to the 2003 observations and recommendations of a USAID crop biotechnology consultant. Significantly, the stakeholders in question are not cotton farmers but key policymakers responsible for giving the green light to biotechnology research. In other words, the problem is seen as one of providing "accurate information," by translating the literature on biotechnology from English into French and thereby improving "the quality of thinking about biotechnology in Mali, but also to the entire French-speaking community worldwide" (De Greef 2003, 17).

Created in the wake of a deliberate donor effort to dismantle an Africa-centered research network, SAFGRAD, the donor-led Forum for Agricultural Research in Africa (FARA),[22] has also recently, and not surprisingly, taken a similar position. The executive secretary, Dr. Monty Jones, called on African governments to create "supportive environments" to facilitate the widespread adoption and use of agricultural biotechnology. One of FARA's programs, DONATA (Dissemination of New Agricultural Technologies in Africa) is specifically designed to respond to this call "by accelerating dissemination and uptake of new technologies." Similarly, the promotion of crop biotechnology has been front and center for a working group on Capacity Building for Science and Technology supported by the Partnership to Cut Hunger and Poverty in Africa.[23]

Science and Democratic Development

WHERE HAVE ALL THE FARMERS GONE?

At a time when African cotton farmers have finally found a voice in the global debates on cotton production and marketing, the absence of their direct involvement, as well as their muted and sometimes conflicted voice, in addressing the challenges of crop biotechnology should provoke both questions and concerns.

The final declaration issued at the establishment of the African Cotton Producers Association (Association des Producteurs de Coton Africain, AProCA) is noticeably silent on agricultural research in general and specifically on crop biotechnology. Even François Traoré, the "José Bové of Africa,"[24] while welcoming the GE cotton trials in Burkina as a way in which science can improve production without harming the environment, also sees GE cotton as an unnecessary complication.

On the other hand, in late 2004 the Malian National Coordination of Farmers' Organizations (Coordination Nationale des Organisations Paysannes du Mali, CNOP) issued a call for a moratorium on cotton biotechnology. With a focus on their concern for biodiversity protection, the CNOP stated, "the hazardous nature of biotechnology and its control by a few multinationals obliges us to call for a minimum five-year moratorium on the introduction of genetically engineered crops in order to implement a participatory approach to evaluating the risks the introduction of these crops pose for our countries" (1). More recently, in September 2005 the African Biodiversity Network and the Coalition for the Protection of Africa's Genetic Patrimony hosted representatives from nineteen African countries in Nairobi for the Seminar on the Strategy of Civil Society on Agricultural Biotechnology in Africa. At the end of this seminar, the Nairobi Declaration on Crop Biotechnology and African Agriculture called for stopping the introduction and patenting of crop technology in Africa (GRAIN 2005a).

Despite these calls of concern, the lack of attention to agricultural research issues by farmers' organizations in West Africa is not new. In considering the types of policies that would attract the attention of farmers' groups, technology policies rank lower than the perceived gains from dealing with economic, fiscal, and financial policies. Furthermore, when faced with the promises to cut costs and exposure to toxic pesticides, a wait-and-see attitude, as expressed by François Traoré, seems understandable.

Recent studies of cotton farming in West and in South Africa suggest that agricultural biotechnology research deliberately excludes farmers because the researchers know their trials do not respond to farm-level problems. In West Africa, Deveze and Fontaines (2005) found that improving the livelihoods of cotton farmers depended on: improving functional literacy, developing natural resource protection programs, strengthening grower organizations, and improving the socioeconomic environment.

Moreover, some evidence suggests that donor agencies either seek to manipulate, co-opt, or deliberately exclude greater involvement by grower organizations. With reference to issues of privatization, USAID's "rapid assessment" identified one of the underlying dilemmas that is equally relevant to research. "Capacity building for the large number of private agricultural organizations is likely to be a massive, expensive, slow undertaking. Yet if it is not done, the privatization process will simply mean a change from a single parastatal to a cartel of several private enterprises acting in a similarly imperious, non-transparent manner" (USAID 2005, 19–20).

If USAID's follow-through to support farmers' groups falls in the footsteps of the World Bank's once highly publicized Strengthening Producer Organizations initiative, there is little hope for farmers to become more directly involved in biotechnology research. Some anecdotal evidence even suggests there are subtle yet deliberate efforts to suppress the new initiatives on the supply and distribution of input to cotton farmers that have arisen. The case of the Upper Niger River Valley Union and Associated Farmers' Enterprises (Union des GIE de la Zone OHVN et Associés, UGOA) is illustrative. After two years of successfully showing how cotton farmers in one region of Mali could manage their own input supply system, reports circulate about both direct and indirect ways in which its activities and accomplishments are being undermined and discredited. If these reports are correct, this should raise serious concerns about the depth of the roots of democratic development in Mali and elsewhere in West Africa.

As McAfee observes, "a high-stakes battle continues over whether food, farming, and biotechnology will be understood and governed as a problem of corporate technoscience, economic efficiency, and universal legal standards, or whether the broader issues of who really benefits and who loses from genetic engineering of crops, privatization of research, and world-scale consolidation of agro-economic power will be addressed by emerging institutions of global governance" (2003, 192).

The question and concern is simple but profound: if empowered grassroots groups are challenged for activities they have been encouraged to pursue, then where are the incentives for research scientists to include farmers in defining and implementing their research? The scientization of politics undermines democratic accountability and threatens the foundations of democratic development.

Notes

1. See Daouda Mané, *Adoption du coton transgénique au Burkina Faso: Des pas de géant pour l'envol de l'or blanc.* Dakar: Le Soleil. http://www.lesoleil.sn/imprimer.php3?id_articles=4940.

2. This chapter focuses on Bt cotton (see next section). The term *genetically engineered (GE) cotton,* sometimes referred to as *genetically modified (GM) cotton* and *biotech cotton* will also be used.

3. The ICAC is an association of more than forty governments of cotton-producing, -consuming, and -trading countries. Its mission is to assist governments in fostering a healthy world cotton economy by raising awareness, providing information, and serving as a catalyst for cooperative action on issues of international significance. http://www.icac.org.

4. Jeuneafrique.com. "Décevant 'coton Bt.'" May 29, 2005. http://www.jeuneafrique.com/gabarits/articleJAI_online.asp?art_cle=LIN29065dcevatbnotoo.

5. "Bollgardization" refers to the replacement of conventional cotton varieties by Bollgard. In addition to these farmer concerns, there is an international coalition of women, Diverse Women for Diversity (DWD), calling for a boycott of Bt cotton and clothing made from it.

6. The heading of this section and the next are from the lyrics of the popular 1950s song "Teach Me Tonight" by Sammy Cahn and Gene De-Paul, originally recorded in 1953 by Jo Stafford.

7. Bollgard carries the Cry1Ac gene from Bt while Bollgard II contains two "Cry genes." The Cry gene family is a coding for an endotoxin that is highly specific to certain insects and that accumulates as an insecticidal crystal in a cell compartment.

8. This section draws heavily from a similar discussion in the chapter "Pesticides, Politics and Pest Management: Toward a Political Economy of Cotton in Sub-Saharan Africa" (Bingen 2003b).

9. These mixtures commonly include dimethoate (an organophosphate and a general use pesticide) as well as either cypermethrin or deltamethrin (synthetic pyrethroids whose use is restricted because of their toxicity to fish).

10. Similarly, Eicher, Maredia, and Sithole-Niang point out that even if a multitude of scientific and regulatory issues are resolved, "the rise and decline of smallholder Bt cotton in South Africa shows that sustainable adoption of Bt crops requires a number of institutional problems to be solved such as seed and fertilizer input systems, access to markets and favorable economic and trade policies" (2005, 11).

11. This represents an elementary resistance management strategy in which the refuge becomes an area where Bt-susceptible insects breed with those that have developed Bt resistance. In principle, and assuming the genetic trait for resistance is partially recessive, the offspring of this mating would be susceptible to Bt toxins.

12. This call in many ways mirrors the 2002 recommendation by the U.S. National Research Council to do a better job of screening of GE crops for environmental effects, to find ways for more public involvement in the review process, and for continued ecological testing and monitoring after GE plants are on the market.

13. Also see Greenberg's concerns related to the realignment of local needs with "dominant global interests" that "binds African producers into a social and economic model in which they will forever be producers of primary goods and consumers of processed goods" (2004, 1). It has been recognized for some time that the first green revolution left a very small footprint across Africa.

14. U.S. trade representative Rob Portman, cited in "U.S. Announces Launch of West Africa Cotton Improvement Program." USDA News Release 0486.05.

15. The WACIP is a useful reminder that political support for U.S. foreign assistance has been frequently based on the ways in which foreign aid programs can either directly promote U.S. private capital flows or protect U.S. capital interests.

16. Originally reported by Scott Kilman and Roger Thurow in the *Wall Street Journal*, August 5, 2005; yaleglobal.yale.edu/article.print?id=6112.

17. There are also reports that the World Bank has offered to drop ten years of pressure to privatize the cotton sector on the condition that gov-

ernments would allow the introduction of Bt cotton. Such decisions strengthen the observation that cotton is just a new Trojan horse for a joint U.S. government–private strategy to introduce other GE crops, including regulatory policy supportive of biotechnology.

18. As a result, even a regional ministerial-level conference was convened in June 2005 in order to focus on the need for the appropriate regulatory structure.

19. Without considering a long history of smallholder dependence on "publicly available" seed through the national companies, the consequences of this "nonpolitical" regulatory approach for the future control of cottonseed in West and central Africa are equally troublesome. In South Africa, Monsanto now controls 40 percent of the seed market. Are West African governments willing to put their smallholders in a similar position?

20. My appreciation to Norman Uphoff (pers. comm.) for his observations on the Ecoagriculture Partners.

21. See http://www.i-sis.org.uk/CHSA.php.

22. In 2000 FARA replaced the Special Program for Agriculture in Africa , which had been supported by the World Bank. SPAAR helps national, international, and subregional institutions "deliver more responsive and effective services to its stakeholders . . . [by playing] . . . advocacy and coordination roles for agricultural research for development." http://www.fara-africa/or/aboutus.htm.

23. http://www.africanhunger.org/?location=front&aid=10.

24. *Le Monde.fr,* "François Traoré, héraut de la révolte des cotonniers africains," July 9, 2005. www.lemonde.fr/web/article/0,1-0@2-3212,36-671196 @51-669395,0.html.

References

Adjovi, Emmanuel V. 1998. "Quand l'or blanc intoxique ses producteurs." *SYFIA International* . www.syfia.info/fr/article.asp?article_num=273.

Bingen, Jim. 2003a. "Community-Based Producer Organizations: A Contribution to the West Africa Regional Program Action Plan for the Initiative to End Hunger in Africa." Agricultural Policy Development Program. Report prepared for USAID AFR/SD (PCE-I-00-99.00033-00, Order No. 5). Bethesda, MD: Abt Associates.

———. 2003b. "Pesticides, Politics, and Pest Management: Toward a Political Economy of Cotton in Sub-Saharan Africa." In *African Environment* and Development: Rhetoric, Programs, Realities, ed. B. I. Logan and W. G. Moseley, 111–26. Burlington, VT: Ashgate Publishing.

———. 2005. "A Question of Quality: Cotton in West Africa." In *Agricultural Standards: The Shape of the Global Food and Fiber System*, ed. Bingen and L. Busch, 219–42. Dordrecht: Springer.

Bingen, R. James. 1998. "Cotton, Democracy, and Development in Mali." *Journal of Modern African Studies* 36:265–85.

Bingen, R. James, and Derick W. Brinkerhoff. 2000. *Agricultural Research in Africa and the Sustainable Financing Initiative: Review, Lessons, and Proposed Next Steps.* Washington, DC: USAID/Africa, Office of Sustainable Development/Agriculture, Natural Resources, and Rural Enterprise Division.

Brulle, Robert J. 2000. *Agency, Democracy, and Nature. The U.S. Environmental Movement from a Critical Theory Perspective.* Cambridge, MA: MIT Press.

Buttel, Frederick H. 2003. "The Global Politics of GEOs: The Achilles' Heel of the Globalization Regime?" In *Engineering Trouble: Biotechnology and Its Discontents*, ed. Rachel Schurman and Dennis Kelso, 152–73. Berkeley: University of California Press.

Camara, M., F. Haïdara, and A. Traoré. 2001. "Étude socio-économique de l'utilisation des pesticides au Mali." Institut du Sahel, Bamako, AGROSOC / Sécurité Alimentaire—Gestion des Ressources Naturelles; Université de Hanovre, Institut des Sciences Économique—Projet Politique des Pesticides; FAO, Projet Gestion des Pesticides au Sahel.

CNOP (Coordination Nationale des Organisations Paysannes du Mali). 2004. "Atelier de réflexion des leaders paysans sur les enjeux des ogm au Mali: Déclaration de l'atelier." Document published 27 October. www.penserpouragir.org/article.php3 ?id_article=139.

De Greef, W. 2003. "Biotechnology and Agriculture: Capacity Building Projects." Draft report prepared at the request of USAID Mali.

Deveze, J. C., and D. H. d. Fontaines. 2005. "Le devenir des agricultures familiales des zones cotonnières africaines: Une mutation à conduire avec tous les acteurs : A partir des cas du Bénin, du Burkina Faso, du Cameroun et du Mali." Paris: AFD, EVA/STR.

ECOWAS (Economic Community of West African States). 2005. "Rapport de la réunion des experts de la Hôtel de l'Amitié, Bamako, Mali, 21–23 juin 2005." Paper presented at the Conférence Ministérielle des Pays de l'Espace CEDEAO sur la Biotechnologie, Bamako.

Eicher, Carl K. 1995. "Zimbabwe's Maize-Based Green Revolution: Preconditions for Replication." *World Development* 23:805–18.

Eicher, Carl K., Karim Maredia, and Idah Sithole-Niang. 2005. "Biotechnology and the African Farmer." East Lansing: Department of Agricultural Economics, Michigan State University.

Evans, Peter. 1979. *Dependent Development: The Alliance of Multinational, State, and Local Capital in Brazil.* Princeton, NJ: Princeton University Press.

Fischer, Frank. 2000. *Citizens, Experts, and the Environment: The Politics of Local Knowledge.* Durham, NC: Duke University Press.

Gillham, Fred E. M., T. M. Bell, T. Arin, G. A. Matthews, C. L. Rumeur, and A. B. Hearn. 1995. "Cotton Production Prospects for the Next Decade." World Bank technical paper 287, Washington, DC.

GRAIN. 2004. "Bt Cotton at Mali's Doorstep: Time to Act!" www.grain.org/briefings/?id=162.

———. 2005a. "Déclaration de Nairobi sur 'Les OGM dans l'agriculture africaine.'" http://www.grain.org/semences/?id=45.

———. 2005b. "USAID: Making the World Hungry for GM Crops." Barcelona, Spain: GRAIN.

Greenberg, S. 2004. "Global Agriculture and Genetically Modified Cotton in Africa." Paper. African Centre for Biosafety.

Grossholtz, J. 2004. "The Cotton Campaign Brought to You by Diverse Women for Diversity." *Capitalism Nature Socialism* 15:81–87.

Hillocks, R. J. 2005. "Is There a Role for Bt Cotton in IPM for Smallholders in Africa?" *International Journal of Pest Management* 52:131–41.

ICAC. 2000. "Report of an Expert Panel on Biotechnology in Cotton." International Cotton Advisory Committee, Washington, DC.

———. 2004. "Report of the Second Expert Panel on Biotechnology in Cotton." ICAC, Washington, DC.

ISAAA. 1996. Annual Report 1996. Advancing Altruism in Africa. www.isaaa.org/Resources/Publications/about_isaaa/Annual_report96/Annual_report96_2.htm.

———. 2007. ISAAA in Brief. www.isaaa.org/inbrief/pdf/isaaa-inbrief.pdf. Accessed September 2007.

ISAAA AfriCenter. 2007. Key AfriCenter Projects. http://africenter.isaaa.org/keyprojects/default.html.

James, C. 2004. "Preview: Global Status of Commercialized Biotech/GM Crops: 2004." Report 32 ISAAA Briefs. International Service for the Acquisition of Agri-Biotech Applications, Ithaca.

Kneen, B. 2003. "GE Cotton Quality." *Ram's Horn* 211 (June): 6–7.

Laxminarayan, Ramanan. 2003. "On the Economics of Resistance." In *Battling Resistance to Antibiotics and Pesticides: An Economic Approach,* ed. Laxminarayan, 1–14. Washington, DC: Resources for the Future.

Mali, Ministère de l'Agriculture, de l'Élevage et de la Pêche. 2004. "Développement de la culture du coton génétiquement modifié au Mali," ed. I. d. E. Rurale.

McAfee, Kathleen. 2003. "Biotech Battles: Plants, Power, and Intellectual Property in the New Global Governance Regimes." In *Engineering Trouble: Biotechnology and Its Discontents*, ed. Rachel Schurman and Dennis Kelso, 174–94. Berkeley: University of California Press.

Mensah, R. K. 2002. "Development of an Integrated Pest Management Programme for Cotton." Part 2, "Integration of a Lucerne/Cotton Interplant System, Food Supplement Sprays with Biological and Synthetic Insecticides." *International Journal of Pest Management* 48:96–105.

OBEPAB. 2000. "Les accidents causés par les pesticides chimiques de synthèse utilisés dans la production cotonnière au Bénin." Cotonou: Organisation Béninoise pour la Promotion de l'Agriculture Biologique.

Sklar, Richard L. 1987. "Postimperialism: A Class Analysis of Multinational Corporate Expansion." In *Postimperialism. International Capitalism and Development in the Late Twentieth Century*, ed. David G. Becker, 19–40. Boulder: Lynne Rienner.

USAID. 2005. "Summary and Findings of the West African Cotton Assessment." Washington, DC: U.S. Agency for International Development.

Waibel, Hermann, Jan C. Zadoks, and Gerd Fleischer. 2003. "What Can We Learn from the Economics of Pesticides? Impact Assessment of Genetically Modified Plants." In *Battling Resistance to Antibiotics and Pesticides. An Economic Approach*, ed. R. Laxminarayan, 137–57. Washington, DC: Resources for the Future.

Wilkins, T. A., K. Rajasekaran, and D. M. Anderson. 2000. "Cotton Biotechnology." *Critical Reviews in Plant Sciences* 19:511.

10

Organic Cotton in Sub-Saharan Africa

A New Development Paradigm?

Brian M. Dowd

COTTON PRODUCTION IN SUB-SAHARAN AFRICA (SSA) is the result of centuries of interactions between global and local actors. Trade contact with Asia and the Americas gave rise to the cultivation of all four domesticated varieties of cotton (*Gossypium* spp.) in SSA by the nineteenth century. The early twentieth century brought a series of interventions by European colonial powers seeking to increase cotton exports. Colonial administrators enacted forced labor camps, disrupted local markets, and disseminated intensive cropping strategies and new crop varieties in order to fill demand for the burgeoning European textile industry (Bassett 2001).

More recently, in the late twentieth century, the independent states of Africa, international lending institutions, and nongovernmental organizations (NGOs) pushed to further modify cotton production strategies through the promotion of green-revolution technologies. They championed the adoption of intensive agricultural methods, including animal traction and synthetic inputs in order to boost yields, increase regional development, and combat rural poverty. Furthermore, advocates claimed that an increase in rural incomes would allow farmers to invest in resource conservation and thus increase environmental stewardship and protection (see Cleaver and Schreiber

1994). Heavy financial assistance supported the development of national cotton industries (e.g., World Bank 1988) as the scope of cotton cultivation grew throughout the region. As a result of these efforts, cotton production increased by nearly 300 percent since 1980, reaching 1,543,000 metric tons in 2004. SSA is now the third-largest cotton exporting region in the world after North America and Central Asia (ICAC 2005). This impressive growth leads many analysts to proclaim cotton one of the continent's agricultural success stories (Gabre-Madhin and Haggblade 2004).

Despite the apparent success at improving production and incomes, many analysts point out the negative impacts of cotton production on the livelihoods of rural African farmers. Recent scholarship demonstrates that intensive cotton production may lead to soil degradation rather than soil conservation (Moseley 2005), potentially threatening regional food security. Reports published by NGOs document the sickness and at times death of cotton farmers and their family members due to exposure to cotton pesticides (Ton, Tovignan, and Vodouhê 2000; Tovignan, Vodouhê, and Dinham 2001). Furthermore, experiences from other cotton production regions in the global South, including the contamination of cattle due to the grazing of pesticide-laden cotton plants, and the full-scale abandonment of cotton growing due to pest resistance to chemicals, raise concerns that similar circumstances could occur in SSA (Myers 1999).

The emergence of organic cotton projects is in part a response to these critiques and in part an attempt to exploit a global niche market for organic fiber. Certified organic cotton cultivation first began in 1994 in Uganda and Tanzania and has since spread to Benin, Senegal, Mali, and Burkina Faso. Although certified organic cotton production still represents only 0.15 percent of total cotton exports from SSA (Organic Exchange 2005; ICAC 2005), interest among farmers, international NGOs, and buyers is expanding rapidly. Organic cotton differs from conventional cotton because it is produced without the use of synthetic chemicals or genetically modified organisms (GMOs). Advocates claim that organically produced cotton can improve rural livelihoods better than conventionally produced cotton by (1) increasing rural incomes through price premiums, (2) decreasing health risks by eliminating the use of synthetic chemicals, and (3) decreasing environmental and soil degradation through the use of synthetic-free, locally available soil fertility enhancing techniques. Despite the presence of organic projects for over a decade, very little research has been published that analyzes their presence and activities in SSA, nor their claims of improved rural livelihoods.

A History of Organic Cotton Production and Certification

An Englishman, Lord Northbourne, is the first person credited with using the term *organic* to refer to a type of farming (Rigby and Cáceres 2001). Northbourne referred to a whole-systems approach to agriculture, integrating crops, animals, and social structures (Lotter 2002). As the origin of the term implies, organic farming often suggests a style of agriculture that goes beyond simply not using synthetic compounds. Definitions for organic agriculture can also include goals for sustainability, worker justice, and ecological awareness (Edwards-Jones and Howells 2001). Accreditation organizations such as the International Federation of Organic Agriculture Movements (IFOAM) balance what is proscribed under organic guidelines and what is aspired to in organic agriculture by including both standards and goals in their published organic guidelines. Only the standards, however, are required when meeting the guidelines for certification. I will return to this distinction between standards-oriented and goal-oriented definitions of organic production when I analyze the environmental impacts of organic cotton production.

While the concept of organic farming has its origins in the global North, many of the production strategies in SSA can be viewed as organic by default, since farmers do not use synthetic inputs. However, in order to access markets and gain premium prices for their goods, farms must be certified as organic. The first serious attempt at certified organic cotton production took place in Turkey in the late 1980s, by a European cooperative consisting of five different organic food importers (Myers 1999). Turkish farmers were already exporting other organic food crops and wanted to incorporate cotton into their crop rotations. Certified organic cotton production for export has since expanded throughout the world, reaching 25,733 tonnes in 2004 in over fifteen countries (Organic Exchange 2005). A report issued by Organic Exchange (2005), an NGO that analyzes developments in the organic cotton sector, estimates that although organic cotton production is expected to continue to increase, demand is projected to outpace production by over twelve thousand tonnes beginning in 2007 (see fig. 10.1). This projected gap between supply and demand of organic cotton represents almost half of current worldwide production.

The cultivation, purchase, ginning, and selling of organic cotton requires the coordination of a number of different actors in each country. Since organic cotton is still relatively new in SSA, all these functions are coordinated by an organic cotton project directed either by a small group of organizations or by a single entity. This chapter is mainly concerned with the cultivation and purchase of organic cotton at the farm level. One main cause for the consolidation of the organic sector into a project is the cost of certification. Most farmers are unable to afford the costs of certification, thereby requiring organic cotton projects or cotton exporters to pick up the costs. Since the organization that pays for certification retains the title, farmers must sell their product back to the holder of the certification in order to obtain a price premium. Despite this arrangement, certification

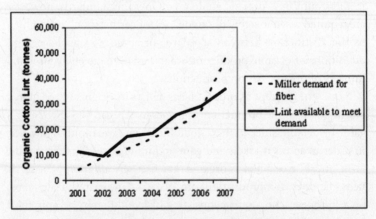

Fig. 10.1. Availability of organic cotton lint on the global market, compared with demand from miller/spinners, 2001–7. (Organic Exchange 2005)

costs are still relatively high for the various projects and can vary between an estimated 2 to 10 percent of product value for larger projects (e.g., Uganda, Tanzania) and 20 to 50 percent for smaller projects (e.g., Benin, Senegal) (Ton 2002).

One significant way in which projects save money on certification is through the implementation of an internal control system (ICS). An ICS is a web of organic growers that essentially police each other in order to ensure the proper use of certifiable techniques. This allows for the certifier to validate the ICS and sample just a small percentage of the farms in order to certify all the farms in the project. The French firm EcoCert is the largest certifier active in SSA and uses this technique to certify organic cotton projects. For example, in Uganda, EcoCert certifies the organic cotton project by validating the credibility of the ICS through the inspection of a small sample, generally 10 to 20 percent of contracted farms (Kidd, Tulip, Wagala 2001; Tulip, pers. comm., 2005).

Two common concerns with certification are the seed source and the conversion period during the transition from conventional to organic agriculture. European Union organic standards require that seeds come from an organic source when available (Riddle and Coody 2002). State cotton agencies in most SSA countries coordinate the selection of cotton varieties in order to reduce contamination by inferior strains and therefore restrict the use of alternative sources for organic seed. Such state regulation requires most organic cotton projects to buy seed directly from the state and have it be exempted from noncertified chemical pretreatment (Ton 2002).[1] European Union standards also require a two-year conversion period if the field where organic production is to begin was under conventional cultivation during the prior growing season (Riddle and Coody 2002). This requirement would force farmers to either leave the field fallow during the conversion period or practice organic farming without being able to sell their product as certified organic. Such a situation could exclude farmers for two reasons. First, farmers may not be able to afford to set aside fields as fallow. Second, since organic cotton yields are generally lower than those for conventional cotton (Ton 2002),[2] farmers may not be able to absorb the lost economic returns during the conversion period. Most organic projects get around this problem by concentrating their efforts in areas of the country where fallowing is still practiced. Entrance into the project is then restricted to only those farmers who have fields that have been fallow for two to three years (Franck Merceron, pers. comm., 2005). This limits the geographic dispersion of organic projects since it excludes areas where farmers no longer fallow their fields.

Organic Cotton Project Trends and Key Components

The Lango Organic Project in Uganda,[3] organized by the Dutch trader in organic textiles Bo Weevil BV, and the BioRe project in Tanzania, initiated by the Swiss yarn trader Remei AG, are by far the two largest organic cotton projects in SSA (see figs. 10.2, 10.3). These two projects alone contribute 92.8 percent of total organic cotton lint production from SSA (Organic Exchange 2005). The remaining organic cotton exports from SSA are divided among four smaller projects: the Organisation Béninoise pour la Promotion de l'Agriculture Biologique

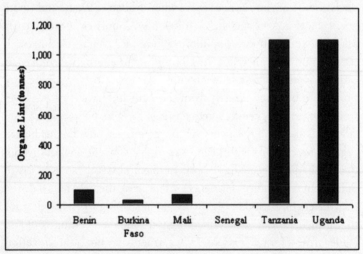

Fig. 10.2. Total production of organic cotton lint in sub-Saharan Africa by country, 2004/5 season. (Organic Exchange 2005; Traoré 2005)

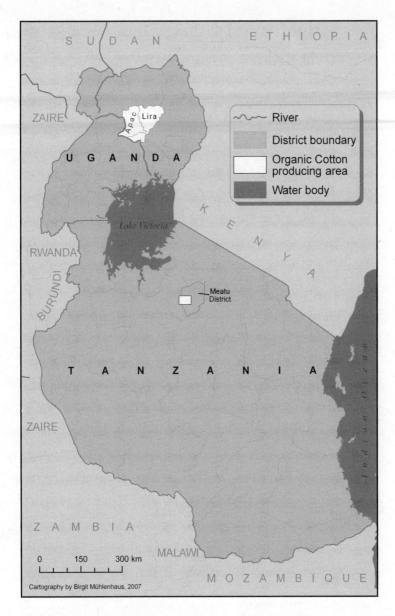

Fig. 10.3. Approximate locations of the Lango Organic Project in Uganda and the BioRe project in Tanzania.

(OBEPAB) project and the Farmers' Federation project in Senegal, both initiated in 1996, and two projects run by the Swiss NGO Helvetas, one in Mali initiated in 2002, the other in Burkina Faso initiated in 2003. Although by comparison West African organic cotton projects are much smaller than those in East Africa, they are drawing a considerable amount of attention from international NGOs and development organizations for their potential to address the problems associated with chemically intensive cotton cultivation in that region. Other projects in Zimbabwe, Mozambique, Togo, and Senegal failed shortly after start-up for a host of reasons, including political turmoil, lack of development assistance, and mismanagement (Ton 2002; Ebeh Kodjo, pers. comm., 2005).

Two factors largely determined where and how organic cotton projects began: the style of conventional cotton production practiced in each country and the local environmental conditions. For example, the Export Promotion of Organic Product from Africa (EPOPA) project began the Lango Organic Project in 1994 in the Lira and Apac Districts of Uganda (Dankers 2003). This area was targeted due to its fertile soils and to the presence of black ants (*Lepisiota* spp.), which are natural predators of cotton pests (Malins and Nelson 1998). The BioRe project in Tanzania also took advantage of relatively abundant and rich soils to begin its project in the Meatu District of the Shinyanga region of Tanzania in 1994 (Ratter 2002). Furthermore, the conventional cotton sectors in Uganda and Tanzania, at the time of project initiation, were relatively disorganized and consequently lacked a reliable system to distribute mineral fertilizers and synthetic pesticides (Ratter 2002; Tulip and Ton 2002).[4] This meant that conventional cotton production largely took place without the aid of synthetic inputs, making it relatively easy for farmers to switch to certified organic production.

The generally favorable environmental conditions and disorganized conventional cotton sectors found in East Africa contrast with the less favorable environmental conditions and centralized conventional cotton sectors found in the West African nations of Mali, Burkina Faso, and Benin. West Africa lacks the black ants found in Uganda and has no beneficial insects that control cotton pests at a comparable scale. Also, West African soils are generally less fertile than those found in Uganda and Tanzania (ISRIC 2002).[5] The conventional cotton sectors in West Africa are much more organized by comparison, have a legacy of heavy state involvement in the promotion of cotton production, and distribute synthetic inputs on credit. For decades farmers have used mineral fertilizers and synthetic pesticides to cultivate conventional cotton. As a result, the input-intensive cotton cultivation in West Africa produces much higher yields on average than conventional cotton farmers in East Africa. Conventional cotton yields in crop year 2004/5 for Mali and Benin were 434 and 431 kilograms of seed cotton per hectare, over twice as large as Tanzania (186 kg) and Uganda (156 kg) (ICAC 2005). Furthermore, total mineral fertilizer use in 2002 in Mali and Benin is over five times the amount used in Tanzania and Uganda (FAOSTAT 2005).[6] As these figures demonstrate, organic cotton has been developed largely in East Africa, where the use of chemical inputs is not yet a dominant factor in the conventional cotton sector and environmental conditions are generally favorable to organic production.

Impacts on Rural Livelihoods

The conventional cotton practices and environmental context of each country largely influence the organic cotton projects' impacts on rural livelihoods. These impacts can be categorized into three main groups: economic, health, and environmental. The limited amount of systematic research makes it difficult to fully assess the impacts of organic cotton projects on rural livelihoods. However, the available evidence suggests that while organic price premiums are helping alleviate rural poverty, current organic practices may not be improving soil quality.

ECONOMIC

The clearest impact of organic cotton on farmers is improved incomes. All organic cotton projects strive to improve the incomes of farmers, and it appears that this is being achieved. Organic cotton improves the income of farmers through price premiums and reduced input costs. High premiums paid to organic farmers for their product appears to be the largest single contributor to improved incomes, and the biggest reason for farmers to become certified organic producers (Ton 2002; Tulip and Ton 2002). Price premiums can be from 10 to 50 percent higher than locally purchased conventional cotton. The addition of a fair trade certification in the Helvetas projects in Mali and Burkina Faso has increased the price premium to nearly double the price paid for locally purchased conventional cotton (Merceron, pers. comm., 2005). Furthermore, since organic production does not use synthetic inputs, production costs in organic systems are lower. In many cases input costs for conventional cotton can run up to 30 percent of the total cost of production (Agro Eco 2004). The benefits of reduced input costs and price premiums appear to outweigh any reductions in yields in organic systems. A systematic cost-benefit analysis in Benin confirmed that even with the reduction in yield of organic cotton, the price premium and lower production costs made organic cotton cultivation more profitable that conventional production (Gbesso 2000). It should be noted that organic systems generally require more farm labor. Since this comes predominately in the form of family labor, the costs are often not incorporated into economic analyses.

Two other components related to income generation from organic cotton are the timeliness of payment and added income through the sale of other organic crops. In most SSA countries, payments for purchased cotton in the conventional sector can take months, even years.[7] In the most extreme cases, payment is never received by farmers (Ton 2002). Organic cotton projects have generally benefited from a more timely payment schedule, which most often varies on a scale from days to months.[8] This is most likely due to the fact that organic projects are considerably smaller than the conventional cotton sector. Income generation has also been influenced by the selling of other organic products for export. Organic farmers incorporate these crops into their field rotations and then collect a premium payment upon purchase by an exporter. This is currently being practiced with peanuts in Senegal and sesame in Uganda and Mali (Simon Ferrigno, pers. comm., 2005; Merceron and Traoré 2005; Ton 2002; Tulip, pers. comm., 2005).

In areas where chemically intensive conventional cotton production is practiced, improved farmer health is a main goal of organic cotton projects. Organic cultivation prohibits the use of synthetic chemicals during production. Since synthetic pesticides can cause harm to human health, synthetic-free production most likely improves the health of farmers. This is very important in countries like Benin, where exposure to synthetic pesticides has caused sickness and death among rural farmers and their family members. In fact, the documented problems with synthetic chemicals was one of the main reasons OBEPAB began the organic cotton project (Ton 2003). Many organic cotton farmers in Benin mention that health improvement is one of the reasons that they decided to farm organically (OBEPAB 2002). Organic plant protection strategies employed in West Africa use botanical sprays principally derived from locally available trees.[9] Although these sprays are effective in reducing pest populations, they do not appear to harm the health of project farmers. While

Fig. 10.4. A student researcher with OBEPAB in Benin conducts field trials with biopesticides made of locally available plants and products.

there have been no reported deaths due to chemical exposure and farmers report feeling better, health improvements have not been measured systematically.

ENVIRONMENTAL

The environmental impacts of organic cotton production in SSA are difficult to assess and have yet to be systematically studied. Often the most important environmental variable in SSA is soil quality, due to its importance in sustaining continued agricultural productivity. Although there is no lack of organic techniques to improve soil quality and limit erosion, not all organic farmers nor projects in SSA implement these strategies. Cultivation strategies vary widely due to a number of factors, including awareness of techniques, soil fertility, access to manures, and the level of attention from project extension services.

While it is difficult to measure differences in the relative level of importance of soil quality for each organic cotton project, one potentially useful indicator is the number of extension workers per hectare of organic area under cultivation. Research suggests that in order to achieve adequate yields and soil nutrient levels in organic systems, farmers must apply adequate inputs of organic matter (Pimentel et al. 2005). Thus a key factor in determining impacts on soil quality will be the amount and quality of organic soil amendments used in the production process. Extension workers are the primary transmitters of agricultural techniques and management strategies to project farmers. More extension workers may result in better attention to the needs of individual farmers, and to better transmission of improved techniques. At the least, the number of extension workers represents the level of attention of each organic cotton project to issues of organic crop management. The number of extension workers in each project varies considerably. The project in Mali employs one extension worker for every 28 hectares in organic cultivation, compared to 42 hectares in Benin, 182 hectares in Tanzania, and 605 hectares in Uganda (Ton 2002; Merceron, pers. comm., 2005).[10] The differences in numbers of extension workers suggest more attention to organic crop management and soil quality in the West African nations than in East Africa. This would be

Fig. 10.5. Michel Atekokale applies biofertilizer made from wood ash and crushed palm nut shells to young cotton plants in southern Benin.

expected, given that soils are generally poorer and farmer perception of an adequate cotton harvest may be higher in West Africa.

A different but related factor influencing the impact of organic cotton projects on soil quality is to what extent farmers achieve the goals of organic agriculture rather than simply the standards of organic certification. Many studies in the global North suggest that organic agriculture can outperform conventional agriculture in improving soil quality. When compared to conventional systems, organic systems are less vulnerable to soil erosion (Siegrist et al. 1998) and increase organic matter and biological activity in soils (Bulluck et al. 2002). These results, however, may not be applicable to the situation in SSA, due to differences in soil structure and cultivation technologies. The organic and conventional agriculture referred to in these studies differs vastly from the organic and conventional agricultures presently being practiced in SSA. The most important difference, as far as this analysis is concerned, is that the organic agriculture practiced in these studies used high-quality organic inputs applied in adequate levels at appropriate time intervals. These organic best-management practices, more in line with the goals of organic agriculture, may improve soil quality. However, if these best-management practices are not being implemented, and farmers simply comply with organic standards, they may not achieve improvements in soil quality.

A good example illustrating the complexities of soil quality assessment and the potential consequences of a standards approach to organic production is found in Mali. Many organic cotton producing families in Mali also produce conventional cotton. Their conventional fields are generally much larger and account for the vast majority of total cotton and food production. With the introduction of organic cotton, many farmers now concentrate manure applications on organic fields instead of spreading them across all their cotton- and food-producing fields. By concentrating manure on a relatively small subset of the entire farm, farmers may be sacrificing overall farm sustainability for increased organic cotton yields. While these farmers are meeting organic standards, they may not be improving the overall soil quality of all their fields, since their production is not integrated into a whole-systems model congruent with the goals of organic agriculture. Irrespective of concerns at the farm scale, the level of manure applications may not even be adequate to replenish soil nutrients and improve soil quality on organic fields. Further research into the impacts of organic cotton on soil quality at both the field and farm scale is needed in order to address these concerns.

A complete assessment of the environmental sustainability of organic cotton–producing farmers in Mali, however, would not be complete without taking into account all the soil quality–enhancing activities these projects have inspired at the farm and community levels. In the same Malian project, farmers are beginning to invest in resource conservation by building animal enclosures adjacent to organic cotton fields. While this is not a novel development concept in SSA, its adoption has never been fully realized. Perhaps the substantial price premiums for organic cotton (almost twice as much as for conventional in 2005) are giving farmers an added incentive to increase the conservation and use of their manure resources. There are also signs that organic production is increasing the value of other local manure resources. Observations in southern Mali suggest that organic cotton production may be stimulating a trade in the seasonally collected manure of the oxpecker (*Buphagus* spp.), a species of bird that follows cattle.

The case of Mali illustrates the potential differences in soil quality between an organic-standards approach to growing cotton and a production strategy more congruent with the goals of organic agriculture. It also demonstrates the difficulty in choosing the proper scale at which to assess the environmental impacts of organic cotton production. By not incorporating all fields into a whole-systems approach, organic farmers in Mali may not be reaping the full benefits of organic production, including improvements in soil quality across all fields. Although attempting to achieve the goals of organic agriculture may be the most beneficial for soil quality, the environmental, economic, and social context of production may, in fact, not allow for such an approach to be fully implemented. For instance, there may not be adequate levels of organic inputs in order to achieve benefits in soil quality across all fields. This example also demonstrates the inherent issue of scale in assessing the broader environmental impact of organic cotton production. If environmental sustainability is assessed solely at the field level, it will miss the potentially negative consequences at the farm level of focusing manure applications to organic fields. Similarly, a farm-level assessment may miss the development of manure markets at the community scale.

The Future of Organic Cotton in SSA

Organic cotton cultivation continues to grow and attract significant attention. The international market for organic cotton fiber is increasing, and development organizations are drawn to organic cotton as a means to improve rural livelihoods. Even the World Bank has stated that organic cotton can play an important role in reducing the negative externalities of cotton production (World Bank 2001). With the addition of projects in West Africa, and projected global demand increases for organic fiber, the number of organic cotton projects and total exports are likely to continue to rise. However, at least two main factors will determine the ability for projects and exports to continue to grow in the near future: adequate financing and institutional capacity.

Securing sufficient funding is probably the most significant element necessary for the continuation and expansion of organic cotton in SSA. Funding allows for the continued maintenance of project management, for an extension in project services, and a continued issuance of sufficient price premiums to attract farmers. Funding sources for different organic cotton projects include international cotton buyers and international development organizations. Projects in Tanzania and Uganda have integrated almost all the cost of management and extension into the prices paid by buyers for organic cotton. Other projects, in Burkina Faso and Mali, are funded by a host of international development organizations and cotton buyers. These projects aim to ultimately incorporate the costs of the project into the price paid by cotton buyers. If the demand for organic cotton continues to increase, the expansion of the projects will require additional funding. Funding is also important to finance the purchasing of cotton. This normally comes in the form of a line of credit to a local institution to coordinate the purchase. Due to lack of adequate crop financing, nearly all cotton projects at one point in time, including the OBEPAB in Benin and the Lango Organic Project in Uganda, either had to sell their cotton on the conventional market or refused to buy all the available organic cotton (OBEPAB 2002; Tulip and Ton 2002). Funding also allows for significant price premiums to be paid to farmers. Since yields are generally lower in organic cotton systems, this price premium ensures adequate return for a farmer's investment and continued interest in cultivating organic cotton. Lower premiums, or no premiums altogether, will most likely diminish farmer interest.

Building the capacity of local institutions is also a key element of organic cotton projects in SSA. In Uganda, where essentially all the national and local-level administration of the organic cotton project is run by Ugandan organizations, efforts to build institutional capacity deal primarily with increasing their visibility and role in promoting organic cotton at the international level. Promotion at the international level is currently managed by the Dutch trader Bo Weevil. In other organic cotton projects where local institutions are not yet coordinating a significant part of national and local-level administration, a project goal is to create and build the capacity of local organizations to take over these responsibilities. In Mali the project coordinator, Helvetas, is aiding in the development of a new Malian producer organization, MOBIOM, or Movement Biologique Malienne, with the hope that they will take over management of the organic cotton project in the near future (Merceron, pers. comm., 2005).

If demand for organic cotton lint rises, institutional capacity is increased, and adequate funding is available, it is likely that organic cotton projects will continue to grow in SSA. However, even if such projects significantly expand their area of intervention, organic cotton will still impact only a small number of the cotton growers in the region. In this regard, organic cotton is a different kind of development project. Can organic cotton expand into areas where price premiums are not paid and organic practices are adopted simply for their health and potential environmental benefits? That seems unlikely, given that organic cotton yields are often much less than conventional yields and price premiums appear to be the largest pull for farmers to join organic cotton projects. Also it remains to be seen whether organic cotton from SSA will be able to tap into increased global demand, or if that gap will be filled by other organic cotton–producing nations.

There are many potential pitfalls to organic cotton cultivation as a development strategy. World cotton price fluctuations and the demand of organic cotton may change to the extent that price premiums no longer are sufficient to make organic production more profitable than conventional. The potential introduction of GM cotton will undoubtedly complicate efforts to continue and expand organic cotton production. Differences between a goals-oriented organic agriculture and a standards approach may lead to nutrient mining on organic fields. Furthermore, organic production, in its targeting of nutrient inputs exclusively on organic fields, may be reducing the overall soil quality at the farm level. This could leave organic cotton production vulnerable to the same criticisms as for conventional cotton—that increasing the incomes of rural farmers is happening at the expense of resource extraction and long-term sustainability.

Notes

Research for this chapter was funded in part by the Center for Tropical Research in Ecology, Agriculture and Development (CenTREAD) and the Environmental Studies Department, University of California, Santa Cruz. I thank Daniel Press and Robin Dautricourt for valuable comments and edits on earlier drafts.

1. Currently the BioRe project in Tanzania is the only organic cotton project in SSA using seed from an organic source (Ton 2002). A new venture by Bo Weevil to provide organic seeds for production in Uganda should be ready in 2006 (Bo Weevil 2005).

2. Although some organic cotton yield numbers exist, I have chosen to leave them out of this analysis primarily due to their wide variability and questionable accuracy.

3. According to Tulip and Ton (2002), the project in Uganda is referred to as the Lango Union Organic Promotion, and outside Uganda as the Bo Weevil Lango Organic Project. Before 1999 it was referred to as the Lango Union Organic Project. For simplicity, and in convention with the name used by Tulip and Ton in their country report, the project is referred to here as the Lango Organic Project.

4. Uganda recently began to distribute pesticides for free to cotton farmers, although it appears that farmers are not applying them, perhaps because farmers are aware that the pesticides kill beneficial insects as well as pests (Tulip, pers. comm., 2005).

5. In general, regional and global soil comparisons are extremely problematic. However, for the purposes of this coarse-level comparison,

soil data can be useful to gain a general understanding of the environmental conditions affecting each location.

6. Data for 2002 were the most recent available. Data for pesticide use were not available.

7. Uganda is the one exception, where both organic and conventional payments occur at the time of purchase (Tulip, pers. comm., 2005).

8. The BioRe project in Tanzania is the only organic project in SSA to have had serious problems with late payments to farmers (Ton 2002).

9. Sprays used in Mali rely on two botanical oils (*huile de m'peku, huile de koby*) produced from three native tree species: *Lannea acida, L. microcarpa* (m'peku), and *Carapa procera* (koby). Botanical sprays in Benin are made primarily of neem (*Azadirachta indica*) leaves and seeds mixed with papaya leaves, hot peppers, garlic, and locally produced soap.

10. The figure for Mali is for 2005; all other figures are for 2001.

References

Agro Eco. 2004. *Benin Organic Cotton Project.* Bennekom, Netherlands: Agro Eco.

Bassett, Thomas J. 2001. *The Peasant Cotton Revolution in West Africa: Côte d'Ivoire, 1880–1995.* Cambridge: Cambridge University Press.

Bo Weevil BV. 2005. "Uganda, Lango Organic Project." http://www .boweevil.nl/bw_fr_agricult.htm.

Bulluck, L. R., M. Brosius, G. K. Evanylo, and J. B. Ristaino. 2002. "Organic and Synthetic Fertility Amendments Influence Soil Microbial, Physical and Chemical Properties on Organic and Conventional Farms." *Applied Soil Ecology* 19 (2): 147–60.

Cleaver, Kevin M., and Götz A. Schreiber. 1994. *Reversing the Spiral: The Population, Agriculture, and Environment Nexus in Sub-Saharan Africa.* Washington, DC: World Bank.

Dankers, Cora. 2003. *Environmental and Social Standards, Certification and Labelling for Cash Crops.* Rome: Food and Agriculture Organization of the United Nations.

Edwards-Jones, G., and O. Howells. 2001. "The Origin and Hazard of Inputs to Crop Protection in Organic Farming Systems: Are They Sustainable?" *Agricultural Systems* 67 (1): 31–47.

FAOSTAT. 2005. *Fertilizer Data.* Rome: Food and Agriculture Organization.

Gabre-Madhin, Elini Z., and Steven Haggblade. 2004. "Successes in African Agriculture: Results of an Expert Survey." *World Development* 32 (5): 745–66.

Gbesso, C. Albert. 2000. "Étude comparée de rentabilité socio-économique du coton biologique et du coton conventionel." Master's thesis, National University of Benin, Cotonou.

ICAC (International Cotton Advisory Committee). 2005. *Cotton Statistics, 1980–2005*. Washington, DC: ICAC.

ISRIC (International Soil Reference and Information Centre). 2002. *ISRIC-WISE Global Soil Profile Data Set*. Wageningen, Netherlands: ISRIC.

Kidd, Andrew D., Alan Tulip, and Charles Wagala. 2001. *Benefits of Globalization for Poor Farmers: A Story of Organic Produce Exports from Uganda*. Lindau, Switzerland: BerterInnen News.

Lotter, Donald W. 2003. "Organic Agriculture." *Journal of Sustainable Agriculture* 21 (4): 59–128.

Malins, Annabelle, and Valerie Nelson. 1998. *Farmers Fair Trade (Uganda) Ltd., Organic Cotton Trade Case Study*. Medway, England: Natural Resources Institute.

Merceron, Franck, and Djibril Traoré. 2005. *Programme de promotion du coton biologique au Mali: Rapport annuel d'activités 2004*. Bamako: Helvetas.

Moseley, William. 2005. "Global Cotton and Local Environmental Management: The Political Ecology of Rich and Poor Small-Holder Farmers in Southern Mali." *Geographical Journal* 171 (1): 36–55.

Myers, Dorothy. 1999. "The Problems with Conventional Cotton." In *Organic Cotton: From Field to Final Product*, ed. Myers and Sue Stolton, 8–20. London: Intermediate Technology Publications.

Organic Exchange. 2005. *Organic Cotton Industry Statistics*. Berkeley: Organic Exchange.

OBEPAB (Organisation Béninoise pour la Promotion de l'Agriculture Biologique). 2002. *Le coton au Bénin: Rapport de consultation sur le coton conventionnel el le coton biologique au Bénin*. London : Pesticide Action Network.

Pimentel, David, Paul Hepperly, James Hanson, David Douds, and Rita Seidel. 2005. "Environmental, Energetic, and Economic Comparisons of Organic and Conventional Farming Systems." *Bioscience* 55 (7): 573–82.

Ratter, Saro G. 2002. *The Cotton Sector in Tanzania: An Evaluation of Conventional and Organic Production*. London: Pesticide Action Network.

Riddle, Jim, and Lynn Coody. 2002. *European Union and United States Regulations for Organic Agriculture*. Bonn: International Federation of Organic Agriculture Movements.

Rigby, D., and D. Cáceres. 2001. "Organic Farming and the Sustainability of Agricultural Systems." *Agricultural Systems* 68 (1): 21–40.

Siegrist, S., D. Schaub, L. Pfiffner, and P. Mader. 1998. "Does Organic Agriculture Reduce Soil Erodibility? The Results of a Long-Term Field Study on Loess in Switzerland." *Agriculture Ecosystems and Environment* 69 (3): 253–64.

Ton, Peter. 2002. *Organic Cotton Production in Sub-Saharan Africa: The Need for Scaling Up.* London: Pesticide Action Network.

———. 2003. *Organic Cotton in Sub-Saharan Africa.* London: Pesticide Action Network.

Ton, Peter, Silvère Tovignan, and Simplice Davo Vodouhê. 2000. *Endosulfan Deaths and Poisonings in Benin.* London: Pesticide Action Network.

Tovignan, Silvère, Simplice Davo Vodouhê, and Barbara Dinham. 2001. *Cotton Pesticides Cause More Deaths in Benin.* London: Pesticide Action Network.

Traoré, Djibril. 2005. "Organic Cotton Cultivation in Mali." Proceedings of International Conference on Organic Textiles, Chicago, May 1–3.

Tulip, Alan, and Peter Ton. 2002. *Organic Cotton Study: Uganda Case Study.* London: Pesticide Action Network.

World Bank. 1988. *Cotton Development Programs in Burkina Faso, Côte d'Ivoire, and Togo.* Washington, DC: World Bank.

———. 2001. *Project Appraisal Document: Cotton Sector Reform Project, Benin.* Washington, DC: World Bank.

———. 2005. "White Gold in Burkina Faso." http://web.worldbank.org/ WBSITE/EXTERNAL/COUNTRIES/AFRICAEXT/BURKINAFASOEXTN/ 0,,contentMDK:20532614~menuPK:343882~pagePK:141137~piPK :141127~theSitePK:343876,00.html.

Conclusion

Hanging by a Thread
The Future of Cotton in Africa

Leslie C. Gray and William G. Moseley

AFRICAN COTTON IS A CROP with meaning that goes beyond its status as a fiber plant. This crop, and its associated commodity chain, is a key thread in the complex fabric connecting African and global economies. Perhaps not so surprisingly, scholarship on African cotton, like that on globalization more broadly, arrives at very different conclusions on the prospects and possibilities for cotton-led development. For some, cotton is at the heart of concerns about unequal globalization, environmental degradation, technology transfer, and poverty (Kutting 2003; Oxfam 2002, 2004). Many debates have centered on the role of developed country subsidies in reducing world prices. Indeed, cotton prices have plummeted by 50 percent in the past several years. Estimates by the International Cotton Advisory Committee have predicted that if the United States alone were to remove subsidies, world cotton prices would increase between 6 and 11 cents per pound (or 2.7 and 5 cents per kg) (Baffes 2004). Recent failures of international trade negotiations make this unlikely, putting the livelihoods of many African cotton farmers, among the poorest populations in the world, at risk. Declining prices are not the only problem facing African cotton cultivators. Farmers also complain about declining land availability and reduced soil quality. Cotton is a resource-intensive crop, demanding high levels of fertilizers and pesticides. Despite these problems, national cotton production levels are at their peak. Not only is cotton expanding into new frontiers, but cotton farmers are cultivating larger and larger areas in the attempt to keep their income high in spite of declining world prices.

In contrast, cotton is also portrayed as an engine of economic growth for African countries, an example of sectoral growth, technological innovation, and marketing successes. Several studies indicate that cotton production has decreased poverty rates for cotton producers (e.g., World Bank 2004; Sians and Wodon, this volume). Cotton production has led to improvements in infrastructure: better roads, more schools, and better communications. In many cotton villages, new types of enterprises are spurred by the influx of money from cotton production.

Successful collective action by farmers has also been common in the cotton sector. For example, West African cotton farmers historically have shown great agency in the face of price fluctuations and institutional problems. Farmers often responded to low prices by protest and withdrawal from the cotton market (Bassett 2001). Recent trends in African cotton have shown producer cooperatives to be powerful in forcing democratization in the cotton sector. Networks of farmers and international NGOs are an integral part of the story of cotton production.

With 8 percent of the world's cotton being produced in sub-Saharan Africa, and 15 percent of global exports, global cotton has firmly rooted itself in African soil (Baffes 2004). While Africa's share of global trade for many of its other major commodities has been declining, Africa's share of the cotton trade has been rising. The chapters in this volume shed light on the global/local nature of African cotton production by examining the complex intersection of cotton, poverty, and development at different scales. Chapters range from examinations of the cotton crisis, cotton reforms, cotton livelihoods and the introduction of new technologies that have the potential to change the landscape of future cotton production.

Several broad themes emerge from the chapters in this volume. While declining world prices are a serious issue, the ability of farmers to weather declines in prices is often determined by national and local issues. These include government policy, institutions that provide marketing and supply services, access to resources such as land, labor, and agricultural inputs, and individual decision making. Despite declining world prices, some cotton growing economies have had success with cotton production while others have not fared well. In particular, the failure of cotton institutions in many countries is striking. Whether it comes to managing input distribution, new technologies, or marketing, cotton institutions are failing African farmers. Prices offered to farmers in West Africa declined from 2003 to 2007 at the same time that input prices increased in many countries, making cotton production precarious for local producers. Problems with corruption, particularly in the marketing and transportation of cotton, have made cotton difficult for poorer farmers, who are cash constrained. Late payments, a theme of many chapters in this book, have put farmers in a bind, constraining them to sell food crops (which must often be repurchased later in the season for a higher price) in order to settle debts. One of the results of this squeeze has been high levels of indebtedness. Cotton farmers must borrow large amounts of money for inputs, sometimes equaling almost half of what they expect to gain at the end of the season. The risks of crop failure are high, for many reasons, from household labor shortages to late pickup, to unforeseen natural disaster. These risks become less and less justifiable as cotton prices decline.

One of the striking observations is the differential ability of wealthier and poor farmers to engage in cotton production. Without sufficient inputs of labor, land, manure, and agro-chemicals, it is difficult to be a successful cotton producer. Thus while some farmers can do well with cotton, poorer farmers who produce cotton are at great risk of falling into debt. Recent declines in world prices have put the vulnerability of poorer farmers in stark relief. Given declining profit margins, cotton farmers can do most things right and still risk indebtedness. Several chapters illustrate how cotton institutions tend to benefit larger and wealthier farmers more than poorer farmers.

Despite problems in the cotton sector, cotton is central to the well-being of cotton growing countries and to the livelihoods of many African farmers. Several African countries are dependent on cotton production to balance budgets. African households in these countries are likewise dependent on cotton production to supplement their budgets and to make their farming systems work. Remarkably, in spite of all the problems farmers face, they continue to grow cotton. This is partly because cotton is one of the few crops for which farmers can get inputs on credit, inputs that are necessary not just for cotton but increasingly for food crops as well. With declining access to land and falling soil quality in many areas, farmers are increasingly dependent on cotton production as a vehicle for accessing fertilizers needed for both cash and subsistence cropping. Cotton production has become embedded in the economic and social life of many African farmers and affects their livelihoods in significant ways. Decisions about whether to grow cotton go beyond the income-earning potential of this crop and are often related to larger livelihood needs. Farmers are frequently motivated by reasons that go beyond prices: whether this be access to inputs on credit or diversification of crops in order to manage risk. Cotton is also important in the broader social fabric of life in Africa, providing economic opportunities that allow young men to stay in villages rather than migrate and stimulating broader economic development.

Finally, Kutting (2003) argues that West African farmers are too poor to pollute. Several chapters in this volume that explore the environmental dimensions of cotton production show that this perception is not quite correct. While cotton production in Africa has not led to the types of widespread landscape change and pollution that it has in other parts of the world, African cotton has many environmental consequences, particularly in the effects of pesticides on human health or the effects of cotton on soil quality. Several of the chapters demonstrate that cotton production is affecting local environments and local people quite significantly. Despite the claims of the state cotton company, Moseley (chapter 3), for example, shows how in Mali cotton production has resulted in reduced soil quality and that the soils management practices of large cotton farmers in Mali are no better, and arguably worse, than the practices of those who farm little or no cotton. Gray (chapter 2) illustrates how pesticide poisoning is a significant problem for farmers using handheld pesticide sprayers. Organic cotton is often thought of as a solution to the environmental problems surrounding cotton. Dowd (chapter 10) shows that things are not quite that simple. While organic cotton may be beneficial for the environment, Dowd points to the potential side effect that organic cotton producers may use all their manure on organic fields, leaving conventional fields without any inputs of organic matter.

The Future of African Cotton

African cotton has many different effects, but clearly it is embedded in the life of those who produce it. Will African farmers continue to grow cotton in light of continuing declines in world prices? Recent interviews with farmers in Burkina Faso, where prices paid to farmers have eroded over the last five years, show that there is a limit to how low prices can go. Farmers indicate that they will significantly reduce their production of cotton but not stop it altogether because they need the inputs for their other crops. Given the drastic decline in producer prices, it remains to be seen how cotton will fit into the livelihoods of farming villagers. Will it go the way of peanuts, which declined rapidly in importance after the 1970s, or will it remain an important link to the global economy in places where farmers have few other options?

What does the future hold for African cotton? African governments are anxious to keep cotton production high, given its importance to the fiscal situation and a history of institutional support. Producers, under the pressure of declining world prices, are questioning whether to continue growing cotton. The question should not be whether cotton will continue to be a major export crop in Africa. Rather, we wonder if African governments and communities will be able to parlay cotton revenues into real development gains. Could wisely invested cotton revenues lead to a more diversified and sustainable set of economies or will cotton simply be a source of income in the medium term? Worse yet, could a temporary boost in world cotton prices simply perpetuate the "resource curse" phenomenon whereby cotton receives increasing institutional support to the detriment of other sectors in the economy?

Several trends will continue to affect African cotton. The most glaring issue is the decline in prices that African producers receive. While most of the focus is on subsidies, the decline in the dollar vis-à-vis the euro is an equally important factor. Because cotton is sold in dollars on the world market, the exchange rate determines how much sellers receive for their cotton. From 2002 to 2007, the dollar declined about 30 percent in relation to the euro; this has meant that the costs of cotton inputs have increased at the same time that the prices received have declined.

Despite the depreciation of the dollar, much of the debate about threats to African cotton will continue to be linked to subsidies. Although there was an outcry against industrialized country subsidies in the last round of international trade talks, it is unlikely that subsidies will be removed in the short-term (at least in a meaningful way). In the United States, the politically powerful agricultural lobby has prevented any discussion of subsidy decreases. Four countries in West Africa (Mali, Benin, Burkina Faso, and Chad) have put forward demands to the World Trade Organization for compensation for their economic losses directly caused by subsidies, but so far these demands have not been greeted favorably. This is partially because giving compensation would create a precedent for demanding compensation for other subsidized commodities, something the industrialized countries want to prevent (Goreux 2005). Industrialized country policies to influence cotton therefore look to increase the productive capacity of African farmers. They argue that African farmers must increase yields in order to remain competitive. The industrialized countries, while unwilling to cut subsidies or give direct aid to the cotton sector, have invested in agricultural research in Africa. The United States Agency for International Development gave 20 million dollars to support West Africa cotton, with the goal of increasing productivity through activities such as technical support, reform of the cotton sector, and promotion of biotechnology.

One proposal for cushioning African countries from world price volatility is to create a cotton price support fund. This would be a form of self-insurance in which countries would create funds to stabilize the year-to-year volatility in world prices (Gergely 2005). In the past several years, though, the low prices of cotton have forced countries with support funds to abandon them. In 2005, the government of Burkina Faso stated that their support fund would prevent the producer price for cotton from ever going below 175 FCFA/kg. By 2007, the support fund was bankrupt and cotton had reached 145 FCFA/kg. Since industrialized countries are unwilling to contribute to cotton support funds, the sustainable formation of such funds seems unlikely given declines in world cotton prices and the depreciation of the dollar.

A cornerstone of some future policies is the introduction of genetically modified cotton. Many African countries are testing genetically modified cotton and intend to introduce it in the next few years. While Bt cotton failed among smallholders in the Makhathini Flats in South Africa, West African governments are holding out high hopes for Bt cotton, both to increase yields and to reduce pesticide use. Reports from both India and China have shown mixed results with genetically modified cotton, with high yields in some studies and low yields in others. Indonesia has abandoned genetically modified cotton due to problems with drought resistance, pest infestations, and reduced yields (Villar 2007).

Another future emphasis of many governments and international donors is the continued reform of the cotton sector in Africa, particularly though liberalization and privatization. Several chapters illustrate how reforms influenced the performance of cotton economies. Many cotton economies have been able to weather shifts in world prices, particularly in some southern Africa countries, because increasing local efficiencies allowed farmers to receive higher prices, have functioning input markets, and receive more timely payments. However, national level reform may have its limits. Gouse, Shankar, and Thirtle (chapter 4) illustrate how liberalization can jeopardize the cotton sector, an industry where vertically integrated supply chains were historically used to guarantee prices and delivery. Indeed, if we look at the countries where cotton production has increased most rapidly (Burkina Faso and Mali), these are the areas where neoliberal reforms in the cotton sector are the least advanced (Goreux 2005). Goreux suggests that holding up liberalization and privatization as panaceas for the African cotton sector is a diversionary tactic. The real focus should be on removing subsidies, improving productivity, and creating safety nets for farmers when the market price declines. Indeed, some of the recent neoliberal reforms proposed for West Africa may decrease the broader development goals and social safety net of the cotton sector in West Africa, which were some of the reasons why cotton was so popular among farmers.

One bright spot for the future is the role of producer groups in asserting their power. Unions of cotton growers are using their influence to determine local price policy by bargaining with national governments and international policymakers. Thus, West African farmers are going global. Mirroring the fair trade movement in other commodities such as coffee, West African cotton producers are utilizing alternative networks to create new markets for cotton production. For example, while members of West African farmers' unions were attending WTO meetings to change policy, they were also attending international meetings of organic farmers, marketers, and textile makers seeking to move away from chemical-intensive cotton production toward organic production. These initiatives work side by side with their more conventional efforts to change the pricing policies of developed countries.

These alternative networks have been spurred by members of the NGO community. For example, OXFAM has pushed its "Make Trade Fair" campaign for cotton and other commodities. The promotion of organic cotton is another aspect of the alternative trade movement. Dowd (chapter 10) illustrates how European NGOs are organizing organic cotton cooperatives in East and West Africa. While the area under organic cotton is minuscule, nongovernment organizations and fair trade activists see organic cotton as a potential tool for getting African farmers higher prices for their commodities. Organic cotton also has the potential for decreasing the environmental degradation associated with cotton production, particularly a reduction in the use of toxic pesticides and an increase in applications of organic soil amendments. Notably, organic cotton production has been easier to establish in areas where the state is less active in the promotion of conventional cotton production, making East Africa more favorable for this type of production than West Africa.

African Cotton and Globalization

The implications of this volume for our understanding of globalization in relation to Africa would appear to be several. In the introduction, we broached three broad and interrelated themes related to globalization that might be informed by a study of African cotton production: (1) To what degree is Africa involved in the globalization process? (2) What is Africa's relationship with global trading regimes? (3) What is the nature of African agency (at the national and local levels) in the globalization process?

First, Africa definitely is not operating outside the globalization process. The problem is that the touted benefits of globalization appear to be mixed and very unevenly distributed. Engaging with the global market presents the smallhold African cotton producer with certain opportunities and risks. Wealthier, relatively well capitalized farmers seem better able to ride out the risks and take advantage of opportunities. Second, global trading regimes have been managed to the advantage of more powerful producers. Powerful constituencies in the global North have, until very recently, been successful at keeping subsidies for their producers off the table in international negotiations. But this has all changed in recent years as African governments, farmer unions, international NGOs, and the news media all seem to have become more effective at influencing debates on international trade. Third, this increasing effectiveness is a testament to the agency of African governments and African farmer unions on the global stage. But African actors should also be wary. The more recent push for GM cotton in Africa may represent global capital's attempt to usurp the farmers' role in defining the problems and solutions of African agriculture.

References

Baffes, John. 2004. "Cotton: Market Setting, Trade Policies and Issues." World Bank Policy Research Working Paper, February.

Bassett, Thomas J. 2001. *The Peasant Cotton Revolution in West Africa: Côte d'Ivoire, 1880–1995*. London: Cambridge University Press.

Gergeley, Nicolas. 2005. "A Proposal for the Implementation of a Mechanism for Mitigating Volatility in Cotton Prices." In *International Trade Negotiations and Poverty Reduction: The White Paper on Cotton*, ed. Eric Hazard. Dakar: Enda Prospectives Dialogues Politiques, Occasional Paper 249.

Goreux, Louis. 2005. "Cut Subsidies, Beware Diversionary Tactics and Don't Miss the Hong Kong Window of Opportunity." In *International Trade Negotiations and Poverty Reduction: The White Paper on Cotton*, ed. Eric Hazard. Dakar: Enda Prospectives Dialogues Politiques, Occasional Paper 249.

Kutting, Gabriella. 2003. "Globalization, Poverty and the Environment in West Africa: Too Poor to Pollute?" *Global Environmental Politics* 3 (4): 42–60.

Minot, Nicholas, and Lisa Daniels. 2005. "Impact of Global Cotton Markets on Rural Poverty in Benin." *Agricultural Economics* 33 (3): 453–66.

Oxfam. 2003. "Cultivating Poverty: The Impact of U.S. Cotton Subsidies on Africa." Oxfam Briefing Paper 30.

———. 2004. "Finding the Moral Fiber: Why Reform Is Urgently Needed for a Fair Cotton Trade." Oxfam Briefing Paper 69.

Villar, Jose Lopez. 2007. "The Introduction of GM Cotton in the World." *Friends of the Earth International: Agriculture and Food*, no. 111 (January): *Who Benefits from GM Crops? (1996–2005)*.

Index

CNRA. *See* Centre National de
Recherche Agronomique
Coalition for the Protection of
Africa's Genetic Patrimony, 243
coercion, 68–69; state-sanctioned, 130
commercialization, 138; in Kita, 200
commission agents, 49–50
commodities: agricultural, 20; export value of SSA agricultural, *7;*
production of, 21, 23, 99, 198. *See
also* commodity chain
commodity chain, 4, 36, 37, 272;
analysis, 42–46; cotton, *39, 41;*
global, 20, 37–40, 57–58; West
African cotton, 40–42
common property, *95*
Compagnie Cotonnière (COPACO),
40, 49–50
Compagnie Malienne de Développement des Fibres Textiles (CMDT),
40, 48–49, 60n5, 61n12, 85, 178, 181,
182, 183, 186, 204n8, 208, 212–13;
AV credit system restructuring
by, 213; benefits of, 196; blacksmith
training program of, 192–93,
204n10; cotton expertise of, 198;
infrastructure, 199; late payments
to farmers and, 185, 204n4; new
system of, *209;* peanut cultivation
and, 198; privatization of, 201; as
RDO, 200–201, 202; resources
provided by, 193–94, 200–201
Companhia Nacional de Algodão
(CNA), 148, 155n17
Compaoré, Blaise, President, 2
competition, 118
concession companies, 147
consumers, international, 3
consumption: alternative, 4; of cotton
producers, 171; cotton production
v., 159–60; income v., *168–70*
contamination, 50; of cattle, 252; of
lint in Tanzania, 134, 154n10; of
lint in Uganda, 134, 154n10;
polypropylene, 143, 155n14, 236
contract farming, 124, 154n3
coopératif pour les producteurs cotonniers (CPC): AV v., 216–17,

220; in Dissan, creation of two,
217–18; households v. other households, *219;* poverty v. system of,
220–22; rules of, 214–15; system, 221
Cooperative Act, 134
cooperative unions, 127
COPACO. *See* Compagnie Cotonnière
corporations, 3
corruption, 75–76
Côte d'Ivoire, 43, *51,* 68–69; commodity chain in, *39;* farmers, delayed
payments to, 57; privatization of
cotton sector of, 49–50; seed
production in, 47
Cotlook A price, 51–52, 54–56
Cotpro, 139
Cottco, 138, 151; Gold Club membership of, 140; management of,
155n11; outgrower scheme of,
139–40, 152; yield of, 148
cotton: in Africa, future of, 272–80;
auction system in Tanzania,
136–37; basin, move from old to
new, 96; belt, 145; broils, 36–37;
competitive market model in, 134;
dependence on, 99; environment
and, 14–18; ginning, 48–53, 148–49,
155n17; GL7, 61n8, 70; grading, 54,
61n11, 212; hand picked v. machine
picked, 12; household farming in
Kita, 182; marketing of, *39,* 47,
48–53; monopolies, 42; pest problem, 229–31; plants, root system
of, 14–15; poverty and, 13, 65, 273;
purity of varieties of, 126; quality
v. price, 50–51, 54, 75–76, 126–27,
134, 154n10; reaction against, 186;
reasons for growing, 190–92;
scramble for, 141–42; sector, privatization of, 174; seed to fiber
conversion of, 61n11; shipping
price of, 54, 57–58; "stacked-gene,"
104; U.S. foreign aid agenda for
biotechnology and, 238–39. *See
also* Bt cotton; cotton companies;
cotton price(s); cotton producers;
cotton production; farmers; har-
vest(s); organic cotton; organic

cotton (*cont.*)
  cotton production; world market price; yield(s)
Cotton Act, 134–35, 145, 155n19
Cotton, Colonialism, and Social History in Sub-Saharan Africa (Isaacman and Roberts), 5
cotton companies, 127; costs of, *49*; cotton producers v., 48–49, 61n10; farmer debts to, 57; hidden profits of, 48–49, 58; private, 135, 136, 146; of West Africa, *52*; World Bank v. West African, 236
cotton cultivation, 77; benefits of, 186; drawbacks of, 183–86; for fertilizer, 191; strategies, 262; ulterior motives for equipment of, 187–88; wealth and, *87*, 88, 94
Cotton Development Fund (CDF), 135, 136, 152
Cotton Development Organization (CDO), 137, 152
Cotton Development Strategy, 146
Cotton Development Trust, 144
Cotton Famine, 6
Cotton Marketing Board (CMB), 129, 138
Cotton Outgrower Fund, 143, 151, 153, 155n15
Cotton Outlook index, 50–51
cotton price(s), 22, 45, 52–53, 55–59, 60n8, 61n11, 72–73, 125, 154n5, 177, 196, 213, 272, 277; floor, 61n12, 184; local and world seed, *163*; poverty v., 65; quality v., 50–51, 54, 75–76, 126–27, 134, 154n10; two parts of, 184; U.S. policies of, 24; U.S. subsidies v. world, 36, 60n2. *See also* Cotlook A price; world market price
cotton producers, 59, 162, 174; artificially competitive, 160; benefits for, 186–92; in Benin, 162, 164, *165*, 167; consumption of, 171; cotton companies v., 48–49, 61n10; income of, 58; management practices of, *90*; non-cotton producer households v., 167, 174; poverty

of, 167; price-setting, 55–56; world market price and, 53–54, *55*, 56, 61n11. *See also* organic cotton production
cotton production, 8–9, 10–12, *11*, 21, *39*, 46–48, 80, 159; AV system of, *218*; benefits of, 273; in Benin, 162, *163*, 171; Bt smallholder, 228; in Burkina Faso, 66, *67*, 68–71, 73; challenges of, 126–27; changes in wealth and, 98; CMDT, 201; coercion for, 68–69; collective, 212–16; consumption v., 159–60; in Dissan, 211; extra work of, 184; farmer perceptions of, 71–72; future of, 276–80; gendered division of labor in, 13; household, 221; indirect effects of, 91–95; input levels v., 60n8; institutional setup for, 127, *131*; intensification of, 207, 217, 252, 261; low cost of, 124, 154n2; in Mali, 84–86, 100; map of, *107*; in Mozambique, 130, 147; new markets for, 26–27; peanuts v., 220; potential of, 177; Siwaa v. Djitoumou, 88, *89*, 90–91; in South Africa, 105; specialized benefits of, 192–94; SSA, 123, 251–52, 259; sustainability of, 97, 100; systems of African, 5–9; in Tanzania, 137; in U.S., 12–13, 23; in West Africa, 52; in Zambia, 141
cottonseed, 43–44, 194
Coulter, Jonathan, 161
CPC. *See* coopératif pour les producteurs cotonniers
credit, 145, 207; access to, 186–87; AV system of, 213; default, 146, 149; dependence on, 108–9; equipment on, 187; failure of, 124; inputs on, 70, 73, 74, 108–9, 139, 140, 143, 144, 189, 213, 275; managing, 220; output marketing and, 125; repayment rates, 142; size of cotton fields v., 191; subsidized, 135–36; supplier, 44, 46, 60n7
crop(s), *173*; as collateral, 109; household evaluation of, 177–78;

equipment, 94, 186–87, 211; CMDT, 189; CMDT blacksmith use for, 192; labor v., 187–88; loans to buy, 187, 189; ownership of, 188

euro, dollar v., 53, 58, 277

European Union organic standards, 255

export: cotton, increase of, 22–23; European colonial powers increase of cotton, 251; revenues, 20–21, 99

Export Promotion of Organic Product from Africa (EPOPA), 258

extensification, 48, 60n8

extension workers, 262

fair trade certification, 260

FARA. *See* Forum for Agricultural Research in Africa

Farm Act, 37

farm community, 178

farmers, 144; in agricultural research, exclusion of, 243–44; American, 22–23; biotechnology research and, 244; Bt cotton v. Non-Bt cotton costs for, *112*; in Burkina Faso, 66; competition between, 118; competition v. price, 135; Cottco's technical support to, 139; cotton production, perception of, 71–72; on CPC system, perspective of Dissan, 216–17; debt of, 14, 57, 73–75, 274; Dissan, 209, 212–13, 214, 216–17, 219, 220; family v. corporate, 24, 60n4, 65, 129; free-riding, 70; health of, 79, 261–62; income of African cotton, 36–37, 56–59, 273; income of organic cotton, 259–60; income of U.S. cotton, 37; inputs to, *39, 132–33*; international economy and cotton, 3; Kita, 179, 180, 182, 183, 186; Mossi, 78; needs of, 178, 202; oxen, 77; payment of, 57, 66, 75–76, 185, 204n4, 260, 269nn7–8; politics and, 18; power of, 22; practices, 209–10; resource-poor, 105; rights of, 236; sedentary, 183;

smallholder cotton, 114–15, 129, *132–33*, 235, 247n19; soil quality v. wealth of, 89–91, *92–93*; SSA, 242–45; technology fee, 235; union, 26; wealth of cotton, 12; wealthy, 94

Farmers' Federation, 258

farming, contract, 124, 154n3

farm policy, 23, 25

farms, efficiency of, 115–16

Faso Cotton, 41–42, 45

favoritism, 139

FCFA. *See* Francs de la Communauté Financière Africaine

fertilizer, 43, 45, 58, 70, 126, 273; cotton cultivation as means to acquire, 191; inorganic, 90; mineral, 259; monopolies, 44. *See also* biofertilizer

filière approach, 4, 38, *39*

first-grade cotton, 54, 61n11

floor price, 61n12

FOB. *See* free on board

Forum for Agricultural Research in Africa (FARA), 242, 247n22

France, Max Havelaar, 202

Francs de la Communauté Financière Africaine (FCFA), 43, 60n6, 162, 183, 204n4

free on board (FOB), 48, 53–54, 61n9

French Company for the Development of Textile Fibers (CFDT), 40, 69, 85

French Textile mills, 207

funding, organic cotton production, 266

GATT. *See* General Agreements on Tariffs and Trade

GCC. *See* global commodity chain

GE cotton. *See* Bt cotton

gene flow, Bt cotton and Non-Bt cotton, 234

General Agreements on Tariffs and Trade (GATT), 21

genetically modified cotton (GM), 17–18, 44, 111. *See also* Bt cotton

Gergely, Nicholas, 48–49, 56

Ghana, 17
G. hirsutum, 40
Gibbon, Peter, 154n7
GIE. See Gini income elasticity
Gini income elasticity (GIE), 172, 173
ginning: cotton, 48–53; output ratio,
148–49, 155n17
gins, protection of, 146
global commodity chain (GCC), 20,
37–40, 57–58
global corporate science, 238–39
globalization, 4, 5, 15, 18–21, 24–27:
African cotton and, 280; disen-
gagement from, 23–24
Global Network of the Crop
Biotechnology Knowledge
Center, 241
Glover, David, 154n1
GM. See genetically modified cotton
GM cotton. See Bt cotton
GMO(s): legislation, 104; uncertainty
of, 231. See also Bt cotton
Goreux, Louis, 22, 160, 279
Gossypium arboreum, 5
Gossypium herbaceum, 5
Gouse, Marnus, 18, 278
GPC, 70, 74, 75
Gray, Leslie C., 276
Greenberg, Stephen, 231, 246n13
green revolution, 237, 246n13, 251
Guere, Orou, 2
GV, 69–70

"Hanging by a Thread," 81n1
harvest(s), 77–78, 94; CMDT collection of village, 220; dependence
on, 199; Dissan, 209, 219; in
Mali, 188
"Harvesting Poverty," 25, 83
health: costs, pesticide usage and,
126; organic cotton production
and, 261–62
Heckman, James J., 171
Helvetas, 267
Hillocks, R. J., 231, 232
Hofs, Jean-Luc, 108–9, 117
household(s): agricultural production, 209–10; CMDT, 211; cotton

production, 221; CPC v. other,
219; definition of Dissan, 210–11;
farms, Mali's RDOs and, 182;
head of, 177; income, 167, 203n2;
wealthy, 197
Howard, Julie, 222
Huang, Jikun, 116, 117

IAM. See Instituto do Algodão de
Moçambique
ICAC. See International Cotton
Advisory Committee
Ichimura, Hidehiko, 171
ICS. See internal control system
IFI. See international financial institutions
IFOAM. See International Federation
of Organic Agriculture Movements (IFOAM)
IFPRI. See International Food Policy
Research Institute
illness, pesticide related, 16
IMF. See International Monetary
Fund
income(s), 160, 172; annual Dissan,
212; consumption v., 168–70;
cotton as main source of SSA
cash, 123; cotton grower's, 47,
56–59; of cotton producers, 58;
debt v., 189–90; household, 167; of
Kita farmers, 186; organic cotton
and rural, 259; other sources of,
173, 174; recommended inputs v.
low, 47
India: Bt v. Non-Bt cotton in, 231;
crop management in, 232
Indonesia, Bt cotton in, 228
inequality, 160, 174; in Benin, 172
INERA. See Institut Nationale d'E-
conomie Rurale
inputs, 15, 39, 42–46, 58, 76–78, 98,
115, 123–24, 155n13, 161; boycotts
and, 57; Cargill's voucher for, 140;
chemical, 79; cost of, 260; cotton
production v. levels of, 60n8; on
credit, 70, 73, 74, 108–9, 139, 140,
143, 144, 189, 213, 275; distribution
of, 161; to farmers, 39, 132–33;

labor, 184; Bt cotton v. cost of, 113;
in cotton production, gendered
division of, 13; equipment v.,
187–88; exchanges, 92–93; family,
154n2; force of Africa, 3; organic
cotton production, 260; yield v.,
76–78

Laboratoire d'Analyse Régionale et
d'Expertise Sociale (LARES), 164

Lacy, Scott M., 14, 188, 204, 204n7,
205n13

land: availability of, 273; communal
ownership of, 109; fertile, access
to, 78; wealth of farmers v. management of, 91–93

The Land Bank, 106, 108

The Lango Organic Project, 256, 257,
258, 266, 268n3

Lango Union Organic Promotion,
268n3

Larson, Marianne, 135

Ledermann, Samuel T., 26

legislation, GMO, 104

Lerman, Robert, I., 172

liberalization, 118, 135; economic, 180;
in Kita, 200; of Mozambique, 147

Lint Company of Zambia
(LINTCO), 128, 141

Lint Marketing Board, 137

loan(s), 142, 187, 204n5; AV v. individual loans, 212; CMDT, 188,
204n6; equipment, 187, 189; repayment of, 187; repayment rates in
Zambia, 142, 155n13

LOMACO, 148–49

"The Long Reach of Cotton," 81n1

Lonrho Africa, 106

Lonrho Cotton, 141, 142, 148

maize, 76, 199; herbicide-tolerant,
104

"Make Trade Fair," 22, 27, 279

Makhathini Cotton, Ltd (MCG), 108

Makhathini Flats, 105–8; Bt cotton
in, 110–15; yield increase in, 116–18

Mali, 24–25, 26, 43, 48, 84–86; cotton
company costs in, 49; cotton-
growing areas in, 86; environ-

mental sustainability of, 97, 100;
fertilizer monopolies in, 44;
government of, 96, 100, 178,
179–80, 181, 201; harvests in, 188;
inputs in, 187; organic v. conventional cotton production in,
264–65; poverty in, 90; railroad
in, 178–79; seed production in, 47;
village banks in, 187; wealth distribution in, 97–98; wealth v.
cotton cultivation in, 87, 88

Malian Company for Textile Development. See Compagnie Malienne
de Développoment des Fibres
Textiles (CMDT)

Malian National Coordination of
Farmers' Organizations (CNOP),
243

Mali's National Agricultural Research
Institute, 242

Manatali, loans in, 204n5

Mané, Daouda, Adoption du coton
transgénique au Burkina Faso,
245n1

Maredia, Karim, 246n10

marketing, output, 125

marketing systems, 126–27

Marxism, 161

MCG. See Makhathini Cotton, Ltd

McKenzie, C., 161

Ministry of Agriculture, 145

Minot, Nicholas, 13, 164, 174

mixed seed strategy, 233–34

MOBIOM, 267

Monsanto, 44, 103, 104, 110, 114, 229,
235, 247n19

Moseley, William G., 15

Movement Biologique Maliene, 267

Mozambique, 151; Civil War of, 130,
146; concession model of, 145–49;
cotton concession of, 130; cotton
production in, 130, 147; cotton
sector reform of, 131; cotton sectors of, 150; input delivery to
smallholder cotton farmers of,
132–33; liberalization of, 147; open
concession system of, 147–48;
yields, 148

Mpumlanga, 105
Murphy, Sophia, 53
Museveni, Yoweri, President, 35

Namala, 183
Nampula, 146, 148
National Agricultural and Environmental Research Institute. *See* Institut Nationale d'Economie Rurale (INERA)
National Corporation for Agricultural Promotion (SONAPRA), 161, 164
National Cotton Council, 37
National Union of Burkinabé Producers, 227
natural disasters, 75, 77
New York Cotton Exchange, 51
New York Times, 24, 25, 65, 81n1, 83
NGO. *See* nongovernmental organization
nongovernmental organization (NGO), 4–5
NorskHydro, 44
Northbourne, Lord, 253
NuCOTN 37-B, 110
NuOpal, 110

OBEPAB. *See* Organisation Béninoise pour la Promotion de l'Agricuture Biologique
ODIMO. *See* Opération de Développement Intégré du Mali Ouest
Oerke, Erich-Christian, 15
Ofiço, Alfonso Osorio, 155n16
OHVN. *See* Upper Niger River Valley Union
Opération de Développement Intégré du Mali Ouest (ODIMO), 180, 181, 183, 187, 189, 190, 192, 195
opérations de développement rural, 178
opérations de développement rural (RDO), 180, 181, 182
organic agriculture, 263–65
organic certification, 253, 254–55, 260, 263–64

organic cotton: availability of, *254;* Bt cotton v., 268; future of, 266–68; project trends and key components, 256–59; on rural livelihood, impact of, 259–65; supply and demand for, 254, 266, 267; yield of conventional v., 255–56, 260, 266–67, 268n2. *See also* organic agriculture; organic certification; organic cotton production
organic cotton production, 10, 17, 27, 100, 252, 279–80; conversion period into, 255–56; East Africa v. West Africa, 259; on environment, impact of, 253–54, 262–65; funding for SSA, 266; GMO v., 234; health and, 261–62; history of, 253–56; labor of, 260; price premiums for, 260, 265, 266–67, 268; soil quality and, 262, 264–65; SSA, *256;* in Uganda, 268n1; West African v. East African, 259; World Bank on, 266
Organic Exchange, 254
organic manure, 191
organic plant protection, *261,* 269n9
Organisation Béninoise pour la Promotion de l'Agriculture Biologique (OBEPAB), 256–58, 261, 266; student researcher of, *261*
organochlorine, 16
organophosphate, 16
Ouattara, Mamadou, 60n1
outgrower schemes, 124, 139, 142, 155n12; of Cottco, 139–40, 152
output: marketing, credit and, 125; ratio, ginning, 148–49, 155n17
overgrazing, 95
oxen, 77, 80, 187, 193
Oxfam, 20, 22, 27, 65, 279

Partnership to Cut Hunger and Poverty in Africa, 242
patents, 234–35, 243
Paul Reinhart, 42, 50
PCS. *See* primary cooperative societies
peace clause, of U.S. farm bill, 25

peanuts, 180, 195–97, 199, 205n14; cotton v., 220; in Kita, 180–81, 182, 205n14; shelled v. unshelled, 197–98

peripheral commodity production, 20–21

Pest Control Act of 1983, 104

pesticide(s), 15–18, 45–46, 58, 70, 78–80, *80*, 90, 100, 243, 273; Bt cotton v. use of, 116–18, 227, 232–34; in Burkina Faso, 66; cost of, 111–12; death from, 16, 230, 252, 261; management of, 126, 230; natural, 104; productivity, 116–18; smallholder farms v. corporate farms use of, 115; treadmill, 230; in Uganaa, 268n4

"Pesticides, Politics and Pest Management: Toward a Political Economy of Cotton in Sub-Saharan Africa," 246n8

pirate buying, 144, 146, 147–48

pisteurs (merchants), 57

Plexus, 148

policy, 99; AV, 216; Burkina Faso cotton, 66; farm, 23, 25

politics: scientization of, 237–38; SSA farmers and global, 18

pollution, insecticides and groundwater, 230

polypropylene contamination, 143, 155n14, 236

Pongolapoort dam, 106

Porter, Phillip, 6

Portman, Rob, 246n14

Poulton, Colin, 135, 140

poverty, 83, 162, 164; cotton and, 13, 65, 273; CPC system v., 220–22; environmental degradation v., 96–97; in Mali, 90; reduction, 160, 165–66; in rural households of Benin, trends of, *166*

price: competition, 134; Cotlook A, 51–52, 54–56; cotton quality v., 50–51, 54, 75–76, 126–27, 134, 154n10; exchange rates and formation of, 53; floor, 61n12, 184; FOB cost, 48, 53–54, 61n9; Kita's

rising grain, 183–84; premiums for organic cotton producers, 260, 265, 266–67, 268; producer, 54–55, *56*, 61nn11–12; U.S. subsidies v. world cotton, 36, 60n2; variability of peanut, 196; world market, 53–56, 59, 71. *See also* cotton price(s); world market price

pricing policies, international, 13, 66

primary cooperative societies (PCS), 128; privatization of, 134

private goods, 127

privatization, 41–42, 49–50, 52, 59, 138, 162, 244; of CMDT, 201; of cotton sector, 160–61, 174; of inputs, 125, 159; of Ivorian cotton sector, 57; PCS, 134; of research, 245

production: commodity, 21, 23, 99, 198; of cotton, systems of African, 5–9; global commodity, 20, 37–40, 57–58; household agricultural, 209–10; simultaneous cotton and peanut, 197

property rights, 240

public goods, 127

pyrethroids, 16

Qaim, Martin, 114–15, 116, 117

rainfall, 46, 77; debt and, 190; in Dissan, 211; too much, 185; yield v., 113

RCU. *See* regional cooperative unions

RDO. *See* opérations de développement rural

rebate, 184–85

reform, cotton sector, *131*, 160

reform process, 130

regional cooperative unions (RCU), 128; privatization of, 134

Remei AG, 256

research: of Bt cotton trials of, 227, 233, 237, 243; international networks for, 240–42; privatization of, 245; resistance management, 232–33, 246n11; enforcement of, 235

Rhodesia, 129
Rhodesia National Farmer's Union, 129
road network, of Kita, 195, 197, 200, 205n11
Roberts, Richard, 68, 69; *Cotton, Colonialism, and Social History in Sub-Saharan Africa*, 5
rock lines, 191, 204n9
Rodney, Walter, 1
rural development, 202

SAFGRAD, 242
Sahel drought, 180, 203n1
Sangare, Siaka, 213, 216, 220, 221
SAP. *See* structural adjustment programs
Saphyto, 45
Sara, 74, 78, 79
Schwartz, A., 69
second-grade cotton, 54
seed: chemically treated, 126; exchange, Bt cotton and, 235; Monsanto and market for, 240; production, *39, 47*; quality, 126; smallholder dependence on publicly available, 247n19; source, 255
SENCHIM, 44, 45
Senegal, Farmers' Federation in, 258
Senegal River Basin Authority, 181
Senko, 183
Serrano, Alex, 222
Shankar, Bhavani, 18, 116, 278
shipping price, 54, 57–58
Siaens, Corinne, 13
Sianesi, Barbara, 171
single-channel marketing monopolies, 127
Sithole-Niang, Idah, 246n10
Siwaa, 85; cotton production in Djitoumou v., 88, *89*, 90–91; inequality in, 98; soil quality v. wealth of farmer in, *92*; wealth distribution in, *97*–98; wealth v. cotton cultivation in, *87, 88, 94*
SOBA, 42
Société Tropicale d'Engrais et de Produits Chimiques (STEPC), 44, 45
SOCOMA, 42

Sofitex, 40, 41–42, 45, 46, 50, 69, 71, 73, 74, 75
soil, 14, 15, 78, 100, 268n5; degradation of, 89, 252; erosion, 264; fertility, 98, 177; management, *90, 91*; organic cotton production and quality of, 262, 264–65; quality of, 88, *92–93*, 268, 273; quality v. wealth of farmers, 89–91, *92–93*; West African, 259
SONAPRA. *See* National Corporation for Agricultural Promotion
sorghum production, Dissan, *211*
South Africa, 10, 17, 104, 111
South African Committee for Genetic Experimentation (SAGENE), 104
The South African Development Trust Corporation, 108
The South African Genetically Modified Organisms Act, 104
Sow, Moussa, 203n1
SPAAR. *See* Special Program for Agriculture in Africa
Special Program for Agriculture in Africa (SPAAR), 247n22
SSA. *See* sub-Saharan Africa
"stacked-gene" cotton, 104
STEPC. *See* Société Tropicale d'Engrais et de Produits Chimiques
Strengthening Producer Organizations, 244
structural adjustment, Kita, 200
Structural Adjustment Period, 161
structural adjustment programs (SAP), 21
sub-Saharan Africa (SSA), 2, 27n1; agricultural research in, 237; cotton as main source of cash income, 123; cotton production in, 123, 251–52, 259; export value of agricultural commodities in, *7*; farmers, 242–45; global politics and farmers of, 18; organic cotton production, 256, 266. *See also* Africa
subsidies, 53, 58–59, 71, 79–80, 99, 125, 154n4, 228, 277; agricultural,

UNPCB. *See* Burkinabé cotton growers' union
Upper Niger River Valley Union (OHVN), 244
U.S. *See* United States
U.S. Agency for International Development (USAID), 238, 239; public information campaign of, 240
USAID. *See* U.S. Agency for International Development
USDA, survey on pesticide use with Bt cotton, 232
U.S. farm bill, 22–23, 25
U.S. farm policy, 23
U.S. Foreign Assistance Act, 238
U.S. National Cotton Council, 239
U.S. National Research Council, 246n12
U.S. secretary of agriculture, 238

village associations (AV), 187, 189, 208–9; CMDT meeting with, 213–16; cotton production under system of, *218*; CPC v., 216–17, 220; credit system of, 213; debt absorption, 189, 204n7; Dissan, 220–21; individual v. loans from, 212; policy, 216; presidents of, 190, 194; responsibilities of, 212
Vunisa, 106, 108, 110

WACIP. *See* West Africa Cotton Improvement Program
Waibel, Hermann, 231
Walet, Mariama, 49
Wall Street Journal, 65, 81n1, 246n16
WCA. *See* West and Central Africa
wealth: agricultural equipment as sign of, 188; cattle holdings v., *94*, 95; cotton cultivation v., *87*, 88; CPC system v., 220–22; distribution in Mali, 97–98
weeding, 77–78
West Africa: commodity chain of, 40–42; cotton companies of, *52*, 236; organic cotton production of East Africa v., 259; soil of, 259; World Bank v. cotton companies

of, 236; yields of East Africa v., 259. *See also* cotton production
West Africa Cotton Improvement Program (WACIP), 238, 239, 246nn14–15
West and Central Africa (WCA), 10, 27n3
wet growing season, 118
whiteflies, 230
WideStrike cotton, 229
Wodon, Quentin, 13, 175n1
World Bank, 6, 19, 23, 38, 41, 56, 59, 61n12, 84, 96, 100, 244, 246n17; on organic cotton production, 266; support of SPAAR, 247n22; West African cotton companies v., 236
world market price, 23, 160, 162, 164, 174; in Burkina Faso, 56; cotton producers and, 53–54, *55*, 56, 61n11; government pricing v., 72–73; subsidies v., 154n4; synthetic fibers v., 159; U.S. cotton farmers and, 37, 60n3
World Trade Organization (WTO), 21, 25, 27, 35–36, 53, 83–84, 238; Hong Kong meetings of, 36, 60n1
WTO. *See* World Trade Organization

Yara, 44
yield(s), 48, 60n8; in Benin, *163*; Bt cotton, 111, 113–14, 227, 231–32; Burkina Faso cotton fiber, *67*; of Cottco, 148; increase in Mahathini Flats, 116–18; insects v., 229–30; labor v., 76–78; livestock and, 78; Mozambique, 148; organic v. conventional cotton, 255–56, 260, 266–67, 268n2; rain v., 113, 185; West African v. East African, 259
Yitzhaki, Shlomo, 172, 175n1

Zambia, 153; Cotton Act of, 134–35, 145, 155n19; cotton sector of, *131*, 141, *150*; government of, 141; input delivery to smallholder cotton